Covert Propaganda and Molding the Mass Mind

Covert Propaganda and Molding the Mass Mind

HOW OUR THOUGHTS ARE BEING SECRETLY SHAPED

Chad Hill

ISBN: 151230557X
ISBN 13: 9781512305579
Library of Congress Control Number: 2015908470
CreateSpace Independent Publishing Platform
North Charleston, South Carolina

Contents

Introduction

THIS BOOK IS ABOUT A highly secretive and practically invisible world populated by covert (secret) propagandists, a realm created to protect and grow the financial interests of the economic power elite by influencing and molding our thoughts and behavior.

These molders of the mass mind are highly trained artisans who painstakingly and secretly shape our attitudes and behavior much like a ceramic artist or potter sculpts supple clay, massaging and manipulating it into a desired shape. Covert propaganda is the primary tool these mind potters deploy to make us malleable for molding.

The word "propaganda" is going to throw off a lot of readers because the word itself has been highly propagandized to make us think propaganda is something used by other countries, not something we would employ.

The reality is we're one of the most propagandized countries in history. We invented modern mass-persuasion propaganda techniques. It's no mistake that propaganda is misunderstood. It was planned that way.

Propaganda, simply put, is the attempt to influence attitudes and behavior. Education informs. Propaganda persuades. Propaganda is not inherently unethical when it is open and aboveboard, like most advertising and public relations. The problem arises when it's practiced behind closed doors, away from public scrutiny, and is designed not to be detected.

This book is about the propaganda techniques covert propagandists secretly use to manipulate, mold, and control us. Clandestine mind manipulation is not directed primarily at individuals, but at the mass mind or public opinion, which, in turn, influences us.

This highly secretive molding and manipulation of the mass mind is conducted primarily by propagandists and other operatives working covertly for a myriad of big business interests and government entities, including intelligence, security, and surveillance agencies. They're so secretive that Edward Bernays, one of the founders of covert propaganda, called them an "invisible government." These covert operatives are invisible because we don't know who they are, where they work, what they do, or what their agenda is. We do know, however, that their primary allegiance is to the economic power elite.

Propagandists will immediately attempt to discredit the phrase "economic power elite" because they don't want the average American to believe there's an elite, oligarchic/plutocratic class that controls our country. They'll also likely try to diffuse and discredit revelations, such as mine, about the elite's invisible government by screaming "conspiracy theory." This book is not based on theory, but on facts and my personal experience at the highest levels of propaganda.

I've spent many years as a propaganda servant of the economic elite. I plan to share with you what I've learned so you'll be better prepared to recognize covert propaganda techniques that are designed to obliterate clear and critical thinking. Why, you might ask, would anyone want to discourage clear thinking? The answer is simple. If we can't think clearly, others can think for us.

My experience has included being a journalist on four daily newspapers, working ten years for the world's largest public relations/propaganda firm, teaching mass communications at a major university, and owning my own PR firm for several decades.

I managed a campaign in the early eighties to help introduce the world to personal computing and, after that success, was hired by a consortium of top technology firms to introduce the public to faxing and e-mailing. In short, I know quite a bit about the game of mass persuasion. I have no problems with it as long as it's overt and transparent. When it slips into the shadows of secrecy and deception, I start to worry. You should, too.

Some of the things I reveal will shatter many of your stereotypes. Our country has done a lot of clandestine things that will shock you. Stick with me. There's light at the end of the tunnel provided we get a lot more transparency. We, the people, need to retake the country that has been stolen from us in what has been a century-long and secret propaganda war.

CHAPTER 1

Whose Thoughts Are They?

On August 6, 1945, the United States dropped a nuclear bomb on Hiroshima, Japan. Three days later we dropped another atomic weapon on Nagasaki. We've been taught for seventy years that dropping the bombs was a military decision based on the need to save American lives and to end the war.

Evidence from leading historians, numerous top military leaders (including General Eisenhower), and a report from the US Strategic Bombing Survey Group, which studied the bombing decision in detail, have called those explanations into question. It becomes clearer why we took such drastic action if you analyze the decision from a purely propaganda standpoint. I'm not aware of anyone who has done that. Until now.

Both the bombing survey group and the historians determined that President Truman ignored repeated advice from his top military leaders that Japan was ready to surrender, that the war was over, and that there was no military reason to drop the bombs that killed between 150,000 to 200,000 men, women, and children. The evidence suggests, as I will show later, that Truman dropped the bombs anyway. Truman wanted to send the Soviet Union and the entire world a simple message: don't mess with us; we have the bomb and will not hesitate to use it. Dropping bombs is typically an act of war and not propaganda. When bombs are deployed to scare people and to send a message, it becomes propaganda.

Truman and his advisers knew we were in a race with the Soviets, a sprint to the oil fields. We were also in a race to grow empire and to protect the financial interests of the economic power elite. We needed a scared and submissive public, domestic and worldwide, to win those races. We still do.

The best way to win the sprint for oil and empire is by manipulating and controlling public opinion. The primary weapon for doing that is covert (secret) propaganda.

If true, as the evidence indicates, that Truman dropped nuclear bombs to send a propaganda message, we've been told one of the biggest lies in history concerning arguably the biggest event in history. It wouldn't be the first or last time we were lied to or deceived. Propagandists don't use the word "lie." Instead they soften it with the euphemism "disinformation."

As soon as Japan surrendered, Congressman John E. Rankin, a member of the House Committee on Un-American Activities, began issuing press releases on "Communist intentions to dominate the world." The Cold War and its scare campaign had begun. We scared not only Japan and the Soviets; we scared the entire world with the bombings. Now it was time to launch a propaganda war in the United States and to drop secret weapons of mass mind destruction on the American people in order to obliterate critical thinking and to create a malleable mass mind or, in other words, to scare us into submission so that we would acquiesce to the needs of the economic power elite.

In a spring 1947 private meeting with President Truman, Senate Foreign Relations Committee Chairman Arthur Vandenberg urged the President to "scare the hell out of the American people."[1]

On July 23, 1951, covert operatives for the CIA and the intelligence divisions of the army, navy, air force, and FBI held a joint meeting "to explore coordination of mind control research."[2]

A few years later, covert operatives sent President Eisenhower a secret memorandum in which it was noted that the propaganda campaign required "an aggressive covert, psychological, political and paramilitary organization."[3] This aggressive, covert organization has become what amounts to an "invisible government" of covert propagandists and intelligence and surveillance operatives.

How could I possibly know about an invisible government and its covert propagandists if they operate in secrecy? Because I've been a propaganda servant of the economic power elite. Covert propagandists are invisible because we don't know who they are, where they work, what they do, or what their agenda is. They can do anything they want, and we won't know about it because they operate far away from public scrutiny.

Buckle your seat belts for a journey into a secret realm few have visited. What I reveal will be an eye-opener. Many readers will likely have lifelong stereotypes shattered and will have difficulty fathoming how the country they love could have done some of the things I'll document. I'll unveil numerous propaganda techniques that have been and are currently being used to influence events at home and abroad and to obliterate clear and critical thinking so others can think for us. I'll show how a lot of the things we take pride in as our own beliefs, sometimes arrived at by in-depth and critical thinking, are often only predictable by-products of well-planned and highly secretive propaganda programs that have been deployed for many decades to influence our thoughts and behavior.

Who we are, how we act, how we dress, our political viewpoints, our sexuality, our relationships, our emotional state, and even our religious beliefs or nonbeliefs are among the things that can be influenced by propaganda.

Ironically, the word "propaganda" itself has been propagandized through a secret campaign that was designed to associate propaganda with something evil, something enemies use, but not us. The reality is that we invented modern propaganda. Even Adolf Hitler credited us with teaching him propaganda techniques.

Propaganda, simply put, persuades. Education informs. There are basically two types of propaganda: open or overt propaganda and closed or covert propaganda. Advertising and public relations are overt propaganda.

I'll give many examples of overt propaganda throughout the book, but I'm primarily interested in covert or secret propaganda, the kind that goes on behind the scenes, far away from public scrutiny. Covert propagandists don't want you to know what they are doing. In fact, they don't want you to think for yourself. They want to think for you. They do this by getting you to feel first and think second.

I bet you've often told someone, "That's how I feel about it." If so, you were feeling first and thinking second. Our innate need to feel first and think second, our emotional attachment to things, is exactly what propagandists exploit.

By the time you finish this book, you'll be shocked at the many ways covert propagandists have learned to secretly manipulate us. They've created an environment in which we don't know what we don't know. I should note that most covert propaganda is not directed at us as individuals. There aren't people sitting behind closed doors secretly conspiring to determine the best ways to influence you as an individual. There are, however, many highly professional mass mind molders in covert government and private agencies researching and implementing motivational and psychological techniques to mold and manipulate public opinion which, in turn, influences you.

The primary purpose of this mass mind manipulation is to protect and grow the financial interests of the economic power elite. Covert propagandists learned decades ago that this is best accomplished, not by totalitarian strong-arm tactics, but by persuading people to adopt acceptable "self-censorship."

This self-censorship is primarily accomplished by providing acceptable parameters of thought and behavior or, to put it another way, by drawing lines in the sand that we learn instinctively not to cross for fear of consequences. This book will identify those who secretly draw these lines in the sand. I'll give you advice on how to detect and protect yourself from their unrelenting assault on your senses, attacks that are designed to mold your thoughts and to obliterate clear and critical thinking so others can think for you. These techniques are also unleashed to numb your sensitivities and to neutralize and co-opt potential dissent so that you remain in the status quo sandbox.

I should point out that our country's deepest problems are systemic and are not, in most cases, because of the failings of politicians or government functionaries. Most of them have never heard of covert propaganda.

It's not politicians who are out of control. It's the economic power elite and its invisible government that are out of control. These invisible operatives have no political allegiance. They don't care about political parties or conservative vs. liberal ideology. They don't even care about facts. They deal in emotions.

These covert propagandists are, in most cases, answerable to no one outside their invisible realm. This gives our top leaders, including presidents, plausible deniability (a common propaganda technique).

The beauty of having what amounts to a secret government is that you can't catch someone you can't see. As of 2015 the United States had seventeen covert agencies, with tens of thousands of covert operatives who are sworn to secrecy. These covert agencies, such as the CIA and NSA, also hire private contractors who are sworn to secrecy.

This book is a journey into the secret world of covert propaganda, a world that most of my readers likely never imagined existed. But the invisible operatives have been among us for many years. Covert propagandists are like dark matter. We can't see it, but it's there. The fingerprints of these propagandists and their partners are all over our history. I'll show you their handiwork. They're like ghosts; they're invisible, and they exist to scare us into submission, to get us to acquiesce to whatever our invisible government believes it must do, no matter how repugnant or unethical, to grow and protect the financial interests of the economic power elite. One of the primary instruments for growing and protecting these financial interests is war.

For most of its brief history, the United States has had a love affair with war. War has become such an obsession that we may now be in what an Obama administration official said could be "an endless war." That sounds omnibus, but it's not an aberration.

• • •

Since its birth in 1776, the United States has been at war 93 percent of the time (222 out of 239 years). We've never had a decade without at least one war. To support this nearly continuous state of war, we have over seven hundred military bases in more than one hundred countries and spend 41 percent of the world's total military expenditures (next are China at 8 percent and Russia at 4.1 percent).[4]

We've also been involved in many covert military operations and have incited, directed, and funded the overthrow of numerous democratically elected governments throughout the world.

Even when there was no blood spilled on the battlefields, we've had an almost manic-obsessive need to create some type of war, such as the so-called war on drugs.

There's one war we've been fighting nonstop for a century. It's the biggest war of all, a war that all of our other battles fall under. It's the propaganda war. You probably haven't heard of it because, well, you aren't supposed to know about it.

I noted at the beginning that Senator Vandenberg advised President Harry Truman that the government needed to "scare the hell out of" the American people. Truman heeded his advice and launched the Cold War, which has been a key battle in the propaganda war. The purpose of the Cold War was to scare us by manipulating our emotions, primarily the emotion of fear. To scare us Truman deployed a cadre of covert propagandists whose charge was to create a malleable mass mind, that is, a consensus of opinion that would acquiesce to the postwar ambitions of the economic power elite, which were to aggressively expand its growing empire.

One of the key weapons in both the Cold War and the propaganda war has been mass mind manipulation. That phrase might cause some readers to conjure up thoughts of "conspiracy theory." They would be wrong. My book is based on facts, not theories. Ironically, the labeling of controversial or hard-to-believe information as conspiracy theory is, in itself, an act of propaganda. Conspiracy theory was put into the popular vernacular (as was the word "brainwashing") as part of Operation Mockingbird, which was kicked off in the fifties by covert propagandists following the secret meetings on mind control that I noted earlier. Conspiracy theory was used extensively after the assassination of President John Kennedy to discredit non-government versions of his death. Conspiracy theory is a subset of demonization, a propaganda technique to destroy, deny, degrade, and disrupt enemies by discrediting them.[5]

General Douglas MacArthur, one of the most respected military leaders in our history, acknowledged the existence of a covert propaganda campaign when he noted in 1957 that:

> Our government has kept us in a perpetual state of fear—kept us in a continuous stampede of patriotic fervor—with the cry of grave national emergency. Always there has been some terrible evil at home or some monstrous foreign power that was going to gobble us up if we did not blindly rally behind it (our government).[6]

Keeping us in a "perpetual state of fear," stirring up "patriotic fervor," and getting us "to blindly rally behind" government is the role of covert propaganda.

Covert propagandists learned many years ago from motivational researchers and psychologists that people are most vulnerable to manipulation and persuasion when they're aroused emotionally and feel insecure. The easiest emotion to manipulate is fear. Covert propagandists are experts at scaring us. That's their job.

An aroused and scared populace, covert propagandists believe, is more likely to passively accept and even to trust whatever messages the economic power elite need to implant in the group mind. A scared public is more likely to accept and support war, repression, loss of freedom, and acquiescence to the elite's pursuit of profit and empire.

Propaganda pioneer Edward Bernays said, "Propaganda is the executive arm of the invisible government."[7] Bernays (more on him later in the chapter) wasn't the only one to alert us to the invisible government. Supreme Court Justice Felix Frankfurter said, "The real rulers in Washington are invisible, and exercise power from behind the scenes."[8] John F. Hylan, mayor of New York from 1918 to 1925, noted: "The real menace of our

Republic is the invisible government which like a giant octopus sprawls its slimy legs over our cities, states and nation."[9]

I love the former mayor's simile and agree that the invisible government is "like a giant octopus," but since it's invisible, it needs covert propagandists to help sprawl its slimy legs over our nation. These shadowy propagandists, in turn, need secrecy to work their magic for the economic power elite.

President Franklin Roosevelt warned about the economic elite: "The real truth of the matter is that a financial element in the large centers has owned the government of the U.S."[10]

Another warning came from Senator William Jenner, who said in a 1954 speech that "we have a ruthless, power-seeking elite. This group is answerable neither to the President, the Congress, nor the Courts. It is practically irremovable."[11]

Senator Daniel Inouye of Hawaii said in 1986 congressional testimony that "there exists a shadowy government with the ability to pursue its own ideas of national interest from all checks and balances and free from the law itself."[12]

Major General Smedley Butler, one of the most decorated marines, described the economic elite and its intentions when he wrote: "War is a racket. Only a small 'inside' group knows what it's about. It is conducted for the benefit of the very few, at the expense of the very many. Out of war a few people make huge fortunes."[13]

From mid-2014 to spring 2015, the State Department approved military sales to Egypt, Jordan, Iraq, and Saudi Arabia, including Hellfire missiles, tanks, Patriot air defense weapons, and rocket launchers. The United States sold a billion dollars of weaponry just to Saudi Arabia in 2012–2013.

Making and protecting "huge fortunes" for the economic power elite is not only the bottom line for fighting wars, as General Butler noted, but also the rationale for covert propaganda at home and abroad.

• • •

So far, I have given evidence of the economic power elite's invisible government and its covert propaganda campaign from the father of modern propaganda, from a US president, from three senators, from a Supreme Court justice, from a big-city mayor, and from two of our top generals. There's much more evidence to come.

Before going into more detail about this covert propaganda war, I want to share with you a few examples of how our minds have been manipulated and molded and how covert propaganda has influenced numerous events at home and abroad.

The three things General MacArthur warned us about are good examples of mind molding: arousing our emotions and keeping us in a perpetual state of fear, stirring up patriotic fervor, and getting us to blindly rally behind government. Another example of mind molding is the decades-long propaganda campaign to bring about the marriage of capitalism and democracy by persuading us you can't have democracy without capitalism. Other examples include self-censorship; discrediting and demonizing anything that smacks of collectivism through a massive and continuing anti-Collectivist campaign; getting us to acquiesce to what an Obama administration official said could be "endless war" in the Middle East; and getting us to support overseas aggression and increased surveillance and loss of freedoms at home by creating false-flag incidents, fake atrocity stories, and disinformation (lies). One of the key ways we have been molded will be discussed in Chapter Three when I reveal how SOAP has been used to wash away clear and critical thinking so others can think for us. SOAP is an acronym for **S**ensory overload, **O**bfuscation, **A**wareness diversion, and **P**ursuit of pleasure. The following pages are full of many more examples of mind molding. The propaganda potters have been busy at the wheel shaping our thoughts and behavior for nearly a century.

Some events that have likely involved covert propaganda include using provocateurs to deliberately stir up dissent in order to later crush it at home and abroad (too many to list here); overthrowing democratically elected governments; manufacturing terror incidents and then blaming them on others; dropping two nuclear bombs on Japan; hiring German Nazis, some of whom had committed horrific war crimes, to work for the US government after World War II; government covert agencies working with drug dealers (or looking the other way) when narcotics were brought into the United States; government covert agencies working with organized crime at home and abroad; using sex and violence in media as propaganda tools to manipulate emotions; doing secret research on mind control techniques; and developing a program to send anti-Vietnam war protestors and other "radicals" to internment camps.

One of the most common (and most difficult to detect) covert propaganda techniques is the block and bridge. It has been a favorite covert propaganda technique in the war on communism/Cold War and recently in the so-called war on terrorism. The block and bridge allows you to block or redirect focus from a primary issue or purpose to a secondary issue and then make the secondary issue the main focus in order to hide the primary issue. Most block and bridges are smokescreens designed to hide a true agenda.

For example, the war on communism was allegedly a battle of ideologies (the secondary issue), but the real purpose of the war (from which the focus was shifted or blocked) appears to have been to scare people at home and abroad about the Red Menace so that the economic power elite could grow its empire worldwide primarily by gaining access to and control of world oil supplies. The block and bridge shifted focus from the primary issue and made the secondary issue the focus. The war on terrorism may also be a block and bridge, but the jury is still out, although I will present a lot of evidence that it, too, may involve a lot of block and bridge smokescreens.

• • •

There have been six major battles in the propaganda war and many lesser skirmishes. The major battles include a massive World War I campaign to arouse popular passion in the United States for entering what many thought should be a European war, the dropping of nuclear bombs on Japan, the Cold War, the war on drugs, the war on terrorism, and the thought control war.

There have been numerous other wars, but these six give a good overview of how we have covertly used propaganda at home and abroad to draw lines in the sand. I will give details on all six of these battles in later chapters, but first I want to give you an overview.

The first salvo of the propaganda war was fired by the Committee on Public Information (CPI). The CPI was created by President Woodrow Wilson to garner the support of the American people to enter World War I.

Many people were against our involvement, but that sentiment changed quickly when the propagandists Wilson appointed to the committee, including Edward Bernays and the founder of the public relations/propaganda firm I worked for (Carl Byoir), developed new motivational and psychological techniques to influence the mass mind.

Their pioneer propaganda campaign was so successful that Hitler and his propaganda minister studied and employed our propaganda techniques. Hitler was so impressed with American propaganda that he even hired Byoir during the thirties to handle propaganda for Nazi Germany in the United States.

Ironically, Byoir was an American Jew. But that didn't matter to Hitler. He was more interested in Byoir's propaganda expertise and his ability to convince the American business and financial elite that fascism was going to wipe communism off the face of the earth. Does Hitler hiring an American Jew propagandist seem like strange bedfellows?

It gets even better. President Franklin Roosevelt also hired Byoir several years after he had worked for Hitler. Byoir also did work for President Herbert Hoover, for whom he conducted a "War against the Depression."

Byoir, like me, was practically invisible. He had a major impact on world events for decades, yet he is barely a footnote in history. You certainly didn't read about him in your history books. That's no mistake. Propagandists know the best propaganda is that which is seen the least.

I personally learned this valuable lesson. I've owned my own propaganda business for twenty-five years and worked ten years with the Byoir agency.

During both stints I've never used promotional materials or had a website or used Twitter or Facebook. I've always worked in the background, away from public scrutiny.

The World War I propaganda campaign and the dropping of the nuclear bombs were the first two major battles of the propaganda war. Two other battles, the Cold War and the war on terrorism, may have us locked into "an endless war." This endless war, like our other wars, will likely involve the use of covert propaganda to scare us into supporting a pro-war agenda.

The most effective propaganda for scaring us is to demonize the enemy and to create or manufacture atrocity stories. One step beyond creating fake atrocity stories is to actually create and incite atrocities. Manufacturing and inciting atrocity or terror incidents in order to later blame them on others is called false-flag propaganda. I will give numerous examples throughout the book.

For those who doubt our government would make up false atrocity stories or deliberately encourage and incite violence, keep reading. We've been doing both for decades.

Bernays admitted that he and his fellow propagandists made up false atrocities to incite a public outcry against Germany in World War I, such as the story that German soldiers collected tubs full of human eyeballs and another of Germans cutting off the breasts of nuns (more information later).

These were lies (disinformation) created by propagandists to garner public support for an unpopular war by arousing our emotions, primary the emotion of fear. We have been deploying creative and difficult-to-detect disinformation and false-flag incidents ever since at home and abroad.

False-flags, smokescreens, disinformation, demonization, the block and bridge, and numerous other covert propaganda techniques became widespread during the post–World War II Cold War/Red Scare campaign, which was designed to scare the entire world into submission to protect and expand the financial interests of the economic power elite, primarily, as I have noted, by beating the Soviets to Middle East oil, which an American diplomat said in 1944 was "the greatest prize in history."[14]

The CIA and its operatives and fronts have handled most of the covert propaganda overseas, although the CIA has been involved in some home-front propaganda campaigns, such as Operation CHAOS.

Most of the domestic Cold War propaganda has been handled by the FBI, NSA, and other agencies. In a secret internal memorandum, the FBI told its agents "to enhance the paranoia" of the American people. It has done this in myriad ways, such as using agent provocateurs to infiltrate churches, break up marriages, get people fired from their jobs, and even spy on a deaf, mute, and blind humanitarian. Under its COINTELPRO program that I will discuss later, the FBI often used provocateurs to encourage and incite false-flag incidents in the civil rights and antiwar movements.[15]

Anticommunism has also been used frequently overseas as a smokescreen. For example, CIA documents reveal that the agency engineered a coup and used anticommunism to overthrow the democratically elected government of Iran in 1953 even though the center-left Mosaddegh administration was a long way from being Communist.[16]

In its place we installed the Shah of Iran, an ironfisted dictator who ruled Iran for decades thanks to our support. The CIA documents noted above revealed that the agency had direct involvement in both planning and engineering the coup. Covert propaganda played a key role in the coup. We didn't even have to send in troops. Instead, we clandestinely scared people by inciting violence (what I call "the engineering of dissent") and blamed it on leftists. We were so successful that we would use the same covert engineering of dissent to overthrow a democratically elected leader in Guatemala a year later. We've also used engineering of dissent for decades to stir up Islam radicals in Soviet Muslim countries. Has that come back to bite us?

The Byoir public relations/propaganda firm I worked for represented Iran and the Shah for decades. All evidence indicates that the United

States engineered the coup to put the Shah of Iran on the throne so we would have access to and control Iran's oil interests and so we could block any Soviet interference with our race for oil and empire. Twenty percent of the world's oil travels through the Strait of Hormuz, which Iran borders.

President Eisenhower's secretary of state Dean Acheson even admitted that anticommunism was "a smokescreen" to justify the CIA's involvement in the Iran coup.[17] *New York Times* reporter James Risen uncovered a secret CIA document that described anticommunism as a "rhetorical device."[18]

Middle East historian Ervand Abrahamian found evidence that Iran's oil was the central focus of the coup, "though much of the discourse at the time linked it to the Cold War."[19]

In short, the CIA, a secretary of state, and a leading historian have produced evidence that anticommunism was a block and bridge smokescreen. Our primary goal was getting to Iranian and Middle East oil.

We wanted that oil so badly that we secretly used former Nazis, some who had committed horrendous war crimes, to help in some of the CIA-engineered coups. We've relied on Nazis frequently throughout our history, as I will detail later.

The war on communism is not the only smokescreen or block and bridge. The war on terrorism is supposedly a war against barbaric, savage terrorist extremists, yet we trained, supported, funded, and deliberately incited radical Muslim terrorists in Soviet Muslim countries and in Pakistan/Afghanistan to destabilize the Soviet Union so we could win the race for Middle East oil and, more recently, to secure our access to oil and shipping channels. President Johnson's national security adviser Zbigniew Brezenski has said the stirring up of radical Muslims in Soviet Muslim countries "played a crucial role" in the fall of the Soviet Union.[20]

The so-called war on drugs may have also been a smokescreen/block and bridge. At the same time we were supposedly fighting the war on drugs, the Reagan administration looked the other way or allowed tons of cocaine to move into California during the Contra-cocaine scandal. The block and bridge made it appear we were fighting drugs when, in reality, we were fighting much bigger wars—the war on communism and the propaganda war.[21]

The war on communism, the war on terrorism, and the war on drugs, as I have noted, are mere skirmishes in the propaganda war, a war we started fighting in earnest after World War II, but a war that was first fought during the World War I era.

One of Byoir's propaganda partners shortly after World War I was J. Edgar Hoover, who became FBI director for nearly fifty years.

Byoir, Hoover, and Attorney General Palmer set up a news bureau after World War I to spread the scare message throughout the country that Communists were preparing to invade the United States.[22] The anti-Communist propaganda campaign wasn't just aimed at scaring the American public. There was a more important underlying theme: to pave the way for growing empire.

This post war anti-Communist campaign kick-started the Red Scare movement decades before the fifties (when most people believe the anti-Communist campaign began). Byoir and Hoover's campaign wasn't even the first use of anticollectivism. It was employed extensively during the late 1800's, long before the Soviet Union became Communist, to diffuse, discredit, and demonize a growing labor movement.

Hoover arguably was one of the most powerful men of the twentieth century. Nixon once said Hoover knew so much about covert affairs that "he could bring down the house (government) including me."[23]

Hoover was one of the key architects of the war on communism. He also developed propaganda and surveillance programs to scare the American people, particularly social and political activists, such as Martin Luther King. The FBI used about every covert propaganda trick in the book to discredit, demonize, and destroy King.

The propaganda war may have been the most successful war in history. A strong case can be made that superior American propaganda was the primary reason we won World War I, World War II, and the Cold War. Our propaganda expertise is now fueling the war on terrorism, which Obama administration official Leon Panetta said could be "a 30-year war."

• • •

Dropping the nuclear bombs, as I noted, kick-started the Cold War. I will give details later in the book, but for now I want to share with you how Admiral William Leahy reacted to the bombings. Leahy was the most senior military officer during the war, Truman's chief of staff, and the first naval officer to ever receive five stars. He was at the center of all major military decisions during the war. He reported only to the president.

Admiral Leahy called the bombings a "barbaric act." He said, "In being the first to use it, we had adopted an ethical standard common to the barbarians of the Dark Ages."[24]

However, it wasn't a barbaric act to the economic power elite. They knew that Truman was protecting and enhancing its financial interests by kick-starting a Cold War with the Soviets.

The editors of the nation's top business magazine, *Business Week*, knew what the economic elite had in mind when the magazine came up with the following headline on March 22, 1946: "New Democracy, New Business: U.S. Drive to Stop Communism Abroad Means Heavy Financial Outlays for Bases, Relief, and Reconstruction. But in Return, American Business is Bound to Get New Markets Abroad."

Two pre-bomb events may have influenced Truman's decision to use nuclear bombs as a propaganda weapon to kick-start the Cold War. Both events were related to Middle East oil and the perceived need to take any steps necessary to, as the *Business Week* article noted, "Get New Markets Abroad" in order to fuel what President Eisenhower would later call the military-industrial complex.

The first incident took place in 1944, when an American diplomat visited Saudi Arabia and said the oil there was "the greatest prize in all of history."[25] He wasn't being hyperbolic. His description of Middle East oil made a lot of very wealthy Americans anxious to end the war quickly so they could get on with business. The lust for oil and empire had become irresistible.

A few months later, as a result of the diplomatic visit to Saudi Arabia, President Roosevelt signed an oil-for-security pact with the archconservative king of Saudi Arabia aboard the USS *Quincy* in the Suez Canal. That pact is still in force today.

We pledged in writing to protect the Saudi kingdom from both internal and external enemies in return for access to Middle East oil. We have been working with the Saudis ever since. In fact, the Saudis have secretly funded many of our covert propaganda operations for decades. The Saudi royal family, for example, spent over $70 billion between 1975 and 2002 to spread radical and fundamentalist Wahhabi Islam throughout the world, according to a 2003 article in *U.S. News and World Report.* To spread Wahhabism they set up third-party fronts (a key propaganda technique), such as charities like the Muslim World League and the International Islamic Relief Organizations. The IIRO alone funded 575 mosques just in Indonesia.[26]

During the time that the Saudi royal family was secretly funding and supporting radical Islam, two members of the Bush family, H. W. and George, served as US presidents. Both were very close to the royal family.

George Bush once referred to Saudi Prince Bandar, who spent a lot of time in Texas with the Bush family, as "Bandar Bush." Prior to becoming president, H. W. Bush was CIA director and had become very familiar with the block and bridge and other covert propaganda techniques we were using with the Saudis in the Middle East. This propaganda technique appears to have been used to block the primary focus, Saudi funding of radical Islam and our oil pact with Saudi Arabia, by bridging or shifting the focus to the alleged demonic and barbaric rule of Iran and Iraq leaders and, more recently, to the savagery of radical Islamics, many whom we and/or the Saudis have funded and trained.

"Saudi Arabia's long history as the sugar daddy of Islamic militants around the world didn't complicate their relationship with the U.S. in the past," wrote Carl Gibson in the February 6, 2015, edition of *Reader Supported News.* "In the 1980s, Vice President George H. W. Bush, who had just left his position at the head of the CIA to move into the White House, collaborated with Prince Bandar bin Sultan, Saudi Arabia's ambassador to the U.S., to sell arms to Saudi Arabia at the same time Saudi charities were spending billions on spreading radical Islam."

The February 4, 2015, issue of the *New York Times* reported that imprisoned al-Qaeda operative Zacarias Moussaoui said in a deposition that members of the Saudi royal family were financiers of terrorism in the Middle East and that he was directed in the late nineties by al-Qaeda leaders in Afghanistan to maintain a computer file on donors. He said that list included the head of Saudi intelligence operations, Prince Bandar, and a prominent billionaire investor, plus many top Saudi clerics.

A few years after the discovery of "the greatest prize in history," after the oil-for-security pact with Saudi Arabia, after the dropping of the nuclear bombs, and after Senator Vandenberg's dictum to scare the American people, the FBI, the CIA, and other covert operators aggressively unleashed an anti-Communist propaganda campaign in the United States and in numerous other countries, such as Iran, Guatemala, and Cuba.

Were these incidents connected? In each case, we used anticommunism as a scare tactic to increase and protect the financial interests of the economic power elite. Truman knew no one could stop us. And he wasn't the least bit shy about touting our intentions. Truman revealed the economic motive for this country's Cold War/anti-Communist drive when he said in a March 6, 1946, speech in Waco, Texas, that: "The United States is the giant of the economic world" and would therefore "determine the future pattern of economic relations."[27]

To dominate and control economic relations worldwide after World War II would require aggressive covert propaganda, that is, an invisible government. President Wilson's Committee on Public Information (CPI) had brought together for the first time propagandists, journalists, business leaders, historians, and academics.

Many of these relationships established during World War I were still intact when the Cold War was unleashed after World War II.

CHAPTER 2

The Ultimate Marriage

IN 1939 NEW YORK HOSTED the World's Fair. Edward Bernays, the pioneer propagandist I referenced earlier, was a key consultant to the fair. He recommended that the theme for the fair should establish a link between democracy and American business. To establish this connection, Bernays named a large white dome at the center of the fair "DemocraCity."

Bernays's daughter, Anne, has said: "To my father the World's Fair was an opportunity to keep the status quo. That is, capitalism in a democracy, democracy and capitalism and that marriage. He did that by manipulating people and getting them to think that you couldn't have real democracy in anything but a Capitalist society."[1]

The statement about marrying capitalism and democracy by manipulating the people and getting the public to think you couldn't have real democracy in anything but a Capitalist society is one of the most important quotes in this book because implanting that concept in the mass mind has been one of the primary successes of the mass mind manipulation campaign. Bernays, ironically, was not only involved in promoting the marriage of capitalism and democracy, but in creating and promoting the famous phrase "Make the World Safe for Democracy."

Aldous Huxley warned in his 1958 nonfiction book *Brave New World Revisited* that "by ever more effective methods of mind manipulation, democracies will change their nature; the quaint old forms—elections, parliaments, Supreme Courts and all the rest—will remain. The underlying substance will be a new kind of totalitarianism. All the traditional names, all the hallowed slogans will remain exactly what they were in the good old days. Democracy and freedom will be the theme of every broadcast and editorial."[2]

Huxley was astute enough to recognize that a mind manipulation campaign was underway in the fifties, a campaign that Bernays and his propaganda cohorts started decades earlier. In the above quote, Huxley predicted that a ruling oligarchy and its mind manipulators and thought manufacturers would attempt to bring about the marriage of democracy and capitalism. His prediction has come true.

Bernays and his propaganda partners have worked many decades to implant the marriage between capitalism and democracy/freedom into the mass mind, so much so that to challenge this concept is just about heresy. Calling capitalism antidemocratic is a line in the sand we definitely learn not to cross.

The statement by Bernays's daughter, who is a respected novelist and educator, reflects as well as anything the importance of anticommunism as a smokescreen for the primary goal of growing and protecting the financial interests of the economic power elite.

Bernays wrote a book in the twenties called *Propaganda*. He emphatically stated that there is an "invisible government" in America in the employ of the economic power elite that is secretly "pulling the wires" (as he put it) to manipulate our thoughts and behavior. He should know. He and the early propagandists, with help from psychologists, sociologists, and motivational researchers, such as Sigmund Freud, developed propaganda techniques that are still employed today. Bernays was the nephew of Freud, the founder of psychoanalysis. Freud completely changed how science perceived the mind. Bernays, Byoir, and other early propagandists developed propaganda techniques that were built on Freud's theories.[3]

Freud claimed he had discovered primitive and sexual forces hidden inside our minds. If not controlled, he believed these forces would cause individual and mass chaos and destruction.

Not only was Freudian theory important to covert propagandists; so were later theories, such as Abraham Maslow's hierarchy of needs and the me-oriented theories of the self-help, human potential movement. Bernays was the first person to take Freud's ideas about human beings and use them to manipulate the masses. Bernays and the early propagandists believed in a trickle-down democracy, not the kind of democracy our forefathers envisioned. They believed, as Freud taught them, that the masses were primitive and largely uneducated and had irrational urgings. Most importantly, Freud taught them that the masses needed to be controlled by an enlightened elite.

President Wilson, once president of Princeton University, was the epitome of the economic power elite. Bernays, who himself became very wealthy, was a PR consultant and close confidant to Wilson, so much so that the president invited him to the Paris Peace Conference.

Bernays later said that while at the conference, he came to the conclusion that if you could use propaganda for war, you could use it during peacetime.

The BBC had an excellent series in 2002 that explored the seventies' shift from the socially oriented civil rights and antiwar movements of the late fifties and sixties to the self-help, me-oriented, find-oneself, human potential movements that started in the seventies. The series was called *The Century of the Self.* It focused on how the work of Bernays, Freud, and others influenced the way propagandists, corporations, and governments have analyzed, dealt with, and "controlled" people.

One key thing covert propagandists did was to help co-opt and diffuse the civil rights and antiwar movements by shifting public opinion toward a more me-oriented focus. The self-help, human potential movements didn't magically arise out of thin air. They were created and/or encouraged by covert propagandists, whose charge was to protect the financial interests of the economic power elite.

The elite didn't want an aware, critically thinking, and potentially disruptive populace. They wanted a public that would acquiesce to the status quo and would support their agendas. They wanted a public that would espouse a "my country right or wrong" mantra and who would tell dissenters to "love it or leave it."

They didn't want radicals or people who took to the streets to voice their concerns. Instead they wanted docile, passive people who would be more concerned with mowing the lawn, making money, consuming, keeping up with the Joneses, and pursuing pleasure. They also didn't want poor people and/or people of color pounding the streets for racial or economic equality.

One of the leading journalists and thinkers of the twentieth century, Walter Lippmann, was also a strong believer in an elite group of people leading the masses. In his book *Public Opinion* (1922), Lippmann referred to the majority of us as "a bewildered herd" who "drug themselves with pleasure."[4] Lippmann maintained that the country needed an elite ruling class to manage and control this confused and overwhelmed herd. Control of the masses by the elite, he believed, could best be done by using motivational and psychological techniques that would penetrate and influence the subconscious.

Lippmann realized that this control of the mass mind could be accomplished by the manipulation of symbols, fantasies, myths, and stereotypes (a word he coined). Lippmann defined stereotype as "a distorted picture or image in a person's mind, not based on personal experience, but derived culturally."

Lippmann also noted in *Public Opinion* that "the only feeling that anyone can have about an event he does not experience is the feeling aroused by his mental image of that event." It's the covert propagandist's role to create these pictures and mental images.

These mental images, once firmly established in one's mind or in public opinion, can be very resistant to scrutiny or change and can be passed down from generation to generation.

Lippmann, Bernays, Byoir, and others began enlisting psychologists, psychiatrists, motivational researchers, and others to explore how the brain works so they could tap into the human mind for social control. This was the start of the thought control campaign.

This post–World War I research went on for several decades. It was disrupted for a while during World War II, but was restarted with a vengeance after the war, when our covert agencies began extensive mind control campaigns, which they secretly unleashed on an unwitting American public.

While Freudian theory motivated many of the earlier propagandists, other scientists have had an influence on developing mind control techniques. Swiss psychiatrist Carl Jung said that "in each of us there is another whom we do not know."[5] Jung was describing the subconscious, which is a fertile testing ground for motivational researchers and propagandists. Most of us believe that the conscious is the center of the brain, but neuroscience has shown that "the conscious mind is not the center of the action in the brain" and that "there is a chasm between what the brain knows and what our minds can fathom," as neuroscientist David Eagleman has noted.[6]

This chasm exists because of the lag between perception and conscious awareness. There are 400 billion bits of information a second processed by the brain, but we have awareness of only two thousand bits per second. By the time we're aware of anything, it's in the past. What does this time lag mean for reality? It means that if our thoughts and awareness are always in the past, then reality, as Einstein said, is just an illusion.

Immanuel Kant pointed out that what we see as reality is merely how things appear to us, not how things are in and of themselves. If Einstein and Kant are correct (and no one has proved they're not), then it's no surprise that illusion, like stereotypes, myths, symbols, and fantasies, is fertile ground for covert propagandists.

Just as a magician manipulates reality to create and/or exploit illusions, covert propagandists exploit the limits of our senses, our tendencies to feel first and think second, and our psychological reliance on symbols, myths, stereotypes, fantasies, and illusions as substitutes for reality. They can manipulate us all they want, and we won't know it because illusions trump reality, particularly illusions molded by invisible people working in near-total secrecy.

Most of us have been taught to deal in the world of facts and reality. But Nietzsche said there are no facts, just interpretations based on loosely held opinions. If facts are just interpretations and reality is an illusion, then it's not surprising that an army of lecherous covert propagandists are hovering around us like a swarm of locusts to manipulate facts and illusions.

Propagandists learned long ago, as did magicians, that things aren't always as they appear. For those who still doubt there's been mass mind molding in this country, here are the words from Bernays himself:

> We are governed, our minds are molded, our tastes formed, our ideas suggested, largely by men we have never heard of (or seen). Those who manipulate this unseen mechanism of society constitute an invisible government which is the true ruling power of our country.[7]

He wasn't being hyperbolic or metaphoric. He was describing a reality that has been hidden from the American public for nearly a century.

Besides secrecy, another reason covert propaganda is difficult to detect is that effective propaganda typically avoids facts. Instead, good covert propaganda targets our innermost needs and desires and emotions, particularly fear. That is why a lot of covert propaganda is designed to scare us. Some readers might say to themselves that they aren't fearful of many things and, besides, they are too intelligent to be manipulated. We all have fears, even some we don't know we have.

Intelligent people are often the easiest to propagandize because they have a tendency to analyze things. Analysis doesn't work with covert propaganda because it's practiced in secret by invisible propagandists. How can you analyze or think about what they're doing if you don't know who they are, where they work, what they are doing, or what their agenda is?

Some might find it inconceivable that our government would wage what amounts to a thought control war against its own people, but there's evidence I will reveal later that we are considered "the enemy" in "a just war" by some involved in covert propaganda and surveillance activities. In such a war, these covert intelligence operatives and propagandists believe that the ends justify the means.

For example, Iraqi troops allegedly stormed a Kuwaiti hospital and, in what was called "a savage and barbaric act," threw newborn babies from their incubators and left them to die on a hospital floor.[8] This so-called act of savagery was a planned and rehearsed tear-jerking lie told before a congressional caucus by the teenage daughter of the Kuwait ambassador to the United States, although she was not identified as being part of the royal family. The ruse, which I will unveil in a later chapter, was disinformation and false-flag propaganda in its purest form and was used by the H. W. Bush administration to garner US support for the Gulf War.

Ironically, the words "savage" and "barbaric" and derivations of them are being used frequently in US media during the war on terrorism some thirty years after the Gulf War hoaxes. We also used those terms to label Native American Indians, blacks, and others we wished to demonize. See chapter 11, "Language and Propaganda."

Arousing emotions, particularly fear and hate, becomes of paramount importance prior to and during wars, but our emotions have also been manipulated often during peaceful times. Political scientist and communications theorist Harold Lasswell predicted in the thirties that millions of human beings could be welded into "one amalgamated mass of hate" with "the new hammer and anvil of propaganda."[9]

How many false-flag incidents have been employed to weld us into an "amalgamated mass of hate" using the hammer and anvil of propaganda? Unfortunately, the answer is that our government has engineered numerous false-flag incidents for decades.

• • •

Covert propaganda in America has been conducted primarily by propagandists who work for various covert government agencies and for the economic power elite and its business/financial interests. Educators, politicians, motivational researchers, some law enforcement, and even organized crime and drug kingpins have participated in this mass onslaught on our senses, some knowingly, some unknowingly.

Private intelligence agencies and fronts have also been involved. Participants in the invisible government don't gather in back rooms and conspire to manipulate the American people. They don't have to conspire or plot.

The parameters of thought and behavior and the lines in the sand we learn not to cross were established decades ago. They're embedded in the mass mind and in public opinion. The role of the invisible government today is to keep us in the status quo sandbox.

To do that requires secrecy and numerous covert operations, ranging from propaganda to surveillance. While I'm concerned primarily with the role of propaganda, surveillance also plays an important role in mind manipulation because they both have the same goal—to establish a fear of consequences.

The two together, if they remain cloaked in near-total secrecy, are an extremely powerful force that has the potential to destroy our democracy. Bernays, one of the founders of the invisible government, said:

> In almost every act of our daily lives, whether in the sphere of politics or business, in our social conduct or our ethical thinking, we are dominated by the relatively small number of persons who understand the mental processes and social patterns of the masses. It is they who pull the wires which control the public mind.[10]

Even before Bernays began working his magic on the American people, the elite was laying the groundwork for establishing an invisible government. President Theodore Roosevelt warned at the turn of the century that "behind the ostensible governments sits enthroned an invisible government owing no allegiance and acknowledging no responsibility to the people. To destroy this invisible government, to dissolve the unholy alliance between corrupt business and corrupt politics, is the first task of the statesmanship of the day."[11]

Roosevelt's first task of statesmanship never came true. Not only was the invisible government not dissolved; it grew much stronger during and after World War I. It became firmly in entrenched after World War II and during the Cold War.

Today the invisible government is not only entrenched; it clandestinely controls much of what happens in this country and worldwide. This "invisible government" Bernays and others have described was also examined by Tom Engelhardt in his 2014 book *Shadow Government*. It is also pointed out in a 1964 book by Tom Ross and David Wise, *The Invisible Government.*[12]

These authors describe a secret government of covert agencies embedded inside the visible government. Engelhardt points out that we now have a federal government that keeps just about all important information classified and "in the shadows."

I'll provide names and proof of an invisible government and its activities, not so much from an intelligence or surveillance perspective, but from a propaganda perspective, so that readers will be able to at least get a glimpse of the shadowy world covert propagandists inhabit.

Secrecy, no matter whether it protects propaganda, surveillance, or intelligence activities, gives covert operatives separation from the American people, Congress, and even the president. It was set up that way.

By some of their activities not being answerable to visible government leaders, these covert operatives give our leaders plausible deniability. As I have noted, this is an important propaganda technique. It has been used for nearly a century by leaders from presidents on down so they can claim not to know about a covert activity that might be exposed. Few covert activities ever see the light of day, and those that do are usually heavily redacted.

Covert propaganda has been so successful in this country that even major issues like the Middle East wars, police violence against people of color, and economic inequality barely register on most people's radar, and even if there is public ire, it usually subsides quickly.

In short, we have been so propagandized and co-opted that we don't even know it.

While we've been busy going to school, working at jobs, and raising families, covert propagandists have spent entire careers studying and implementing the most effective ways to manipulate and mold the mass mind. They have over fifty key propaganda techniques in their current arsenal, and they aren't shy about using them because they consider themselves warriors in "a just war." Covert propagandists have mastered thought control. I'm going to show you how throughout the book.

• • •

As I pointed out in the first chapter, the modern covert thought control campaign was kicked off with the June 1, 1951, meeting of covert operatives to discuss Operation Bluebird, which became the MK-ULTRA mind control project.[13]

That meeting was followed by the July meeting of covert propagandists for the CIA and the intelligence divisions of the army, navy, air force, and FBI to explore coordination of mind control research. In 1953 CIA director Allen Dulles stated that "propaganda, censorship and mass indoctrination" were needed "in the battle for men's minds."[14]

How far our government was willing to go in its covert activities was made crystal clear in a highly secretive September 1954 memorandum to President Eisenhower, in which it was pointed out that "there are no rules in such a game. Hitherto acceptable norms of human conduct do not apply. No one should be permitted to stand in the way of the prompt, efficient, and secure accomplishment of this mission (covert actions); long-standing American concepts of 'fair play' must be reconsidered."[15]

Some may dismiss these recommendations for aggressive covert actions as an understandable reaction to the anti-Communist paranoia of the fifties. That's partially true, but anticommunism was used as a propaganda scare tactic long before the fifties.

Propagandists began playing the anti-Communist card to demonize the labor movement during the latter part of the nineteenth century. Carl Byoir teamed with J. Edgar Hoover to disseminate Red Scare propaganda after World War I. In short, anticommunism was used as a propaganda tool long before the Cold War.

The 1954 memorandum to Eisenhower represented a major change in focus for our covert and surveillance operations. Most importantly, it took ethical or moral considerations off the table for covert activities. It set the stage for future leaders like Vice President Dick Cheney to respond "absolutely" with a straight face when asked by a reporter if "anything goes" in the so-called war on terror.

This "no rules" philosophy has justified covert excesses up to the present, ranging from spying on deaf, mute, and blind humanitarian Helen Keller to doing everything possible to demonize and destroy civil rights leader Martin Luther King.

This "no rules" dictum also showed up in FBI and CIA covert mind manipulation programs, such as COINTELPRO and MK-ULTRA, and in the super-secret realm of covert propaganda and special operations run by agencies such as the Special Operations Command (SOCOM), which has elite Special Forces and propagandists in the United States and 134 countries.

I will note later how the head of SOCOM, an agency most have never heard of, has its operatives in thirty-eight agencies throughout our government: from the CIA to the FBI to NSA to the Defense Intelligence Agency.

Another outgrowth of the 1954 memo, which was based on a study of covert activities, has been the proliferation in recent years of paramilitary organizations described in the study report referenced above.

Paramilitary organizations in the United States have taken on numerous forms since that secret document, but a paramilitary focus has raised its ugly head in recent years with the increased militarization of law enforcement, even in small towns. The most recent example is the militarization of police in Ferguson, Missouri.

The 1954 report made it perfectly clear that covert leaders believed Americans needed to be convinced that giving up some of our freedoms was necessary and an acceptable trade-off for the survival of our country.

Here's what one of the clandestine operatives wrote in the 1954 report: "It may become necessary that the American people be made acquainted with, understand and support this fundamentally repugnant philosophy (giving up our freedoms in the name of security)."[16]

How do you make the American people understand and support this "repugnant philosophy"? You do it through mass persuasion, that is, propaganda. Ironically, this same rationale of giving up freedom for security is exactly what is being asked of us today in the war on terror.

What's significant is not just that our covert operatives have adopted many repugnant activities under the cover of protecting us, but that these clandestine manipulators have hidden their operations from the American people. They did this by creating a secret realm, in which they can do whatever they like without us knowing it.

Since establishing its covert operations in the fifties, our clandestine operatives have fought any attempt to make their activities more transparent. There are several reasons for that. One reason is that covert operations depend on secrecy. Another reason is that our covert agencies do a lot more than gather intelligence and conduct surveillance.

A strong argument will be made in this book that intelligence gathering and surveillance are secondary roles and smokescreens for the primary role, which is to protect and grow the financial interests of the economic power elite. The economic elite need secrecy to keep the American public in the dark.

Some may wonder what militarization of police, stirring up dissent, false-flag events, or other police, military, and intelligence actions have to do with propaganda. Everything.

If an event or action is planned and executed with the intent to persuade an individual or group or to influence attitudes and behavior (such as through fear), it is propaganda. I call this type of propaganda "the engineering of dissent."

This technique involves deliberately stirring up dissent in order to later discredit, degrade, diffuse, deny, demonize, dehumanize, disrupt, or destroy the dissenters, whether individuals, groups, or governments. I'll give numerous examples.

Many people will reject the reality that they are victims of a highly secretive mass mind molding and manipulation. No one likes to be taken advantage of or, to use an old Southern cliché, to have "the wool pulled over our eyes." I feel that same way. I don't like being manipulated, and despite decades of experience in the propaganda business, I often get fooled, primarily because those conducting the propaganda operate in near-total secrecy. One thing I know for sure: these covert operatives have spent many years researching the latest psychological, social, and motivational techniques to mold and manipulate the mass mind.

In the following pages, I'm going to provide you with numerous examples of covert propaganda. I, by the way, didn't invent the word "covert." It's part of official government policy.

The Department of Defense has a publication called the "Dictionary of Military and Associated Terms (amended through March, 2015)." It defines "covert operations" as those that "are planned and executed to conceal the identity of or permit plausible denial by the sponsor." In other words, covert operations are specifically designed to "conceal" or hide the truth. If we get too close to the truth, they deploy the propaganda technique of "plausible denial," which usually involves the propaganda technique of "disinformation," a euphemism for lying.

Covert propagandists are highly trained artisans who sit at the pottery wheel of the elite and secretly shape us into what the elite want us to become, much as a ceramic artist or potter sculpts supple clay into a desired shape. We're the clay. Covert propagandists are the potters working on consignment from the elite.

The purpose of this book is to expose some of the techniques these covert propagandists use to mold our thoughts and behavior. Knowledge of these techniques hopefully will allow you to protect yourself as much as possible from propaganda's onslaught on your senses.

Nearly a century of secret, behind-closed-doors propaganda and surveillance has taken our country away from us. We, the people, need to reclaim it. True democracy depends on it.

CHAPTER 3

"SOAP" for the Mind

CHURCHGOERS LISTENING TO THEIR MINISTERS' sermons have likely never suspected that they might be listening to propaganda messages. Religion is one of the oldest forms of propaganda. The primary role of religion is to persuade, that is, to influence our attitudes and behavior. Religion also educates or informs, but a minister who's not adept at persuasion or "selling God" won't last long.

A March 1954 issue of *Public Relations Journal* had an article on how "smart" preachers use good communication techniques to fill their pews and "to maintain a strong financial condition." Preachers were urged to find what "clicked" with their congregation and then to employ "a dignified communications approach." Good communications often involves appealing to our emotions. Our emotions, not our rationality, are often the key target of religion and effective propaganda.[1]

As a teen my favorite minister was Billy Graham. He was obviously a firm believer in his religion, yet he rose to the top of his profession not just because of his faith, but also because of his ability to arouse our emotions and, as the *Public Relations Journal* suggested, sell God. Hundreds of thousands of people were reduced to tears at his Crusade for Christ services.

In most cases religion is open/overt propaganda because you know the source. This kind of propaganda is not dangerous as long as you recognize that it is propaganda since it's trying to persuade you. What is dangerous is propaganda where you don't know the source or the agenda.

The overwhelming success of propaganda in America is due to the fact that few people understand what it is and how it works. There are a lot of powerful people who want to keep it that way.

The producers of propaganda learned long ago that power, primarily power to protect profits and positions of influence, is best obtained by covert actions that prevent us from recognizing that we are even being manipulated in any way. Propaganda has become so sophisticated in this country that we often don't even realize we've been propagandized.

As I've noted, I'm going to give examples of numerous propaganda techniques. These techniques fall under two primary types of propaganda: overt (open) and covert (secret). There are three subsets of covert propaganda: black, gray, and white propaganda. Black propaganda provides one source, but is really from another source. Gray propaganda provides no source. Both black and gray propaganda are very difficult to detect because they're deliberately designed to prevent us from knowing the true source. White propaganda doesn't hide the source, but it's often still covert because the propaganda is so open that it often isn't even recognized as propaganda.

For example, sometimes the very high-speed nature of modern communications technologies, such as smartphones, video games, film, and the Internet, can propagandize us just by their overuse, without the propagandist having to do much of anything. He or she can just sit back and let high-speed media work its white propaganda magic. This type of propaganda, which exploits the very nature of communications tools, usually involves one or more of four propaganda techniques: sensory overload, obfuscation, awareness diversion, and the pursuit of pleasure.

You can remember these by the acronym SOAP. "S" stands for sensory overload. "O" stands for obfuscation. "A" stands for awareness diversion. "P" stands for pursuit of pleasure.

SOAP, if you will excuse the metaphor, is an excellent way for propagandists to wash away critical thinking. I'll go into more detail and give examples of these SOAP techniques later in this chapter and throughout the book.

• • •

There are, of course, other things that influence our attitudes and behavior besides propaganda, but propaganda plays a major, if not the primary, role. Isolated, propaganda rarely has a major effect on individuals. It does, however, have a long-term influence on public opinion and the mass mind, which, in turn, influences us as individuals. Covert propaganda affects all of us—and much more than we realize. In fact, mind molding and mass persuasion have largely defined who we are, what we believe, and how we act.

Some may wonder about the connection between propaganda and surveillance. Surveillance by its very nature creates a climate of conformity and self-censorship because of our fear of consequences. Covert propaganda does the same thing.

Journalist and author Glenn Greenwald, who is one of the world's leading experts on clandestine surveillance, wrote in his best-selling 2014 book *No Place to Hide* that privacy is of paramount importance to our happiness and freedom. "People radically change their behavior when they know they are being watched. They will strive to do that which is expected of them. They want to avoid shame and condemnation. They do so by adhering tightly to accepted social practices, by staying within imposed boundaries, avoiding actions that might be seen as deviant or abnormal."[2]

Greenwald says the primary goal of surveillance is to keep us within "imposed boundaries." Propaganda defines those imposed boundaries. Surveillance keeps us inside the boundaries.

The extensive use of covert propaganda and surveillance is a powerful combination. This duo may be the most powerful weapon ever devised for controlling public opinion and for creating a malleable mass mind. Just as our government hopes that the threat of nuclear weapons will instill fear of retaliation among our enemies, covert propaganda and surveillance keep potential domestic dissenters from crossing certain lines in the sand for fear of the consequences.

Greenwald claims in his book that we're not free to forge our own path as long as we know we are always being watched or judged. He also points out that all oppressive authorities use the fear of consequences and the knowledge of being watched or judged to bring about allegiance to the status quo and to stifle dissent.

Greenwald and others have provided proof that the National Security Agency and other government covert agencies, plus their numerous private surveillance contractors, have gone to great lengths in recent years to control our Internet behavior. For example, NSA's Project X-KEYSCORE is a program that lets intelligence operatives see just about everything we do online in real time. They can see your e-mails, your social media communications, and your Google searches. They can also observe your visit to websites. They can even see the words you are typing. Even more ominous, they can tap into your private conversations as you talk on your cell phone and can listen to private conversations in your home while your cell phone is turned off.

The FBI, according to an October 29, 2014 article in the *Guardian*, has a program called "Network Investigative Techniques."[3] This program, which is being considered as of this writing by an obscure regulatory agency, would give the FBI more powers to hack into computers and carry out surveillance.

Among other things, it would allow the agency to clandestinely install malicious software, or malware, onto a computer that, in turn, would let federal agents effectively control the computer, downloading all its digital contents, switching its camera or microphone on or off, and even taking over other computers in its network.

It's not just the FBI involved in surveillance. The *Wall Street Journal* reported on November 13, 2014, that the Justice Department is overseeing a program in which government-owned airplanes are covertly flying around the country as part of a mass surveillance program that has been kept secret from the public for years. According to the *Wall Street Journal* article, the US Marshals Service has a fleet of Cessna airplanes that are armed with high-tech surveillance gear called "dirt boxes." These are essentially fake cell towers that can trick your phone into connecting to them, and they can then identify the owners and locations of tens of thousands of phones in a single flight.[4]

The Department of Homeland Security (DHS) has a program that can cut off all cell phone activity unilaterally. It's called Standard Operating Procedure (SOP) 303. This cell phone kill switch, as it is sometimes called, was developed in secrecy without any public input. It was put into action in August 2011 when cell phone service was cut off in subway stations in the San Francisco area to quell a demonstration against Bay Area Rapid Transit (BART) for the killing of someone by a BART police officer.[5] In other words, the cell kill switch was used to stop a demonstration. It wasn't because of a terrorist threat.

This book isn't primarily about surveillance and Big Brother, but is about propaganda, particularly covert propaganda. Unfortunately, secrecy permeates not only propaganda and surveillance, but many other government activities. Some might rationalize these intrusions on their privacy by saying they have nothing to hide. They might not have anything to hide, but they have a lot to lose: freedom and democracy. Are we truly free if we are under surveillance?

The key point, however, isn't whether or not we are being watched or listened to, but that the potential of being watched or monitored is enough to keep us from crossing the lines in the sand for fear of the consequences.

That is what surveillance is about: fear. Fear is also the cornerstone of covert propaganda. In propaganda circles this fear of consequences is called the "engineering of consent." Bernays introduced this key propaganda technique shortly after World War I. Subsets of this technique are consensus and conformity propaganda and self-censorship. If we get bombarded enough with conformity/consensus propaganda, we soon latch onto self-censorship without even knowing that is what happened.

Many might say to themselves that they are too smart to be molded or manipulated. That's what a good propagandist wants you to say because research has shown that you will feel superior to a message if you believe it has no influence on you. Once you feel superior to a message, you actually trust it more, not less. Why? Because if you believe you have control over a message, you will react more favorably to it than if the message talks down to you.

Educators and so-called intellectuals are easy prey for propaganda because they believe their "inquiring minds" make them more than capable of judging things themselves. Their rationality and reasoning skills often backfire on them when the propagandist exercises the "end run" propaganda technique, which entails bypassing rationality and appealing to our emotions and innermost needs and desires. Intellectuals often don't realize it, but they, like everyone else, have emotions and are vulnerable to the manipulation of symbols, stereotypes, myths, illusions, and a propaganda technique known as "emotionally laden words."

Often the emotional makeup of intellectuals is even weaker and more vulnerable to propaganda than the average person's. Propaganda involves much more than simply changing attitudes and opinions. Oftentimes it is used to intensify existing opinions, beliefs, and trends.

Propaganda is sometimes used to encourage people to do nothing. Intellectuals often fall for the propaganda technique of obfuscation, which, in simple terms, throws so much complex and often conflicting information at us that we simply don't have time to digest it all.

Many intellectuals, particularly in academia, become specialists. They're often very adept at seeing the trees in the forest, but sometimes they can't see the forest for the trees because they are so immersed in their specialty. Another reason intellectuals have trouble deciphering propaganda is that much of it is done in secret. Many of us know scientists, teachers, researchers, journalists, laborers, architects, and so on, but how many know a propagandist?

By "propagandist," I don't mean someone who works in media or advertising or public relations. Most of these people know little, if anything, about propaganda, particularly the closed or covert propaganda this book is about. Covert propaganda is not a subject taught in college. Journalists and other communications professionals often help implement propaganda, but the vast majority is unwitting or unknowing implementers of mass manipulation programs devised by backroom persuasion experts.

Terrance Qualter, a leading propaganda researcher, has said, "It's impossible to understand the success of propaganda without also understanding how great a part of what men regard as knowledge is in fact no more than a collection of stereotypes."[6]

Propagandists learned long before social scientists and other researchers got in on the act that prejudices, symbols, and stereotypes play a key role in the decision-making process.

Walter Lippmann used "stereotype" to describe the knowledge we think we have of things: the knowledge based on myths, dreams, and fantasies, as distinct from factual knowledge.[7] Lippmann knew that popular passions, religious, racial, or regional traditions, national pride, and other abstract feelings were often more real to people than actual reality.

What Lippmann wrote is key to understanding propaganda. A good propagandist doesn't worry about facts. He or she knows from decades of psychological, motivational, and social research that most people, including the highly educated, often confuse facts with opinions and interpretations of fact.

Philosopher Friedrich Nietzsche said opinion is thought largely based on vanity and hubris, not necessarily based on fact. "There are no facts, only interpretations," he stated.[8]

We often stick to an opinion because we pride ourselves on having come to it on our own or because we have taken great pains to learn it and are proud to have grasped it, and so both come out of vanity, Nietzsche said. He noted that people will often give their opinions freely without necessarily knowing the source. They think the source is in their own head. It's their opinion, after all. They own it, like a piece of property. But when you question them about it, you discover that they cannot tell you how they arrived at their opinion. They cannot even tell you the facts behind their opinion. Very often what facts they can cite are wrong or questionable in some way.

Propaganda encourages people to rely on loosely held interpretations and opinions. These interpretations and opinions are often based on the symbols, stereotypes, myths, and prejudices that propagandists manipulate as substitutes for critical thought and knowledge.

Victor Marchetti, a veteran CIA intelligence agent, said not long ago that clandestine operatives often consider the American people "the enemy" because revelations of the activities of clandestine operatives are perceived as a threat to their ability to operate in secret.

"They don't want us, the people, to interfere. The effectiveness of their programs, they believe, is based on us not knowing about their activities,"[9] Marchetti noted.

"When the public does not know what the government or the CIA is doing, it cannot voice its approval or disapproval of their actions," Marchetti said. "In fact, they (the CIA) can even lie to you about what they are doing or have done, and you will not know it."

If the American people are considered the enemy by our own government, then we are victims of a secret war that we don't even know we're fighting.

Bernays, as I noted earlier, said those engineering this secret war work for an "invisible government." Bernays, according to his memoirs, was keenly interested in how propaganda could be used to manipulate our thoughts and behavior. Bernays was remarkably candid about his manipulative intent: "If we understand the mechanisms and motives of the group mind, it is now possible to control and regiment the masses according to our will without their knowing it," he argued in *Propaganda,* one of his first books.[10]

He also coined the term "engineering of consent" to describe his propaganda technique for controlling the masses.

"Bernays used psychological techniques to mask the motives of his clients, as part of a deliberate strategy aimed at keeping the public unconscious of the forces that were working to mold their minds," according to a review of *The Father of Spin: Edward L. Bernays & The Birth of PR* by Larry Tye.[11]

• • •

Bernays was an expert at covert mind manipulation techniques. For example, he helped the CIA overthrow a democratically elected government in Guatemala (I will give details later).

He also was involved in numerous open and overt propaganda programs, such as the campaign he conceived and conducted in the twenties to remove the "loose morals" stigma from women smoking. A case can be made that this kick-started the women's liberation movement. A woman smoking was frowned upon as unladylike during that period, so Bernays devised a propaganda campaign to make smoking a sign of freedom and liberation. The campaign worked marvelously.

In 1929 Bernays sent a group of young models to march in a New York City parade. He then told the press that a group of women's rights marchers would light "torches of freedom." On his signal the models lit a popular brand of cigarettes in front of numerous eager photographers. The *New York Times* (April 1, 1929) wrote, "Group of Girls Puff at Cigarettes as a Gesture of Freedom." This helped to break the taboo against women smoking in public. Previously, women who smoked in public were considered to have "loose morals."[12]

In short, Bernays persuaded woman to embrace smoking as a symbol of women's liberation by disassociating smoking from "loose morals." He was very careful when picking women to march because "while they should be good looking, they should not look too model-y." He hired his own photographers to make sure that good pictures were taken and then published around the world.

This campaign was an open, overt form of propaganda. Bernays did not hide that he was working for a tobacco company or promoting a brand of cigarettes, but he didn't make an issue of it. He rarely even mentioned the cigarette brand. He was selling smoking.

His goal was to make smoking credible for women. He did this by using classy, wholesome models to disassociate loose morals from women smokers. This campaign, and variances on it, went on for a long time, and eventually the connection between women smoking and loose morals vanished. Disassociation had worked. Women were smoking as freely as men.

The side effect to smoking as a symbol of liberation was addiction to a habit that killed millions of women, including my mother, who had lung cancer. She smoked the same cigarette brand whose manufacturer financed Bernays's propaganda campaign.

My mother had no idea that she likely became addicted to smoking because of a massive mind manipulation campaign that she was exposed to as a teen. Bernays's propaganda didn't promote the cigarette brand itself, but the symbolic act of smoking to make one feel like a cool liberated person. That's what good propaganda does—it appeals to our emotions.

Bernays used his engineering-of-consent propaganda technique to give my mother a socially engineered "consent" to smoke. Did my mother have free choice to smoke or not smoke? Sure, but peer pressures and emotional and psychological manipulations often trump free choice.

Bernays's women's liberation smoking campaign is an example of overt, open propaganda. Although most of the nation's media did not mention that the women's smoking campaign was financed by the tobacco industry, it nonetheless was an open, nonsecretive propaganda campaign.

Other propagandists for the tobacco industry followed Bernays's example and used engineering of consent, combined with another propaganda technique, association, to connect smoking with an emotional issue. One brand, for example, had advertisements for many years to associate smoking with "manliness." It was centered on the theme of "man-sized flavor," which obviously has sexual overtones.

Pitchmen for the brand were macho, rugged individualists, such as tall, lean, and tattooed cowboys and fishermen: the true "Marlboro Man." The campaign sucked me in. I smoked Marlboros for ten years before quitting at age thirty. Why Marlboro's? Probably for the same emotional and psychological reason I bought two Volvos: "the thinking man's car." Driving a Volvo and smoking Marlboros made me a true macho thinking man.

I'm sure many male readers might be thinking they escaped the tentacles of propaganda because they didn't fall for the Marlboro or Volvo messages. And female readers might be telling themselves they weren't victims of overt propaganda because they didn't smoke "torches of freedom" or didn't smoke at all. The reality is that most of us reject overt, open propaganda messages some of the time, but few of us escape covert propaganda at any time because we can't recognize it. Before revealing some examples of covert propaganda, let me give a few more examples of open, overt propaganda. And, yes, you, too, have been influenced by these overt examples if you eat bacon and eggs, use a computer, use e-mail, eat sugar, invest in the stock market, support hands-off capitalism, and so on and on.

If you saw a message from a bacon supplier that told you a breakfast of eggs and bacon is healthy, you might take the message with a grain of salt because it is obvious that the advertisement is a self-serving, paid-for message, and you know both products are loaded with cholesterol. However, if you learned that leading physicians and health professionals around the country recommended eating eggs and bacon as part of a hearty, healthy breakfast, you might take the message more seriously.

In order to promote sales of bacon, Bernays conducted a survey of physicians (using physicians he felt would be favorable to his cause) and then sent the results of that survey to over five thousand physicians. He also sent the survey results to media outlets around the country. How well did this campaign work? Decades later my mother often told me when I asked for cereal instead of eggs and bacon, "It is important to eat a hearty breakfast." She used the very same words Bernays used in his propaganda campaign.

Another example of overt propaganda was a campaign I managed in the early eighties while I was worldwide director of communications for ComputerLand Corporation, the world's largest seller of personal computers. We had over seven hundred stores worldwide. One of my responsibilities was to help introduce the American public to the benefits of personal computing. ComputerLand was, in effect, a third-party front (a key propaganda technique) for the few computer manufacturers in those early years, such as IBM and Apple. They used ComputerLand to front for them and to promote the benefits of PCs because ComputerLand was about the only place you could buy a PC in the early eighties. The job of my PR department was to sell the concept and benefits of personal computing, not the product itself. We conducted a massive nationwide media campaign, in which we appealed to people's emotions and desire to be on the cusp of a new wave of technology, by employing two key propaganda techniques: "conformity propaganda," which is a subset of Bernays's engineering of consent, and "bandwagon propaganda," which delivers the message subtly that everyone is doing it, and you should, too.

Still another example of an overt and open propaganda campaign I directed was when the company I founded after leaving ComputerLand, was selected by the International Computer Fax Association (ICFA) to introduce faxes and e-mail to the world in the late eighties.

ICFA was a trade group of twenty or so companies involved in computing, faxes, and e-mail. I spent a few years blanketing the nation's media and some foreign markets with propaganda I devised to promote faxes and e-mail, but everything I did was open and aboveboard. Nothing was covert. The program was so successful that within two years, e-mailing had caught on. Everyone was doing it.

While at Carl Byoir, I worked on some overt propaganda/PR campaigns for Hallmark Cards, Children's Television Workshop (*Sesame Street*), the sugar industry, the road construction industry, the Three Mile Island nuclear disaster, and numerous associations and trade groups for the economic power elite, such as the New York Stock Exchange, the Securities Industry Association (trade group for investment firms), Business Roundtable (made up of CEOs of the top fifty corporations), and the Intellectual Property Owners Association. I'll give details on most of these propaganda campaigns later. I should note that the five business organizations above were the crème de la crème of trade groups for the economic power elite.

These trade groups had a common and consistent propaganda message: lower taxes on investments and income, less government regulation, and a hands-off, anything-goes, Wild West capitalism. We were promoting all the things that benefit the economic elite. Most of the hands-off, laissez-faire, pro-big business propaganda messages we helped spread decades ago have created an atmosphere today in which big business and financial interests are free to do pretty much anything they want. As Bernays did in the smoking campaign, I promoted concepts and ideas, not a product, when I conducted propaganda for computing, faxing, e-mailing, and the interests of the economic elite.

I didn't hide who I was working for, but the press rarely asked, and they rarely gave readers or their listening audience any information on what organization was funding these public relations/propaganda programs.

Most of the projects I worked on were open and overt. However, I've also handled some covert projects. I did some propaganda for Radio Free Europe and Radio Free Liberty (Cuba). Both radio stations were founded and funded by the CIA, although I didn't know it at the time (nor did the public). In other words I handled CIA propaganda and had no idea I was doing so. This happens often. Our clandestine agencies are very adept at setting up fronts and shell organizations so that their involvement is known only to a few.

Not only did I not know the CIA founded and funded the radio stations to conduct its propaganda; I also didn't know that the Crusade for Freedom, a huge national campaign that raised tens of millions of dollars to support the stations, was a front organization designed to provide cover for the CIA by making it appear that the crusade was self-funding when, in reality, it was fully supported by CIA funds. The crusade did not need public money, but it deceived the American public and took advantage of the public's goodwill.

President Eisenhower, members of both legislative branches, and media throughout the country strongly supported and publicized the crusade and spoke often of the need for Americans to support it with their contributions. Crusade officials blanketed the country with news articles, advertisements, brochures, parades, and campaigns to donate "truth dollars."[13]

The Crusade for Freedom campaign was very similar to a World War I-era propaganda campaign that Carl Byoir helped conduct to garner American support for our entry into World War I. The World War I campaign urged Americans to buy "Liberty Bonds." Some of the same propagandists who thought up that slogan, plus slogans such as "Make the World Safe for Democracy," conjured up "truth dollars" in the fifties as a propaganda slogan.

Another thing both campaigns had in common, although nearly forty years apart, was that they both were created and managed mostly in secret. Unfortunately, secret, behind-closed-doors mass mind manipulation has been the modus operandi for most government propaganda during the past century.

• • •

Earlier in this chapter, I introduced the SOAP acronym and noted it includes the propaganda techniques of sensory overload, obfuscation, awareness diversion, and pursuit of pleasure. Sensory overload overwhelms our senses so that we can't think clearly. It often causes us to tune out. Obfuscation makes things so complex and confusing that we also tune out. Awareness diversion involves getting us to multitask so that we can't fully concentrate on one thing or think critically. Pursuit of pleasure gives us permission to immerse ourselves in self-fulfillment and me-oriented thoughts and activities to such an extent that finding pleasure becomes nearly all-consuming and trumps critical thinking. Let's take a brief look at each of these SOAP techniques.

Sensory overload involves bombarding us with so much stimuli that we can't think clearly. Our senses are daily inundated with an unrelenting and steady bombardment of rapid-fire, high-speed information technologies, such as smartphones, personal computers, the Internet, television, and film. These technologies in large doses can overload our limited perceptual abilities just by their very high-speed nature and, thus, influence our attitudes and behavior, particularly by making it difficult to concentrate on any one thing. Sensory overload encourages us to deal with things on the surface instead of digging deep and critically probing for the truth.

An example of sensory overload is the lack of public protests over our numerous overseas conflicts since 9/11. There certainly have been no large-scale, Vietnam era-type protests. Why? Could it be that we have been fighting so many wars that we are tired of even hearing about them, much less taking any action? Have we been numbed by sensory overload to accept "endless wars"?

A top-ranking official in the Obama administration said in the fall of 2014 that we could be fighting the war on terrorism for decades. There was muted reaction to that statement. Have we been bombarded with so much war and violence that we've tuned out?

In addition to the inherent ability of modern information technologies to overwhelm and overload our senses, we often must also deal with a propaganda technique called obfuscation, which usually involves deliberate complexity in order to hide something or to discourage us from delving into details or going beneath the surface on issues. Have you tried reading an Internet user's agreement or a mortgage agreement or any of the myriad agreements we sign? Complex documents are an integral part of legal, government, and corporate life. One benefit of complex documents is that they keep lawyers in business. Another benefit, particularly to propagandists, is that long, complex communications often cause us to tune out because the information is too complex.

Complexity is a great way to hide intent or to cover up something. It's no accident that legislative bills are often hundreds of pages long. Bankers, Wall Street, and corporate lawyers used obfuscation before and during the 2007–2008 banking crisis to make it very difficult for the press, the average person, and prosecutors to know what was going on. The good propagandist can use complexity to hide things, or at the other extreme, he or she can deploy the propaganda of silence, which entails not giving us any information.

Our defensive reaction to complex and confusing information is often to forget what happened in the past because the information is unsettling and difficult to wade through. This often causes us to dwell on the surface of things.

Good propaganda sometimes deliberately overwhelms us and doesn't give us the breathing room to get our bearings. Another way to get us to lose our bearings is to fragment or divide our ideas and/or actions. Fragmentation doesn't just work with individuals; it can also be an effective propaganda tool to control groups through the divide-and-conquer technique.

One of the leading industrial psychologists, Frederick Taylor, taught big business how to diffuse labor unrest in the latter part of the nineteenth century by dividing worker against worker through job specialization. This division of labor, he believed, would fragment the workforce and do away with past forms of labor collectivization, such as the work gang. Fragmentation is a divide-and-conquer, us vs. them, strategy that divides society into groups, such as unions, religions, class, and political parties.

Sensory overload and obfuscation propaganda exceed our capacities for attention, thus our capabilities of resistance. If people aren't paying attention, others will be able to do what they want without us knowing about it. This is the essence of covert propaganda: getting us to not pay attention, and if we are tuned-in, to make sure we are only paying partial attention.

Covert propagandists learned from extensive motivational and mind control research in the fifties, such as the CIA's MK-ULTRA program, that sensory overload and obfuscation can have drug-like, numbing effects. So can the overuse of high-speed communication tools. This is where awareness diversion comes in. Awareness diversion is often combined with sensory overload and obfuscation to create an environment where we're never fully engaged or tuned-in. We're only partially aware of our surroundings. How many people have you seen driving and texting simultaneously or talking on their cell phone while walking or jogging?

This type of limited or incomplete awareness diverts our attention. The less we pay full attention, the less we think critically. The less we think critically, the easier it is for others to think for us.

A 2013 Pew Research Center poll, as reported in the *Wall Street Journal* on December 30, 2014, showed that 79 percent of baby boomers who own mobile phones are texters and that teens sent an average of sixty texts a day in 2011. They text people in their daily lives more than they call, instant message, or e-mail and even more than they socialize in person outside of school.[14]

Neil Postman, American author and media critic, warned in a speech that "information is now a commodity that can be bought and sold, or used as a form of entertainment, or worn like a garment to enhance one's status." Postman pointed out that we are so overloaded with information that we have lost control of it; we don't know what to do with all of it. With an increasing amount of information available, Postman argued that information has become "a form of garbage, not only incapable of answering the most fundamental human questions but barely useful in providing coherent direction to the solution of even mundane problems."[15]

Sensory overload, obfuscation, and awareness diversion are all by-products of high-speed media and modern communications tools and require only passive involvement of covert propagandists. The other SOAP propaganda technique, the pursuit of pleasure, requires a lot more active involvement by covert propagandists.

Pursuit-of-pleasure propaganda was kicked off in earnest during the fifties after extensive mind control research by government covert agencies showed how critical it was in a postwar economy to shift public opinion from a Puritan heritage of conservation, self-sufficiency, and strict ethical standards to a more hedonistic, fun-at-all-costs morality. This new "manufactured" morality was designed to embrace the pursuit of pleasure and the continuous consumption of rapidly obsolete and nonessential consumer items.

The April 1956 issue of the science publication *Motivations* warned: "We are now confronted with the problem of permitting the average American to feel moral even when he is flirting, even when he is spending, even when he is not saving, even when he is taking two vacations a year and buying a second or third car." The article said one of the most important things is to give people justification for having a good time and enjoying life and to show that being hedonistic is not immoral. This permission given to the consumer to enjoy his life freely, the demonstrations that he is right in surrounding himself with products that enrich his life and give him pleasure must be one of the central themes of every advertising display and sales promotion plan.

This permission to enjoy life freely soon became a central theme of all media, from radio, television, and film to print media. It also became a central theme of secret propaganda campaigns. A study of column inches in thirteen major Sunday newspapers showed general news coverage declined from 1939 to 1959, while coverage of both entertainment and leisure activities nearly doubled during the same period. Anyone who doubts this permission to enjoy life is no longer alive and well only needs to go to one of the popular Internet sites like Yahoo or MSN and observe how much of their home-page content is related to entertainment, sexy models, celebrities, and sports and leisure activities.

Modern mass mind manipulation began in earnest in the early fifties and was kick-started with the CIA's MK-ULTRA mind control research. These thought control efforts began at a time when the economic health of the nation depended on people believing that it was moral and not immoral to surround themselves with products and activities that gave pleasure and instant gratification.

In short, it was a time when combined media, prodded and manipulated by covert propagandists, were used to change the American lifestyle and work ethic to accommodate the special interests of the elite and the new technologies it controlled. These new technologies required a workforce that would submit to the tedium and passive involvement of an automated, high-speed work world for five days a week in exchange for two days of leisure and recreation. Pursuit of pleasure was the primary reinforcement offered to make life in a highly technical and automated work world bearable. The pleasure principle was needed to shake the shackles of our Puritan heritage and to make us feel moral in surrounding ourselves with the fruits of pleasure. It has also been offered to make us captive consumers, conditioned through the acquisitive reflex to consume the nonessential items of the leisure and recreation industries.

By the mid-fifties, American culture was inundated with media-induced sanctions and justifications for consumers to surround themselves with products, from leisure goods to fast cars and sex—things that gave status, pleasure, and instant gratification. This permission to enjoy life fully coincided with heavy media emphasis on drugs (particularly alcohol), sex, high-speed travel, gambling, youth rebellion, rock-n-roll, and other sanctions to "enrich" our lives. It's no quirk of history that *Playboy* and similar sex-related magazines started during this period.

Vance Packard, author of *The Hidden Persuaders* (1957), warned of this major push toward the reorganization of society. He pointed out that massive efforts were underway "to channel our unthinking habits, our purchasing decisions, and our thought processes by the use of insights gleamed from psychiatry and the social sciences."[16]

Typically these efforts take place beneath our level of awareness so that the appeals that move us are often, in a sense, "hidden." This trek into the wilderness of the subconscious mind was of immense interest to the economic elite and the CIA. The CIA collaborated during this period with some of the nation's leading media owners and executives, journalists, educators, and public opinion and motivational researchers to learn how sensory anesthetics, including media, sex, drugs, and violence, could be used to influence conscious and subconscious thought processes and patterns of behavior. In programs like MK-ULTRA, the CIA and its collaborators studied how the body absorbs alcohol and how alcohol and other drugs like marijuana, LSD, and cocaine could be used to numb sense perceptions and to stimulate passive and submissive behavior. They looked into the effects of hard drugs like heroin, and, as I will show later, our covert agencies likely either looked the other way (a propaganda technique called "standing down") or helped spread drugs in the United States, particularly in low-income areas.

When we tune in to high-speed communication tools, are we unknowingly tuning out? Numerous studies have shown that high-speed media overstimulate us, which, in turn, can desensitize and numb us, decrease our ability to concentrate, fragment time, and teach us to think in safe and predictable linear patterns that discourage critical thinking.

In summary, too much information can lead to sensory overload. Too much complication can lead to obfuscation. Too much high-speed media can lead to awareness diversion. Too much pursuit of pleasure can drain energy and divert attention from other matters. Too much of all of these, that is, too much SOAP, can wash away democracy.

If I were still a practicing covert propagandist charged with keeping public opinion within acceptable and manageable parameters, I would do everything I could to encourage extensive use of the Internet, smartphones, video games, and other high-speed media, preferably media with a lot of action, violence, and sex. I would also drown people with information, including publishing hundreds of thousands of books and articles each year, including those with conspiracy-theories so that the crying-wolf syndrome would cause a true conspiracy to be suspect and, even if believed by some, to easily be diffused or discredited. Is that strategy being implemented? Are we drowning in democracy?

Covert propagandists learned years ago that the best way to manage a population is not to restrict freedom of speech or expression, but to encourage more expression (within acceptable parameters) in order to create a façade of openness when the primary objective is to drown us with information. In a May 11, 2015, article in *Reuters,* "Not Outraged by NSA Surveillance? You Probably Just Don't Know How Bad It Is," reporter James Bamford notes that there is a secret NSA program known as TREASURE MAP, which allows NSA to basically map the entire Internet (cell phones, laptops, tablets). Why aren't people outraged? Bamford said it's because of what he calls "NSA fatigue."

In other words, there's acceptance of surveillance as "the new normal," the result of a bombardment of news stories on the topic. This is pure sensory overload, just as deaths are front-page news at the beginning of wars, but after a few months they're no longer headlines.

The amount of information available on the Internet is incalculable. In addition, in the United States, there are some 7,240 magazines, some 1,387 daily newspapers, and hundreds of thousands of TV shows, radio programs, and movies produced each year.

In 2013 between six hundred thousand and one million books were published in the United States, depending on which statistics you look at.

In short, we're drowning in information, and our perceptual abilities are being sunk deeper and deeper underwater. Can we ever come up for air?

This massive bombardment on our senses is a propagandist's dream world. The more trees in the forest, the less likely we will see the whole forest. The more choices we have, the more likely it is that we will miss the truly important things. The more information we have, the more difficult it becomes to think clearly and critically. If we can't think clearly, others can think for us. This book is about how others and their technology tools are doing much of our thinking for us and what we can do to minimize the effect.

If others are secretly molding and manipulating our thoughts and behavior and we don't know about it, then we are at their mercy, as Greenwald warned in *No Place to Hide.* That is a threat to us as free people and to our nation as a democracy.

Ironically, the very secrecy that covert operatives and propagandists rely on for their very existence creates a catch-22. They claim to be champions of democracy, but the secrecy they use to obtain this goal is the antithesis of democracy.

CHAPTER 4

Manufacturing Fear and Scaring the Hell Out of Us

CLANDESTINE MASS PERSUASION EXISTS TO protect and enhance the financial interests of the economic power elite. Propagandists will immediately attempt to discredit the phrase "economic power elite" because they don't want the average American to believe there's an elite wealthy class that controls our country.

For those who doubt such an elite ruling class exists, I recommend they read the book *Who Rules America?* by G. William Domhoff. He gives a detailed historical look at how the upper classes have controlled the federal government, the military, the CIA, and the FBI. He says there's a governing upper class that receives "a disproportionate amount of a country's wealth and contributes a disproportionate number of its members to the controlling institutions and key decision making groups in that country."[1]

What Domhoff describes is what I would call an "oligarchic plutocracy." According to the Merriam-Webster dictionary, an oligarchy is government by the few. Plutocracy is "government by the wealthy—a group of very rich people who have a lot of power." As of the spring of 2015, the top one-tenth of 1 percent owned almost as much wealth as the bottom 90 percent, according, Bernie Sanders, the ranking member of the Senate Budget Committee.

Another good book on the elite is *The Power Elite,* written by sociologist C. Wright Mills. Mills calls attention to the interwoven interests of the leaders of the military, corporate, and political elements of society. He suggests that the ordinary citizen is a relatively powerless subject of manipulation by those entities.[2]

This interwoven interests of the military and big business was the theme of the following statement in *Common Sense* magazine (November 1935) from Brigadier General Smedley Butler, one of the most decorated marines in history:

> "I spent 33 years and four months in active military service and during that period I spent most of my time as a high class muscle man for Big Business, for Wall Street and the bankers. In short, I was a racketeer, a gangster for capitalism. I helped make Mexico and especially Tampico safe for American oil interests in 1914. I helped make Haiti and Cuba a decent place for the National City Bank boys to collect revenues in. I helped in the raping of half a dozen Central American republics for the benefit of Wall Street. I helped purify Nicaragua for the International Banking House of Brown Brothers in 1902–1912. I brought light to the Dominican Republic for the American sugar interests in 1916. I helped make Honduras right for the American fruit companies in 1903. In China in 1927 I helped see to it that Standard Oil went on its way unmolested. Looking back on it, I might have given Al Capone a few hints. The best he could do was to operate his racket in three districts. I operated on three continents."

These "interwoven interests" serve the economic elite and, like Mills said, control the ordinary citizen through manipulation. This manipulation, to be effective, has to be done behind closed doors. And propaganda is the primary tool of manipulation for these interwoven interests. Just about every agency in the government has a propaganda section. Not all of them are covert and operate in secrecy. However, just by the nature of their secrecy, propagandists for covert agencies like the CIA and NSA implement covert propaganda.

The CIA and NSA are just two of seventeen government intelligence agencies as of 2015. All of these covert agencies have in-house staff, and they also often use private contractors, not only for propaganda, but also for spying (clandestine propaganda and spying often go hand in hand).

One of the largest and most secretive government covert agencies is one most people have never heard of—the Special Operations Command (SOCOM), based in Tampa, Florida. According to a January 2014 article in the *Nation* magazine by Nick Turse, SOCOM has elite forces deployed in 134 countries around the globe. These forces consist of everything from our military's most elite special forces to covert propagandists.[3]

SOCOM's activities, Turse said, "are conducted largely in the shadows by America's most elite troops; the vast majority of these missions take place far from prying eyes, media scrutiny, or any type of outside oversight, increasing the chances of unforeseen blowback and catastrophic consequences." Turse pointed out that the Obama administration is using SOCOM to conduct "a secret war" all over the planet. He also revealed that SOCOM in recent years has begun a concerted push into cyberspace and has become deeply embedded inside the Washington Beltway.

"I have folks in every agency here in Washington, DC, from the CIA, to the FBI, to the National Security Agency, to the National Geospatial Agency, to the Defense Intelligence Agency," SOCOM chief Admiral McRaven said during a panel discussion at Washington's Wilson Center last year, according to Turse. McRaven put the number of departments and agencies where SOCOM is now entrenched at thirty-eight. Not only are the CIA, SOCOM, and other covert agencies entrenched throughout government; these covert agencies also have a revolving-door relationship with numerous private contractors.

If a government agency is forbidden by law to engage in certain activities, such as the law that forbids CIA involvement in domestic propaganda, they can simply execute the end-run propaganda tactic by contracting the activity to private third parties or by using front organizations within and outside of government.

In addition to using their own resources and private contractors, clandestine propagandists and the agencies they work for often have a cozy relationship with much of the nation's major media, so much so that media and public relations firms sometimes house embedded CIA, NSA, or FBI agents. An agent posing as a journalist, for example, can get access to information and ask questions without arousing suspicion of his or her motivation.

Government intelligence agencies and their propagandists have nearly a century of close cooperation with media and big business. This revolving-door relationship and interwoven interests have created a secret web of manipulators who weave their magic free and clear from public scrutiny. It was designed that way. This secret web of manipulators is what Bernays called the invisible government.[4]

Many of those in this invisible government who have participated in mind molding other covert operations believe it's justified because they're participating in what one of the propagandists (Robert Maheu) said in congressional testimony is "a just war."[5] The secret CIA memo to Eisenhower that I referenced earlier said "there are no rules."

Former vice president Dick Cheney echoed these same rationales for the Bush administration using torture in its post-9/11 CIA interrogation program. When asked on a December 2014 *Fox News* TV broadcast if he believed the ends justify the means, he replied "absolutely."

This "anything-goes," "a just war," and an "ends justify the means" mind-set is not just the province of conservative Republicans like Bush and Cheney. It has been the mind-set of conservatives and liberals alike for decades in everything from overthrowing democratically elected governments and stirring up domestic and international dissent in order to later crush it, to allowing drugs into our country and working with organized crime.

The anything-goes mind-set is critical to the successful deployment of a propaganda technique I call the engineering of dissent. It has been one of the most effective techniques in the arsenal of covert propagandists. This technique is the opposite of the engineering of consent and involves deliberately stirring up dissent in order to later discredit, degrade, diffuse, deny, demonize, dehumanize, disrupt, or destroy the dissenters, whether individuals, groups, or governments. This technique has been used often at home, including in the civil rights and antiwar movements, and in foreign countries to help overthrow governments and/or to discredit them. It is also often employed as part of false-flag propaganda.

The economic power elite and its propagandists learned an important lesson from the civil rights and antiwar (Vietnam) movements: never again would they allow dissent to get out of control. Radical or aggressive dissent today, such as the Occupy Wall Street movement of 2013 and the 2014-2015 protests over police brutality against people of color, were quickly crushed by an intimidating paramilitary police presence and by agent provocateurs who used engineering of dissent propaganda to stir up dissent in order to later crush it.

What, you might ask, do paramilitary police have to do with propaganda? Everything. One of the primary goals of propaganda is to arouse and manipulate emotions. One of our key emotions is fear. Fear is enhanced when dissenters, domestic or foreign, know that anything goes if you ignore certain parameters of behavior.

Heavily militarized local police forces and surveillance (even just the threat of police action or surveillance) send a strong message: don't cross certain lines in the sand except at your own peril. Those who have crossed these lines in the sand have often paid the price. One of the best examples, which I will detail later, involved Dr. Martin Luther King and our government's decade long campaign to discredit, demonize, and destroy him.

This book will give numerous, verified examples of how our government has used covert propaganda to arouse our emotions, particularly the emotion of fear. I pointed out in the first chapter that the anti-Communist Red Scare campaign was a classic block and bridge propaganda technique, in which you block focus on a primary issue or purpose by bridging or redirecting it to a secondary issue or purpose.

In the anticommunism campaign, concern over protecting and expanding the economic interests of the elite and beating the Soviets to the

Middle East oil fields was redirected to a secondary issue (the Communist threat). The true purpose of the Red Scare campaign, empire building and access to oil, was hidden by scaring us and creating a fear of communism. Anticommunism was always a propaganda tool to arouse our emotions. We were unrelenting in our anti-Communist propaganda. It dominated everything.

Albert E. Kahn noted in his book *High Treason: The Plot Against the People* that "every conceivable promotional device and propaganda technique was galvanized into an intense and incessant anti-Communist campaign which permeated every phrase of the nation's life."[6] Those who doubt that our government would develop propaganda programs to deliberately arouse our emotions and to create a state of fear or terror should keep reading. I give evidence throughout the book that this is exactly what happened.

Abraham Pomerantz the deputy chief counsel to the US prosecution staff at the Nuremberg trials, said in a newspaper interview when he returned from Nuremberg to the United States in 1947 that "I was shocked by the change in the American climate. Judging from the newspaper headlines, you'd think the Communists were already on the march to Washington in a bid for power."[7]

Pomerantz noted in the same interview that our government was sending military equipment and personnel to Turkey and Greece under the pretext of saving them from the Bolsheviks. "If you look beneath headlines, the truth of the matter is that when we speak for Greece and Turkey, we really mean oil," he said. In short, overseas and at home, anticommunism was at various times a smokescreen and a block and bridge, but it was always a great propaganda instrument for spreading fear and scaring us in order to expand the economic interests of the elite and its military-industrial complex.

The Soviet Union was not a serious threat to the United States after World War II. Its infrastructure was devastated, and nearly 28 million of its citizens had been killed. The United States had lost some 420,000 troops and had no attacks on its mainland. The United States emerged from World War II as a strong and powerful nation and a nation that showed it would not hesitate to use nuclear weapons.[8]

I was a victim of the anti-Communist campaign. Communism scared the hell out of me. I even joined the Christian Anti-Communist Society as a teen. I, like many people, feared Communists were everywhere and would soon be invading our country. Ironically, the namesake of the propaganda firm I later worked for was one of the pioneer architects of the Red Scare campaign. Carl Byoir, as I noted, teamed up in 1920 with J. Edgar Hoover to set up a news bureau, from which they blanketed the country with fear messages that Communists were going to invade the United States.

Byoir and Hoover weren't, however, the first to play the anti-Communist card. There were also anti-Socialist and anti-Collectivist movements in the latter part of the nineteenth century to discredit and demonize the labor movement. Even in the nineteenth century, anticollectivism was a rhetorical device and a smokescreen for the real goal of the elite: protecting profits by controlling labor and keeping labor costs as low as possible.

Besides using it to demonize the labor movement and to scare the American people after World War I, Byoir played the anti-Communist card again in the thirties when he handled propaganda in the United States for Hitler. Byoir, an American Jew, was hired by Hitler to convince American business leaders that fascism was a better alternative than communism and that he (Hitler) was going to wipe communism off the face of the earth. That was a "bridge" to divert attention from Hitler's real motive, which was to be able to march unimpeded through Europe. In short, anti-collectivism was used as a propaganda tool against labor in the latter part of the nineteenth century; after World War I to scare the American people by spreading the false message that a Communist invasion was imminent; in the thirties to convince American business leaders that fascism was a better alternative than communism; during the fifties and beyond with the McCarthy-led Red Scare campaign; and overseas as a smokescreen and block and bridge to overthrow governments, such as Iran and Guatemala.

The war on terrorism may also be a smokescreen and block and bridge largely because of our almost-maniacal lust for oil. This lust has caused us to get in bed with some nondemocratic, archconservative Muslim leaders and countries. Have our past cozy relationships with jihadists come back to bite us? Our likely "endless war" on terrorism has an ironic and hypocritical twist to it. We ourselves have a long history of torture and terrorism, both through direct involvement and through the false-flag propaganda technique.

• • •

A false-flag is a manufactured event designed to incite and arouse passions and to make it appear that events were carried out by groups or nations other than those who planned and executed them.

Associated with the false-flag is "standing down" (disassociating from events that governments are aware of and could stop, but choose to let happen anyway by looking the other way or blaming them on another individual, group, or nation). Geraint Hughes uses the false-flag term to refer to those acts carried out by "military or security force personnel, which are then blamed on terrorists."[9]

A good example of a false-flag and standing down is Operation Gladio, a false-flag terrorist operation allegedly set up by intelligence operatives of several countries after World War II to hinder and halt all Socialist influence or inroads in Western Europe, particularly in Italy, where Socialists were gaining in popularity. Gladio, which means "the sword," is the code name for what is now known as a NATO "stay-behind" operation. "Stay-behind" describes the network of covert anti-Communist armies that stayed behind in Western Europe after World War II.

On August 2, 1980, a bomb exploded at the Bologna, Italy, train station. It killed eighty-five people and wounded over two hundred, including numerous women and children. The massacre was blamed on Italian Socialists/Communists, whom the US and Italian governments feared were gaining popular support and could possibly win an upcoming election.

Largely because the voting public associated the bombing with leftists, the leftists lost the election. Years later it was learned that right-wing and

Fascist elements were responsible for the bombing. Several were imprisoned after an Italian prime minister exposed the Italian secret army. Other countries also investigated the roles their intelligence services had in the secret operation.

The United States has never investigated its role. A study by Daniele Ganser shows how these secret armies consisted of CIA and British secret service operatives in collaboration with NATO and other European secret services. Ganser notes in his book *NATO's Secret Armies :Operation Gladio and Terrorism in Western Europe: An Approach to NATO's Secret Stay-Behind Armies* that Gladio units were in close cooperation with NATO and the CIA and that Gladio in Italy was responsible for terrorists attacks against its own civilian population. He said in some countries the secret army linked up with right-wing terrorists who engaged in political manipulation, harassment of left wing parties, massacres, coup d'états and torture in a secret war.[10]

What hasn't been settled is which intelligence organizations were behind the Fascists. The role of the CIA in the Italian operation and its role with Gladio throughout the Cold War is the subject of debate. The CIA, obviously, denies it has been directly involved in Gladio or the Italian bombings. I don't want to speculate whether or not the CIA was involved in Gladio or the bombings, but we do know that the Fascists involved in the bombings were agent provocateurs hired by some organization. The CIA has a past history of using Nazis in their anti-Communist propaganda campaigns. The CIA also has a long history of using agent provocateurs to infiltrate and then stir up dissent in order to later crush it.

Philip Agree, the ex-CIA operative who became well-known worldwide when he wrote the best seller *Inside the Company: CIA Diary*, said that when he operated in Ecuador from 1960 to 1963, "The CIA oversaw the overthrow of two presidents; the infiltration of various political parties and organizations; and the planting of bombs in front of churches and other emblematic sites to frame leftist groups; among other actions."[11]

Planting bombs to frame leftist groups is a classic false-flag manufactured incident. I will give numerous examples later, including the CIA's involvement in coups in Iran and Guatemala. However, my book is not a CIA exposé. I'm more interested in covert propaganda and what we can do to minimize its damage to democracy.

Some might be inclined to defend certain nondemocratic activities because they believe they are necessary to protect us from "terrorism," a word Bush put into the popular vernacular when he declared a "war on terrorism." Bush's manipulation of the word "terrorism" was pure propaganda. Terrorism is what propagandists call an "emotionally laden word," which means a word used to arouse emotions, especially fear. Calling the Middle East conflict a war on terrorism wasn't even unique.

Senator Robert La Follette of Wisconsin gave a speech on the Senate floor in 1917 and warned we were conducting what he said was "a propaganda campaign to throw the country into a state of terror."[12] Among the handful of propagandists conducting this campaign at President Wilson's behest were Carl Byoir and Edward Bernays. It was the first time in our history that a massive mind manipulation campaign was specifically designed to scare the American people. La Follette's observation that the propaganda campaign was designed to create "terror" and to arouse passions was confirmed after the war by none other than the architect of the fear campaign itself, Edward Bernays. Bernays admitted that he and his fellow propagandists used fake atrocities to incite a public outcry against Germany, such as the story of German soldiers collecting tubs full of human eyeballs. Other fake atrocity stories included a nun's breasts being cutoff, a child thrown to the pigs, a German corpse factory where soldiers' bodies were turned into glycerin for weapons, and posters showing German soldiers carrying long bayonets over their shoulders with children's corpses impaled on the bayonet. British atrocity propaganda included German soldiers cutting off the hands of Belgian babies and eating them.[13]

Using atrocities to scare the public and arouse passions was the beginning of a century-long mass mind manipulation campaign, in which propaganda, surveillance, terror, and the threat of terror have been part of what the propagandists consider a "just war." Unfortunately, this war has been conducted in many cases against us, the American people.

The war against communism and the war on terrorism could end up being among the biggest block and bridge and disinformation scams in history, along with the dead-babies hoax that was used to get us into the Gulf War. Each of these three propaganda campaigns was fought to protect the turf of a small group of very wealthy people. The most visible face of anticommunism was Senator Joseph McCarthy, but he likely had no idea who was pulling his strings.

As I noted earlier, Bernays acknowledged that there are those in our "invisible government" who covertly pull the strings and let puppets like McCarthy do their bidding. My focus, however, isn't to take the government or the CIA to task for its activities. My focus is to explain how covert propaganda can work and has worked.

• • •

Propaganda is a fairly simple subject to understand once you learn to discard all the disinformation that surrounds the word itself. However, covert propaganda has become so sophisticated and secretive that it can be tough to recognize. That is no mistake.

Terrorism, torture, military-like police, surveillance, lying, and secret, sophisticated covert propaganda activities, such as block and bridge and false-flag propaganda, are not activities of a democracy, yet we have used all of these tactics for decades, mostly in secret.

A strong case can be made that our government's almost paranoid reliance on secrecy for clandestine propaganda, intelligence gathering, and surveillance has become so pervasive, particularly post 9/11, that we may be losing many of our freedoms and our claims to democracy.

Since World War I, we've had a unique mix of both open, democratic governance and plutocracy-like secret governance. Combined, this duality cleverly obfuscates the reality of mass mind manipulation. It creates a climate in which we, the American people, don't know what we don't know.

Even though this book reveals a lot of abuses by covert agencies and I find much of their work repugnant, I have to admit that it was a stroke of genius to create up to seventeen covert agencies to protect the interests of the economic elite. By working almost entirely in secret (covertly), these agencies can do anything they want, and we won't even know about it. For example, for decades our covert agencies have secretly employed Nazi war criminals.

Six top members of President H. W. Bush's 1988 campaign were forced to resign when a Washington-based Jewish publication revealed they were Nazis and were active in the conservative wing of the Republican Party. H. W. Bush's father has long been thought by many to be a strong Nazi supporter.[14]

On October 29, 2014, *BBC News* reported that CIA officials are said to have turned to Nazis to help serve as propagandists to defeat the Soviet Union during the Cold War according to declassified US records.

The BBC report said academics studying the documents claim America used at least one thousand ex-Nazis after the war, some of whom had committed horrific war crimes. Did our government trust Nazis more than its own citizens because Fascists had shown they were adept at keeping secrets?

Only a small percentage of covert activities ever see the light of day. The few that are revealed, such as the employment of Nazis, are usually discovered decades after the fact. But it's not just the public that is fooled; many of our elected leaders are also kept in the dark. This gives top leaders plausible deniability, a key propaganda technique. How do we truly know what is going on when there are propaganda, surveillance, and intelligence ghosts lurking behind the scenes doing whatever they want? How do we get transparency from this covert mind manipulation?

Public opinion that is numb or apathetic to violence gives the economic elite latitude to use "any means necessary" to protect its assets and power base. An example of this numbing of public opinion to violence was the muted public reaction in December 2014 to evidence that our government authorized the use of horrific torture post 9/11, including disrupting prisoners sleep for days, waterboarding, slamming people against walls, and putting people in a coffin for up to twenty days and releasing insects to crawl over them. Why wasn't there a national uproar?

There are likely many factors, including the belief in an eye-for-an-eye revenge against the alleged perpetuators of 9/11, but another reason could very well be that the American public has been exposed to so much war, torture, and violence in film, video games, television, the Internet, and other media that they have grown accustomed to endless war and violence.

TV shows like *24* feature violence and high-speed action just about every episode.*24* is a highly popular American television series starring Kiefer Sutherland as Counter Terrorist Unit (CTU) agent Jack Bauer. Each twenty-four-episode season covers twenty-four hours in the life of Bauer.

The series begins with his working for the Los Angeles-based Counter Terrorist Unit, in which he is a highly proficient agent with an ends-justify-the-means approach regardless of the perceived morality of some of his actions.

"Is it any coincidence that the #1 movie in America right now is *American Sniper*?" asked journalist Carl Gibson in a January 2015 article in *Reader Supported News*. This is a violence-filled movie about someone who single-handedly killed 150 people in Muslim countries. On *Real Talk with Bill Maher,* Maher criticized the film's portrayal of the sniper as a hero—"American hero! He's a psychopath patriot, and yet we love him."[15]

Although I have no proof, it appears more than a coincidence that violent, terrorism-themed movies and TV shows have been shown during the height of the war on terrorism. Is it a coincidence that numerous so-called "terrorist incidents" happened during the same time frame that potentially damaging revelations about the war on terror were beginning to show up in the fall and winter of 2014? This was a period when the CIA was expecting harsh public criticism and congressional backlash from the late 2014 release of the Senate report on torture, when a bill to reform NSA was gaining momentum in Congress, when Congress was considering a bill to reform the Patriot Act, and when Ed Snowden was making revelations about NSA abuses.

Some of these terrorist incidents included Iran's alleged attempt to kill the Saudi ambassador to the United States in Washington, DC; North Korea allegedly hacking Sony Corporation, which produced the film *The*

Interview; alleged terrorists invading Canada's Parliament; and a twenty-year-old Cincinnati resident allegedly planning to attack the US Capitol.

The FBI was never able to produce proof of an attempt to kill the Saudi ambassador. That "story" quickly died. There still has been no proof that North Korea was behind the hacking incident. The Obama administration claimed later that we hacked them first and, thus, knew they were the hackers. Was this a block and bridge?

In the Canadian incident, Canada's prime minister quickly blamed the Parliament intrusion on savage and barbaric terrorists, but it turns out that the intruder was apparently a mentally deranged individual. It also was later revealed that the prime minister was in the process of seeking increased funding for Canada's security agency.

The Justice Department in January 2015 distributed a press release lauding FBI agents and the Joint Terrorism Task Force for stopping what they said was a domestic terrorism plot. They said the task force arrested a Cincinnati-area man who was planning to attack the US Capitol and kill government officials. Investigative reporters Glenn Greenwald and Andrew Fishman wrote in *The Intercept* that an affidavit filed by an FBI investigative agent alleges the young man had posted comments and information supportive of [ISIS] through Twitter accounts. The twenty-year-old, according to the article, was a "mommy's boy" who lived at home and didn't appear a likely terrorist. "The FBI learned about Cornell from an unnamed informant who, as the FBI put it, 'began cooperating with the FBI in order to obtain favourable treatment with respect to his criminal exposure on an unrelated case,'" according to Greenwald and Fishman.[16]

The authors noted that the informant, with FBI oversight, set up two meetings with Cornell, during which they allegedly discussed attacking the Capitol. The FBI, they said, then arrested Cornell so he couldn't attack the Capitol.

"The known facts from this latest case," they wrote, "seem to fit well within a now familiar FBI pattern whereby the agency does not disrupt planned domestic terror attacks but rather creates them, then publicly praises itself for stopping its own plots."

If the FBI did create or encourage the incident, it would be a classic false-flag/disinformation propaganda action. There have been numerous false flags and lies used by our government during the past century to arouse our emotions and fears. The government apparently even lies to itself.

In a January 17, 2015, *Esquire* article titled "The CIA's Willingness to Lie About Our Torture Regime," Charles Pierce pointed out that journalist Mark Danner in a *New York Review of Books* interview explained how a complicated infrastructure of "mendacity" was constructed and how it became equally as vital to the torture program as waterboarding and rectal feeding.[17]

"Not only did the CIA arrange this infrastructure in order to lie to the American people about what was done in their name, but also the CIA built this infrastructure to provide an institutional basis for the American government to lie to itself," wrote Pierce. Danner, Pierce said, observed that the CIA was actually misleading the Department of Justice.

Pierce warned that the arrest of the troubled teen in Cincinnati, terror sweeps in Europe, and the terror attack in Paris had brought things back to the new normal again, especially within our twenty-four-hour news cycle. "Once again, we are hearing reports from Western intelligence sources about 'imminent attacks' that have been thwarted by the slimmest of margins," Pierce said.

"If the CIA is willing to arrange that the government lies to itself, if it is willing to hack the Congress, I choose to believe that it will feed the public anything that suits its immediate need," Pierce wrote. (Note: My propaganda experience supports Pierce's contention that we've created a secret intelligence, surveillance, and propaganda apparatus so covert and powerful that it can feed the public anything that suits its needs. Not even top leaders in government itself, including presidents, always know everything that is going on. Keeping knowledge of incidents from top leaders, as I have noted, gives them plausible deniability.)

Pierce also reinforces Bernays's observation of decades ago that we have "an invisible government" that pulls the strings behind the scenes.

It's not surprising that this invisible government lies to itself. It was planned that way.

Will we ever see more transparency? Not as long as the public is apathetic and scared. Those pulling the strings know they need an apathetic and scared public in order to carry out what CIA agent Victor Marchetti said that covert operatives believe is a "just war," with us often considered the enemy, particularly those of us who advocate for more transparency and democracy.

Pierce, as a good journalist should, appears to be at least questioning whether our government is telling us the complete truth behind various terrorist incidents. His reluctance to accept government sources, particularly from our covert agencies, as the absolute truth speaks well for journalism.

However, in chapter 5 I will point out how a malleable media has cooperated for decades with the CIA to spread disinformation and other CIA propaganda in a program called Operation Mockingbird. Some believe Operation Mockingbird is still active, but under a different guise.

I will also show that the CIA and other agencies have often fed misleading disinformation to a media that is largely in the CIA's back pocket, particularly the major media outlets.

• • •

The CIA has a long history of involvement with the drug trade and has been involved in behavior modification programs since the early fifties. LSD and numerous other illegal drugs were given to unwitting subjects, including prisoners and the mentally ill, as part of behavior-modification research programs, such as MK-ULTRA. I will show later that our government either looked the other way (standing-down propaganda) or knowingly allowed illegal drugs to be introduced into the US general population during the height of the so-called war on drugs.

Some might say I'm delving into conspiracy theory by even raising these issues and by asserting that some of these (or other) incidents might have been deliberately planned to stir our emotions and to support an underlying agenda. By loosely applying "conspiracy theorist" to those revealing difficult-to-prove incidents, the accusers are aiding and abetting clandestine propaganda operatives because those faced with being labeled conspiracy theorists might exercise self-censorship. Even the best investigative reporters know that being labeled a conspiracy theorist diminishes and discredits their work. My concern is not whether or not there was a conspiracy, but whether or not propaganda, particularly the engineering of dissent or false-flag/standing down propaganda, was involved.

Propaganda is not a good-guy, bad-guy issue. All sides practice propaganda. We're just better at it than everyone else. And we often do it in secret. ISIS does just the opposite. It openly touts its propaganda and makes no secret that it is intended to scare its target audience. Propaganda for ISIS appears to be an instrument of control to scare people into submission. We do the same thing. It's just harder to recognize because we're so good at hiding it. We don't publicly behead people, but we're very good at creating fear. We learned a long time ago that a scared populace is much easier to control.

Fear is one of the easiest emotions to target, partly because most of us have many fears, some of which we don't want to admit even to ourselves. Some of our more common fears are fear of failure, fear of rejection, fear of death, fear of being alone, fear of change, fear of intimacy, fear of sexual inadequacy, fear of commitment, fear of the unknown, fear of God, fear of terrorists, fear of Communists, fear of criminals, and in some countries, fear of drones and surveillance.

These fears are exploited and manipulated by propagandists throughout the world, but as I have noted numerous times, much of our propaganda is covert and conducted by invisible operatives behind closed doors. This makes it much easier for our government to manipulate us and, basically, to do anything it wants without us even knowing what they are doing.

I hope that you, the reader, if nothing else, will also begin to question what you see or hear. That is not being unpatriotic. It's exercising your constitutional rights. It's difficult to know the truth without asking questions and without being aware that things aren't always as they appear. The United States has been involved in so many verifiable examples of engineering of dissent and false-flag/standing-down propaganda that it would be irresponsible for a professional propagandist like me not to at least question how things appear on the surface

CHAPTER 5

Conspiracy and Brainwashing as Propaganda Tools

WITH THE TOTALITY OF THINGS I reveal, some might be tempted to dismiss this book as conspiracy theory, but as I noted earlier, it's not a conspiracy book nor is it theory. It's based on verifiable incidents, some of which I participated in. Interestingly, use of the word "conspiracy" is itself propaganda. The word has been used by clandestine propagandists since the fifties as part of their mind manipulation campaign, usually to discredit a theory or belief.

The word "conspiracy" came into vogue as part of the CIA's Operation Mockingbird program (as did the word "brainwashing," as I will discuss shortly). Operation Mockingbird was a secret campaign begun in the early fifties by the CIA to infiltrate and to influence domestic and foreign media by the use of propaganda and other methods. The CIA recruited leading American journalists to help present CIA propaganda. The CIA even used and funded student and cultural organizations and magazines as fronts for its propaganda. Operation Mockingbird involved over twenty-five newspapers and wire agencies, including some of the nation's leading publications and broadcasting firms.[1]

The word "Mockingbird" is a perfect fit for the CIA's goal to create a malleable media. A mockingbird is a creature with the natural gift to mimic or mirror whatever song another bird makes. CIA official Frank Wisner called Operation Mockingbird his "Mighty Wurlitzer," on which he could play any propaganda tune.[2] This statement shows Agent Wisner had great confidence in "playing" the media and relying on it to do the CIA's propaganda bidding.

The truth of Wisner's statement was verified many years later when Carl Bernstein, who broke the Watergate scandal, identified over four hundred journalists who had CIA ties in an October 1977 issue of *Rolling Stone*. Philip Graham, the publisher of the *Washington Post*, where Bernstein worked when he broke the Watergate scandal, had been in military intelligence during World War II and actively promoted CIA goals in his newspaper for many years. Other top *Washington Post* journalists also had intelligence backgrounds (per Bernstein's article).

When you read, see, or hear a news story, you have no way of knowing if the reporter or commentator is working knowingly or unknowingly for government intelligence agencies, for intelligence front groups, or for big business. In the next chapter, I will reveal the names of some top journalists who have had intelligence ties. Many still do. For example, a prominent national security reporter for the *Los Angeles Times* routinely submitted drafts and detailed summaries of his stories to CIA propagandists prior to publication, according to documents obtained by *The Intercept* and reported by Ken Silverstein in a September 5, 2014, article. Silverstein noted that this reporter explicitly promised positive news coverage for the CIA and sometimes sent entire story drafts to the CIA for review prior to publication.[3]

Not only did Operation Mockingbird involve using media for covert propaganda purposes; it also involved creating new scare words to manipulate the American people, such as the word "brainwashing." The term "brainwashing" was introduced into media and the popular vernacular by CIA propagandist Edward Hunter, who first used the term as part of a fifties anti-Communist propaganda campaign to implant in the mass mind the idea that brainwashing is something the bad guys do, but not us.[4] Brainwashing is an effective tool to implement demonization propaganda, which destroys, denies, degrades, and disrupts enemies by discrediting them.

Hunter simply took an old form of manipulation, physically enforced persuasion, and coined a code word, "brainwashing," and then attached sinister symbols to it to arouse public passions, much like "devil" and "witch" had in the past. I'll point out later how symbol, stereotype, and myth manipulation are key propaganda tools.

Hunter worked closely with trusted media owners and editors to spread the word "brainwashing." For example, on September 24, 1950, the word "brainwashing," invented by Hunter, first appeared in print in the *Miami Daily News*.

Hunter was a veteran of the Office of Strategic Services, forerunner of the CIA, as were future CIA director Richard Helms and Howard Hunt of Watergate fame. Hunter was a journalist turned propagandist, like many propagandists I'll talk about in the following pages.

Hunter followed the Miami introductory article with numerous magazine articles, radio documentaries, films, and a book, *Brainwashing in Red China: The Calculated Destruction of Men's Minds*. Even the title of the book carries the message that brainwashing is something others do, but not us.

Researcher Walter Bowart noted in the book *Operation Mind Control* that "the CIA thought-up the term 'brainwashing' to lead people in the Western World to believe that the inscrutable Orientals had again, like Fu Manchu, invented a revolutionary new technique for controlling the human mind."[5]

About the same time Hunter was working his magic on the mass mind, a very secretive covert wing of the CIA called the "Office of Policy Coordination" was created. OPC sponsored a secret school in Canada for Americans and British involved in clandestine propaganda operations. Ian Fleming, creator of the James Bond spy thrillers, was among those who attended.[6]

It wasn't long before conspiracy spy thrillers such as the James Bond saga began to inundate Western media. These fast-action thrillers were almost invariably cast in a good-guy, bad-guy stereotype mold. James Bond was only able to save the gold at Fort Knox, for example, with the help of the CIA and the US Army (the good guys). Conspiracies and brainwashing were depicted as evil creations of enemies. The term "conspiracy theory" came into vogue after the Kennedy assassination and has been used since as a way to discredit those questioning official versions of events.

Richard Condon's fiction book *The Manchurian Candidate* kept the conspiracy theory and brainwashing stereotype as "forced indoctrination" message alive. Condon's book cemented the idea of brainwashing as "forcible indoctrination," which created people without a free will. Condon had a captured American soldier programmed to be a political assassin for the "bad guys," that is, the Communists.[7]

About this same time, social scientists began to release thousands of scholarly articles, books, and lectures on brainwashing. Many of the social scientists and academics most active in this campaign to cement the brainwashing myth into the public mind were bankrolled, sometimes unknowingly, by intelligence agencies and/or their fronts.

The brainwashing myth is still very much alive. For example, the *Washington Post* carried an article January 16, 2015, titled "North Korea Begins Brainwashing Children in Cult of the Kims as Early as Kindergarten."[8] The article largely consisted of the reporter quoting expatriates now living in South Korea who gave examples of the brainwashing they received while growing up in North Korea.

The article perpetuates the myth that brainwashing is what the bad guys do, but not us. I have no idea if the article was written to reinforce this myth, but "brainwashing" is a word the CIA put into popular usage. The *Washington Post*, as I will unveil later, has a long history of close ties with the CIA.

• • •

The brainwashing myth is a perfect example of how propagandists can manipulate myths, symbols, illusions, and stereotypes to trick us into believing that our beliefs and opinions are the result of careful analysis and study when, in reality, they might be a conditioned response to well-orchestrated campaigns to manipulate our beliefs and opinions.

I don't know of any national survey on the subject, but I would be willing to bet that a large majority of Americans still hold the stereotypical view of brainwashing that Hunter and others worked so hard for many years to infiltrate into the mass mind. Hunter and his propaganda cohorts even fooled those who write our dictionaries and encyclopedias. For example, the Merriam-Webster online dictionary defines brainwashing as "a forcible indoctrination" and as "persuasion by propaganda or salesmanship."

The *Concise Encyclopedia* notes that brainwashing is a "systematic effort to destroy an individual's former loyalties and beliefs and to substitute loyalty to a new ideology or power. It has been used by religious cults as well as by radical political groups."

Let's first look at Webster's definition of "forcible indoctrination." There is plenty of brainwashing that does not require forcible indoctrination. You can brainwash someone without force. Also, "persuasion by propaganda or salesmanship" is not brainwashing; it is propaganda, and not all propaganda is bad.

Webster connects propaganda with brainwashing, just as Hunter wanted. Most propaganda has nothing to do with brainwashing. Advertising, public relations, and many other things in our daily lives (including religion) involve persuasion, but that does not make them brainwashing.

In fact, propaganda *is* persuasion, so to use "persuasion *by* propaganda" is misusing the word "propaganda" and giving the wrong context for brainwashing. That is exactly the stereotype Hunter wanted the American public to develop.

Forcible persuasion has been around probably since humans first appeared on earth. What Hunter did was coin a new word (brainwashing) and connect it to forcible persuasion so that he could demonize propaganda by connecting it with what others do (the bad guys) and not us. This is clever diversion propaganda involving the propaganda technique of block and bridge because it redirects attention from the CIA's propaganda so that more attention is paid to the forcible persuasion of others—that is, the bad guys and "radical groups."

In short, Hunter's efforts were a well-orchestrated campaign using newspapers, magazines, television, radio, movies, books, and other outlets to propagandize the words "propaganda" and "brainwashing." It was one of the best mass mind manipulations in history. Both words are still strong stereotypes. How many of us watching the James Bond thrillers, for example, knew we were being sent some strong propaganda messages that would stay with us the rest of our lives?

The words "conspiracy," "brainwashing," and "propaganda" have all been cleverly propagandized to cover up the clandestine activities of covert surveillance, intelligence, and propaganda operations.

The word "propaganda" itself was propagandized as part of Operation Mockingbird. Our covert agencies have stereotyped and manipulated this word to such an extent that it has become one of the most misunderstood and manipulated words in our language. For example, a December 14, 2014, *Associated Press* story concerned a press conference in North Korea in which North Korea announced they were not going to detain an American who admitted he illegally crossed into the country.

In his comments to reporters, the American strongly criticized the United States for alleged human rights violations in its treatment of prisoners in the CIA's post-9/11 "enhanced interrogation" program. The reporter who wrote the AP story said allowing the American to speak to the media "raised questions of whether Martinez was trotted out to the media for propaganda purposes."

Of course, North Korea trotted out the detainee for propaganda purposes. Every country uses propaganda. This article implies that propaganda is something the bad guys do, but not us. The phrase in the AP article ("raised questions of whether Martinez was trotted out to the media for propaganda purposes") is called "editorializing" or injecting the writer's own interpretation into a news event. By doing this the reporter himself was ironically injecting the stereotype of propaganda into the Associated Press story. The article implies that Martinez was brainwashed. Is it a coincidence that this article was followed by the *Washington Post* article about brainwashing in North Korea and that both were published within a few weeks of the United States accusing North Korea of hacking the Sony Corporation in retaliation for the film *The Interview*?

These articles demonstrate a complete lack of understanding of propaganda and brainwashing; this misunderstanding is why I have written this book. I would hope that I can contribute in some small way to help the reader recognize propaganda. Why is it important? Because propaganda impacts who you are as a person—everything you think, say, and do.

"The public consumed reams of information on the subject (brainwashing), much of it propaganda to serve intelligence, military and executive interests," wrote Alan Scheflin and Edward Opton in *The Mind Manipulators*.[9]

• • •

Scheflin and Opton nailed the purpose of the mind manipulation campaign: that is, to serve intelligence, military, and executive (big business) interests. What the authors likely weren't aware of is that the use of brainwashing as a propaganda tool was modeled after propaganda techniques that were developed prior to and during World War I by President Woodrow Wilson's Committee on Public Information (CPI), the nation's first propaganda agency.

Wilson appointed five people to the CPI and gave these pioneer propagandists almost unlimited power to create and implement propaganda programs to convince a reluctant populace to support America's entry into the European war. In just a few months, they had sent over 80,000 "Four Minute Men" (mini-propagandists) to thousands of communities. By war's end, 7.5 million speeches had been made to tens of millions of listeners. They also created and circulated slogans such as "Make the World Safe for Democracy" and conducted a huge war-bonds program, which was similar to the Crusade for Freedom's "truth dollars" campaign in the fifties. Byoir was involved in both.

Most importantly the Committee brought together for the first time under one roof the leaders of government, media, academia, the military, and big business. They worked shoulder to shoulder on a massive mass persuasion campaign, from which they developed strong relationships with one another, relationships that would prove to be the launching pad for the mass persuasion thought control campaign and would open a revolving door that is still open today. The committee conducted one of the most successful propaganda campaigns in history. So successful, in fact, that Hitler attributed Germany's defeat in the first war to our superior propaganda; in his famous book *Mein Kampf,* Hitler said he and his propaganda minister, Joseph Goebbels, learned much of their propaganda techniques from the CPI.[10]

CPI members used scare words similar to "brainwashing" and associated them with Germans. They also released a lot of disinformation (lies) to arouse the passion of the American people. World War I-era disinformation pales in comparison to the sophisticated lies we unleashed decades later.

On October 10, 1990, a teenage Kuwaiti girl gave tear-jerking testimony before a congressional caucus committee that Iraqi soldiers, guns drawn, invaded a Kuwaiti hospital and took many babies from their incubators and left them to die on the cold hospital floor. The testimony was widely publicized and cited numerous times for months by the media and by members of the US Senate and Congress and by President H. W. Bush as rationale for the Desert Storm military action against Iraq in the first Gulf War.[11]

The problem is the testimony wasn't true. It was a lie. It was an elaborate propaganda ruse designed to arouse our emotions and stimulate support for war. Propagandists don't use harsh words like "lie." They sanitize it, as they do so much of our language, and call lies "disinformation."

Before the 2003 Iraq invasion, there were stories of a wood chipper into whose shredder Saddam fed opponents of his Baathist rule.[12] No evidence of such a machine was ever discovered.

Were the babies-on-the-floor and wood chipper disinformation aberrations, or is lying routinely used to deceive the American public? The answer is they were not aberrations; lying is routine. I will give example after example throughout the book of disinformation, including details about the babies-on-the-floor hoax, which featured numerous deceptive propaganda techniques and might have been one of the most elaborate propaganda disinformation campaigns ever.

Would US government agencies use disinformation and the engineering of dissent to deliberately stir up passions and to overthrow democratically elected governments? Yes. We have done it over and over (in Iran, Guatemala, and Nicaragua to name just a few places).

Would the US government use disinformation and the engineering of dissent to create violent acts that could later be blamed on Communists and other "enemies"? Yes, we have done it over and over.

Would US government agencies use disinformation and engineering of dissent on cooperative projects with drug dealers and organized crime? Yes, we've done it over and over.

Would our government use engineering of dissent and disinformation propaganda to deliberately incite domestic dissent in order to later crush and/or discredit it? Yes. FBI files show these have been done over and over domestically to create a "fear of consequences" for crossing lines in the sand.

Would our law enforcement and intelligence agencies work with ex-Nazis, some of whom committed horrific war crimes, on various propaganda and surveillance projects in the United States in the late forties, fifties, and beyond? Yes, declassified US records, according to an October 2014 BBC report, reveal we secretly used at least one thousand ex-Nazis as spies, propagandists, and informants after World War II. FBI director J. Edgar Hoover dismissed much of the Nazi horrific acts as "just Soviet propaganda."[13]

Would the US government intercept the mail of law-abiding American citizens, listen in on their phone conversations, read their e-mails, and even physically stalk them simply because of their political beliefs? Yes, it has been done over and over, and it was done decades before 9/11, according to the FBI's own files.[14]

Would we use anticommunism and, later, the "war on terrorism" as smokescreens to enhance and protect the profits of the economic elite worldwide, to grow empire, and to gain control of Middle East oil? Yes, the anti-Communist smokescreen was admitted by a secretary of state who helped orchestrate the campaign.[15]

Would we draw up a plan to build detention camps for "radicals" and protestors, a plan that has been called possibly the most undemocratic document in our history? Yes, we did so during the seventies. It was called the Huston Plan.[16] It was drafted by Nixon White House aide Tom Huston, a lawyer, former army intelligence officer, and early leader of the Indiana chapter of the conservative extremist group Young Americans for Freedom. The Huston pan was a 43 page report outlining suggested security operations. It was put together by Huston, a White House aide, in 1970. The existence of this plan was revealed during the 1973 Watergate hearings

Among things the plan called for were domestic burglary, wiretapping, break-ins, no-knock searches, illegal electronic surveillance, and opening the mail of domestic "radicals" (all of which were done). The Huston Plan also called for the creation of camps in Western states where antiwar protesters would be detained. Huston worked closely with the FBI to develop the plan. It was approved at the highest levels of government, but bureaucratic infighting tabled it. However, much of it was implemented in other forms.

The most radical elements of the Huston Plan weren't implemented, but they might have been if the antiwar protests had grown. The plan also called for greatly expanding domestic intelligence gathering by the FBI and other agencies.

Author James Reston Jr., according to HistoryCommons.org, called the Huston Plan "arguably the most anti-democratic document in American history; a blueprint to undermine the fundamental right of dissent and free speech in America."[17]

White House aides Charles Colson and George Bell drew up an enemies list in 1971 that included groups like the National Association for the Advancement of Colored People (NAACP) and the AFL-CIO.[18] These are a long way from being radical groups.

Can the Huston Plan and other covert White House activities during the seventies be dismissed as aberrations, or did the perpetuators just happen to get caught?

Investigative journalist Seymour Hersh noted in a landmark 1974 *New York Times* article that "the Central Intelligence Agency (CIA) has repeatedly, and illegally, spied on U.S. citizens for years."[19] Even though the Huston Plan was eventually rescinded, some believe it remained in effect under the code name COINTELPRO, which I will discuss in the next chapter.

A strong argument can be made that our government's decades-long employment of covert propaganda and surveillance has led to an apparatus that has become so secretive and sophisticated that any mass protests or uprisings, such as the civil rights movement, the anti–Vietnam War movement, and labor movements, would have little chance of success today because they would likely be denied, degraded, dehumanized, demonized, discredited, disrupted, diffused, and destroyed in quick order.

• • •

In addition to the weapons of propaganda and surveillance, those protecting the economic interests of big business and Wall Street also have at their disposal a greatly expanded and militarized police force. An outsider observing the 2014 protests in Ferguson, Missouri, or the April 2015 protests in Baltimore and other cities over police killing young blacks might conclude that the military, not local police, were the ones breaking up the protests. Ferguson and Baltimore police wore military-like camouflage uniforms and personal armor, were armed with automatic military weaponry, and had tanks standing by.

The United Nations Committee against Torture criticized the United States in a November 2014 report that raised concern about racial profiling, the growing militarization of police activities throughout the country, and what it called "a pattern of police brutality and excessive force against racial and ethnic minorities."[20] The report singled out Chicago police for frequent and recurrent police shootings and fatal pursuits of unarmed black individuals. The report noted that no Chicago police officer had ever been convicted for what it termed "acts of torture."

Carl Gibson wrote in the November 18, 2014, issue of *Reader Supported News* that protestors during the civil rights movement faced fire hoses and police dogs just to get the right to vote. He wondered what would happen if similar protests today came up against our current heavily militarized police forces armed with "an arsenal of armoured vehicles, assault rifles, tear gas, flash-bang grenades, rubber bullets, and baton rounds at its disposal." He asked how dissent would even be possible. It wouldn't be possible. Mass protests like those during the civil rights and anti-war movements would quickly be destroyed.

How would our militarized police react today to hundreds of thousands of protestors demonstrating in cities throughout the country, as happened in the civil rights and anti–Vietnam War protests? The military would likely be called in at the slightest provocation. And agent provocateurs would likely be unleashed to stir up dissent so it could be crushed.

In recent years numerous city police departments have been conducting joint exercises with the military. During the week of January 21, 2012, the Los Angeles Police Department conducted joint military exercises in downtown LA. The joint exercises were part of a nationally coordinated campaign by the Department of Homeland Security and other federal law enforcement agencies in collaboration with local police departments. [21] These have apparently been going on since then. What are they preparing for?

The exercises become even more ominous when you consider that the 2001 Patriot Act had a section called the Authorization for the Use of Military Force (AUMF), which authorized indefinite military detention of Americans without charges or a trial. Subsequent National Defense Authorization Acts (NDAA) have allowed indefinite detention to be codified into law. NDAA is a federal law specifying the budget and expenditures of the Department of Defense. Indefinite detention of US citizens would stifle dissent quickly. If things got bad enough, would people start disappearing? We've "disappeared" people overseas. Could it happen here?

Are we getting close to what a police state looks like? It's not paranoia to be alarmed about a huge increase in public and private law enforcement agencies and their militarization or to be concerned that we are being followed and watched nearly everywhere we go. When we drive down the street, traffic cameras keep an eye on us. When we visit a park or go shopping at the mall or visit an ATM or go inside our bank, a camera is likely zeroed in on us. Even our smartphones tell where we are, follow our every movement, and can allow officials to listen in on our conversations. When we are online, information about our personal lives and interests is easily and routinely shared.

It has been thirty years since Orwell's 1984. Is Big Brother here? Does it matter if we lose our privacy? An expert on the subject, Dr. Jennifer Golbeck, wrote in the October 2014 issue of *Psychology Today* that privacy is an intangible asset. "If we never think about it, we may not realize it is gone." She quotes a professor of psychiatry at Stanford University, Elia Aboujaoude, from his book *Virtually You: The Dangerous Power of the E-Personality*: "At its heart this (privacy) is about our psychological autonomy and the maintenance of some semblance of control over the various little details that make us us."[22]

Both surveillance and propaganda insidiously help make us us by setting parameters of both behavior and expectation. Dr. Golbeck also quotes Ian Brown, a senior research fellow at the Oxford Internet Institute, who has noted that "when people think they're being watched, they may behave consciously or not, in ways that comply with what they presume governmental or other observers want." If people treat us differently based on what they have discovered online, Brown believes the result is reduced trust and increased conformity.

As I noted earlier, this increased conformity is not only a by-product of surveillance, but the primary goal of covert propaganda's key technique—the engineering of consent. The reason the engineering of consent is so important is because conformity often leads to self-censorship. If we lack the power to know or control whom we share information with, we can lose a sense of self. And self-doubt, Golbeck noted, can lead to self-censorship "as we begin to fixate on what others will think about every potentially public action and thought."

• • •

I'll give numerous examples in the following pages of secret and covert efforts by government agencies and the economic elite to control our thoughts and behavior and to monitor our every move. Covert propaganda and spying are not hallmarks of a democracy. Can we legitimately claim to be a true democracy? An article on April 17, 2014, in the *BBC News* had the headline "US Is an Oligarchy, Not a Democracy."[23]

Their news article stated off by noting, "The US is dominated by a rich and powerful elite." The article goes on to point out that two professors, Princeton University professor Martin Gilens and Northwestern University professor Benjamin Page, conducted an exhaustive survey on public policy issues between 1981 and 2002 and came to the conclusion that the wealthy few move policy, while the average American has little power.

According to the BBC, the researchers concluded, "Americans do enjoy many features central to democratic governance, such as regular elections, freedom of speech and association and a widespread (if still contested) franchise. But we believe that if policymaking is dominated by powerful business organizations and a small number of affluent Americans, then America's claims to being a democratic society are seriously threatened."

The Merriam-Webster dictionary defines oligarchy as "a government in which a small group exercises control." It defines a plutocracy as a small group that consists of "very rich people who have a lot of power." Putting these two dictionary definitions together makes it appear that we are or are close to being an oligarchic plutocracy. There is overwhelming evidence that a small group of very wealthy people exercise a lot of control and have a lot of power. Covert propaganda has played a major role in allowing a wealthy class to steal or come close to stealing our country.

Everything revolves around protecting the financial interests and security of the economic elite. Members of this ruling class are elitist, but most are also patriotic. They truly believe that what's in their best interest is in the best interest of the country. And they are correct. If the economic elite come under serious attack or are broken up, it will have a huge impact on our country and on all of us because the economic power elite, unfortunately, *is* our country. The interests of the people are secondary to the interests of the economic power elite. Protecting the economic elite's interests is why we fought the Cold War and why we are fighting in the Middle East. The economic elite need enemies to maintain its power base and to feed its insatiable appetite for power and profits. The economy is dependent on the power elite. Their interests are our interests. That is how it was planned all along. That's why there's a revolving door.

In a November 2014 article headlined "Enough Is Enough," Senator Elizabeth Warren gave Citigroup as an example of the revolving door.[24] She pointed out that three of the last four Treasury secretaries under Democratic presidents held high-paying jobs at Citigroup either before or after serving at Treasury.

Directors of the National Economic Council and Office of Management and Budget, the current vice chairman of the Federal Reserve, and the US trade representative also pulled in millions from Citi, Warren said. "That's what the revolving door looks like at just one Too Big to Fail Bank," Warren stated.

What about others, like Goldman Sachs or J. P. Morgan? Shortly before the Eric Cantor episode, another former member of Congress, Democrat Melissa Bean, took the same senior job at JPMorgan Chase previously held by Democrat Bill Daley before his recent service as White House chief of staff.

"Soon after they crashed the economy and got tens of billions of dollars in taxpayer bailouts, the biggest Wall Street banks started lobbying Congress to head-off any serious financial regulation," Warren wrote.

"Public Citizen and the Canter for Responsive Politics found that in 2009 alone, the financial services sector employed 1,447 former federal employees to carry out their lobbying efforts, swarming all over Congress." These lobbyists included seventy-three former members of Congress. Warren also noted that President Obama has repeatedly turned to nominees with close Wall Street ties for high-level economic positions. She gave numerous examples.

Paul Krugman wrote an editorial titled "Our Invisible Rich" in the *New York Times* in September 2014, in which he pointed out that:

> The wealth of the top one percent has surged relative to everyone else; rising from 25 percent of total wealth in 1973 to 40 percent now, but the great bulk of that rise has taken place among the top 0.1 percent, the richest one-thousandth of Americans. [25]

He added that numerous surveys show the average American has no idea how much of a wealth discrepancy we have in this country.

Is unawareness the reason why we, the American people, do not rise up against the elite's theft of our country? Or have we become so propagandized that we are content to lap up the elite's leftovers? "House Negroes" of the Old South escaped working in the fields by attending to their masters' home needs, such as cooking, housecleaning, and gardening. Field hands aspired to these coveted inside positions because the work was easier and they would often be given their masters' leftovers. The plantation owners would fill themselves to capacity and, at times, would give the leftovers to the "house Negroes." Note: They were actually called house "n" word, not Negroes.

Are the elite filling themselves to satiation and then, on occasion, giving the rest of us their leftovers (just enough to keep us in line and coming back for more)?

David Hapgood, author of *Screwing of the Average American: How the Rich Get Richer and You Get Poorer,* wrote that people don't smash the roulette wheel that keeps turning them up losers because they don't want to face the reality that they are among the taken and not the takers. He notes that the average person's cut keeps getting smaller and smaller according to the "trickle-up" theory."[26]

In a similar vein, John Steinbeck said, "The poor see themselves not as an exploited proletariat but as temporarily embarrassed millionaires."[27]

Aldous Huxley said in a speech that "you can do everything with bayonets except sit on them! If you are going to control any population for any length of time you must have some measure of consent. I think sooner or later you have to bring in an element of persuasion (propaganda): an element of getting people to consent to what is happening to them. It seems to me that we are in the process of developing a whole series of techniques which will enable the controlling oligarchy to get people actually to love their servitude!"[28]

The techniques Huxley was referring to were propaganda techniques. It has been over fifty years since his speech. If Huxley were alive today, he would likely consider his prediction accurate about a propagandized population passively accepting their "screwing" (as Hapgood described it) by a plutocracy of very wealthy and powerful people. Getting us to love our servitude is a key goal of covert propaganda.

Modern media's success in making millions of us meekly accept our own screwing is testament to the power of propaganda and, in particular, Bernays's engineering of consent. This propaganda technique has given us the consent to accept our status without protest, to conform, and to exercise self-censorship (and constraint) no matter how far down the totem pole (to use an old cliché) we might be. Propaganda gives us hope that the roulette wheel will someday turn in our favor.

This hope for a better life in the future was a primary propaganda theme that allowed slavery and segregation to thrive in the South for decades. It's still effective in persuading people of color and the poor to passively accept their plight. Media is full of success stories, fiction and nonfiction, of those who have elevated their status. The lottery is also a carrot stick for hope.

Religion has been particularly effective in giving the downtrodden hope. I grew up in the South. While participating in the civil rights movement during the sixties, I attended several black church services. A constant theme in sermons and in the wonderful gospel music (which I still love) was that things would be better in the next life.

The message was, and still is, don't worry; someday the roulette wheel will turn you up a winner, if not in this life, at least in the next one.

• • •

The opposite of the engineering of consent is a phrase I developed. I call it the engineering of dissent. It basically involves deliberately stirring up or inciting dissent, usually to later crush it. It's similar to a false-flag incident. I will give many examples of this propaganda technique but, before doing so, I want to introduce what I call the Eight Ds of dissent propaganda. These include denial, diversion, discrediting, dehumanization, demonizing, disinformation, destruction, and most important, plausible deniability.

These Eight Ds provide nearly foolproof cover for most covert activities. If an enterprising investigative reporter, for example, gets too close to a covert operation or the truth about some secret government action or agenda, he or she is given the Eight Ds' treatment.

First you **d**eny the issue or problem. Next you **d**ivert attention from it. If that doesn't work, you **d**iscredit the person or group. If that fails you **d**ehumanize them and then **d**emonize them. Next you use **d**isinformation (you lie). If all of those Ds fail, you **d**estroy them socially, psychologically, and even physically. Finally there is plausible **d**eniability, which allows those at the top to escape detection.

Deniability (we propagandists call it "plausible deniability"), combined with the propaganda technique of layering, provides near absolute cover and protection for just about any covert activity, although I will give an example of one huge covert activity that employed all of these techniques and was still unraveled, but it took many years after the event.

As long as covert operators work in secrecy, they can do whatever they want and we will not know it, and even if we do, we won't be able to prove anything because you can't finger someone invisible, particularly when they throw in the Eight Ds and other propaganda covers, such as layering.

I have already mentioned the covert propaganda techniques of association, disinformation, layering, diversion, emotionally laden words, the third-party front, block and bridge, the bandwagon, the engineering of dissent, and the engineering of consent. I will discuss these in later chapters, plus other techniques. I will also unveil some linguistic and semantic tools propagandists use to implement these techniques, such as generalizations, specializations, degradation, elevation, euphemisms, hyperbole, minced forms, value-laden words, and unintelligible words.

If you recognize and understand just a few techniques and tools, you will have at least a fighting chance to protect yourself and your loved ones from mass mind manipulation.

CHAPTER 6

Mind Control, Drugs, and a Malleable Media

WOULD THE COVERT WING OF our government and the business/financial interests it supports deliberately attempt to control our political views, social beliefs, moral outlooks, and lifestyles? Yes. And there is proof from many sources, including numerous covert government agency files.

FBI files show that the FBI has been active in covert propaganda activities for many years, including the highly secretive COINTELPRO program; this program reveals a lot about covert propaganda. The FBI files were accidentally uncovered during a break-in at FBI offices.

These files contain information that is startling, particularly because it's hard to believe that some of the FBI's activities took place in a democracy. The Senate Intelligence Committee, headed by Senator Frank Church, conducted hearings on FBI abuses and released a lengthy report on its findings. Here is what the Church Committee wrote in its 1976 report:

> Governmental officials, including those whose principal duty is to enforce the law, have violated or ignored the law over long periods of time (many decades). Groups and individuals have been assaulted, repressed, harassed and disrupted because of their political views, social beliefs and their lifestyles. Investigations have been based upon vague standards whose breadth made excessive collection inevitable. Unsavory, harmful and vicious tactics have been

employed, including anonymous attempts to break up marriages, disrupt meetings, ostracize persons from their professions, and provoke target groups into rivalries that might result in deaths.[1]

Betty Medsger's book *The Burglary: The Discovery of J. Edgar Hoover's Secret FBI* is one of the best exposés ever written on how far the FBI has been willing to go to use engineering-of-dissent propaganda techniques (such as the FBI's dictum to agents to enhance the paranoia of those who disagreed with government policy or injustices).[2]

Medsger revealed from FBI files that FBI director J. Edgar Hoover monitored and persecuted groups or individuals he did not like, such as anyone who smacked of being a socialist sympathizer, an antiwar demonstrator, or an African-American activist. The FBI even opened files on people who simply wrote letters to the editor objecting to the war in Vietnam. The papers also showed that the FBI was encouraging agents to infiltrate schools and churches in the black community using secret informants to turn people against each other.

No one, neither Congress nor successive presidents, could stop Hoover. No one wanted to. He survived eight presidents and had more power than any of them. President Nixon once said long before Watergate, "Hoover could bring down the temple (government), including me."[3]

Some may be tempted to dismiss these repugnant activities by putting the blame on Hoover's right-wing anti-Communist paranoia, but FBI agents have worked with intelligence agencies, corporate and media leaders, the military, and scientists for decades on programs to disrupt, control, and co-opt individuals and groups whose socioeconomic and political beliefs were considered unacceptable.

For those who may doubt our government has had an interest in mass mind manipulation, I suggest looking at the official memorandum "Meeting with IAQ Representatives of Project BLUEBIRD," July 23, 1951. It states that the CIA and the intelligence divisions of the army, navy, air force, and FBI headed a joint meeting to explore "coordination of mind control research."[4]

On March 12, 1955, the National Security Council, on which Nelson Rockefeller served, authorized the CIA, under Directive 5412/I, to "use any means necessary" in its mind control program, including "propaganda, economic warfare, sabotage, antisabotage, subversion and preventive direct actions, demolitions, and deceptive plans and operations." That key directive followed the September 1954 memorandum from the CIA to President Eisenhower in which it was noted that the campaign required "an aggressive, covert, psychological, political and paramilitary organization." The memorandum also noted: "There are no rules in such a game. Hitherto acceptable norms of human conduct do not apply. No one should be permitted to stand in the way of the prompt, efficient, and secure accomplishment of this mission (covert actions)."[5]

You can't get any blunter than these two highly secret memorandums/directives. Operation ARTICHOKE was a mind control program that involved the intelligence divisions of the army, navy, air force, and FBI. Operation BLUEBIRD was also involved in mind control, but was more interested in applying behavior modification drugs to unwitting subjects. Operation BLUEBIRD began in August 1951 and was run by the CIA's Office of Scientific Intelligence. A memo from Richard Helms to CIA director Allen Dulles indicated that Artichoke and Bluebird became Project MKULTRA in April 1953.

The scope of mind control programs was bluntly stated in a memo dated January 1952: "Can we get control of an individual to the point where he will do our bidding against his will and even against fundamental laws of nature, such as self-preservation?"[6]

In 1953, CIA director Allen Dulles, speaking before a national meeting of Princeton alumni, revealed two battle fronts in what he called "the battle for men's minds."[7] He said the first front was mass indoctrination through censorship and propaganda. Dulles said the second front was individual brainwashing and brain changing. This speech was before an audience of fellow Ivy Leaguers, so Dulles likely felt comfortable skipping the usual pieties about freedom and democracy. That same year Dulles approved the

CIA's notorious MKULTRA project and exempted it from normal CIA financial controls.

The MKULTRA implementing documents specified that "additional avenues to the control of human behavior" were to include "radiation, electroshock, various fields of psychology, sociology, and anthropology, graphology, harassment substances, and paramilitary devices and materials."[8]

We have seen many of these avenues to control human behavior implemented in recent decades, particularly the use of paramilitary devices and materials. By 2014 even small-town police forces were often equipped with machine guns, camouflaged military clothing, body armor, and even tanks and armored vehicles.

Some might say that thought control programs like MKULTRA and the proliferation of paramilitary devices are beneficial because they protect us from foreign and domestic "enemies." That might be partially true, but who is the enemy? A top CIA agent, as I noted earlier, said covert operatives often consider the American people "the enemy" because revelations of their clandestine activities is perceived as a threat to their ability to operate in secret. They see themselves as true patriots involved in a just war, in which basically anything goes.

Does the rationalization that propagandists can "use any means necessary" since they are involved in a "just war" extend to rewriting, twisting, or putting a beneficial spin on history? Yes. History has been spun and manipulated for decades in our country, beginning with the World War I era when America's leading historians, such as Dr. Guy Ford, served as mini-propagandists for the Committee on Public Information's propaganda program.

Ford, who was head of the American Historical Association, and his historian cohorts were allowed to avoid military service by serving on the CPI. They were told by propagandists Bernays and Byoir what spin to put on events during the World War I era. I will discuss this in detail in a later chapter.

There are a lot more examples of the distortion of history, including some recent ones. For example, former CIA operator Victor Marchetti wrote a September 2012 article in the *Institute for Historical Review* in which he noted that "the CIA is a master at distorting history; even in creating its own version of history to suit its institutional and operational purposes." He said the CIA can do this because it operates in secrecy.[9]

"When the public does not know what the government or the CIA is doing, it cannot voice its approval or disapproval of their actions. In fact, they can even lie to you about what they are doing or have done, and you will not know it," Marchetti stated.

The article quoted another CIA operative, who said, "We operate in secrecy, we deal in deception and disinformation, and then we burn our files. How will the historians ever be able to learn the complete truth about what we've done in these various operations, these operations that have had such a major impact on so many important events in history?"

Marchetti responded to that statement by noting: "I don't know how the American people will ever really know the truth about the many things that the CIA has been involved in. Or how they will ever know the truth about the great historical events of our times.

"The government is continually writing and rewriting history—often with the CIA's help—to suit its own purposes," he added.

A recent example of an attempt to rewrite history is the Vietnam War Commemoration Project, a $65 million, thirteen-year propaganda project to clean up the image of the Vietnam War in the minds of Americans.[10]

President Obama officially launched the project on Memorial Day 2012 with a speech at the Vietnam Wall in Washington. The project was established by the National Defense Authorization Act. It budgeted $5 million a year for eleven years. It is simply an attempt to put a better spin on the Vietnam War. Which view of the Vietnam War will students of history get a hundred years from now? Will they get a sanitized version or an accurate account of what really happened? What version of history did we get in school of past events? Was it what really happened or what others wanted us to believe happened?

• • •

That last question—what really happened?—can be asked about numerous domestic and foreign events that have involved the clandestine use of propaganda. Another legitimate question is how much mainstream media, often owned by titans of the economic elite, participates in spreading propaganda and/or is manipulated by clandestine propagandists?

In 1996 the *San Jose Mercury News* ran a news series called "Dark Alliance: The Story Behind the Crack Explosion," by Gary Webb. The series reported that in addition to waging a proxy war for the US government against Nicaragua's leftist Sandinista government in the 1980s, elements of the CIA-backed Contra rebels were also involved in trafficking cocaine to the United States in order to fund their counterrevolutionary campaign.[11]

Webb charged that the Reagan administration shielded inner-city drug dealers from prosecution in order to raise money for the Contras. Webb also alleged that this influx of Nicaraguan-supplied cocaine may have sparked and significantly fueled the widespread crack cocaine epidemic that swept through many US cities during the 1980s.

Reporter Ryan Devereaux wrote in the September 25, 2014, edition of *The Intercept* that Webb's bombshell investigation into links between the cocaine trade, Nicaragua's Contra rebels, and African American neighborhoods in California remains one of the most explosive and controversial exposés in American journalism, particularly because Webb reported that the secret flow of drugs and money "had a direct link to the subsequent explosion of crack cocaine abuse that had devastated California's most vulnerable African American neighbourhoods."[12]

The twenty-thousand-word, three-part series by Webb stimulated a backlash against Webb from the nation's most powerful media outlets. These media devoted considerable resources to discredit his reporting and to demonize him even though he was an award-winning journalist.

Although the Webb series was largely ignored by large media outlets, it received considerable coverage on the Internet and in black outlets, including black talk radio. Some of the black radio stations charged that the US government had spread cocaine into black areas as part of its plan to pacify potential protestors and disrupters of the status quo. A declassified article titled "Managing A Nightmare: CIA Public Affairs and the Drug Conspiracy Story," from the agency's internal journal, "Studies in Intelligence," shows that the spy agency was reeling in the weeks after Webb's disclosures. The internal document referenced rumors on talk radio and the Internet that "the Agency was the instrument of a consistent strategy by the U.S. Government to destroy the black community and to keep black Americans from advancing."[13]

One of the nation's leading drug dealers gave sworn testimony at a trial just before Webb's series appeared that in 1981 alone, his drug operation sold almost a ton of cocaine in the United States. He said he was able to sell cocaine at prices lower than other dealers were asking because of his large supply. This allowed him to expand his markets to cities throughout the United States.[14]

Despite this sworn testimony from one of the country's top drug dealers that the CIA was moving unprecedented amounts of cocaine into the United States, where it was reaching the streets in the cheap form of crack and helping lead to an epidemic of addiction in American cities, the nation's major media sat on the information. Webb didn't give up. He continued to investigate the story. The more he investigated, the more evidence he uncovered that the CIA was involved or looked the other way in spreading drugs into the United States.

On December 10, 2004, Webb was found dead in his apartment. He had two .38-caliber bullet shots to the head. His death, despite two gunshot wounds to the head, was ruled a suicide. (Note: Two other investigative journalists also died after investigating covert activities – Michael Hastings in 2013 and Michael Ruppert in 2014.)

Friends of Webb have claimed that Webb told them he was being followed prior to his death. In September 2014, never-before-released CIA documents revealed that mainstream media either completely ignored Webb's story or they did everything they could to destroy his credibility.

Scooped in its own backyard, the *Los Angeles Times* assigned numerous reporters to investigate Webb's reporting.

After Webb's series appeared, Nicholas Dujmovic, a CIA Directorate of Intelligence staffer, wrote a blunt assessment of the potential damage to the agency's image in a document titled "Managing a Nightmare: CIA Public Affairs and the Drug Conspiracy Story."[15] He stated: The charges could hardly be worse. A widely read newspaper series leads many Americans to believe CIA is guilty of at least complicity, if not conspiracy, in the outbreak of crack cocaine in America's cities." The CIA, Dujmovic noted, had "a ground base of already productive relations with journalists.

Did the nation's major media lay off Webb's revelations and then jointly engage in a smear campaign to discredit and destroy Webb because of what this CIA agent called the CIA's "ground base of already productive relations with journalists"?

The online news site *The Intercept* reported in September 2014 that a prominent national security reporter for the *Los Angeles Times* routinely submitted drafts and detailed summaries of his stories to CIA press handlers prior to publication. "Email exchanges between CIA public affairs officers and Ken Dilanian, now an *Associated Press* intelligence reporter who previously covered the CIA for the Times, show that Dilanian enjoyed a closely collaborative relationship with the agency, explicitly promising positive news coverage and sometimes sending the press office entire story drafts for review prior to publication."[16]

In one e-mail to the CIA press officer, Dilanian, according to *The Intercept*, wrote that "I'm working on a story about congressional oversight of drone strikes that can present a good opportunity for you guys," explaining that what he intended to report would be "reassuring to the public" about CIA drone strikes.

How many other reporters have these kinds of close collaborative relations with intelligence and surveillance agencies, but simply haven't been caught? Later in this chapter, I will unveil many more close relationships between the media and our nation's clandestine agencies.

A special Senate Subcommittee, chaired by then-senator John Kerry in 1989, released a 1,166-page report on covert US operations throughout Latin America and the Caribbean. This is from the subcommittee report:

> On the basis of this evidence, it is clear that individuals who provided support for the Contras were involved in drug trafficking, the supply network of the Contras was used by drug trafficking organizations, and elements of the Contras themselves knowingly received financial and material assistance from drug traffickers. In each case, one or another agency of the U.S. government had information regarding the involvement either while it was occurring, or immediately thereafter.[17]

The story of Gary Webb was featured in director Michael Cuesta's fall 2014 film *Kill the Messenger,* which starred Jeremy Renner as the hard-charging investigative reporter. It borrowed its title from a 2006 biography written by award-winning investigative journalist Nick Schou, who worked as a consultant on the film's script. Schou reported in a 2013 article in the *LA Weekly* that Webb's reporting was eventually vindicated.[18]

Major media that were scooped by Webb even continued their demonization of him in their review of the film. Jeff Leen of the *Washington Post* wrote in October 2014 that Webb's articles didn't meet the journalistic standard that "an extraordinary claim requires extraordinary proof."

Robert Parry, who along with Brian Barger first broke the Contra drug scandal in 1985 when Parry was a reporter for Associated Press, responded to Leen's statement that extraordinary claims require extraordinary proof by noting in a *Consortium News* October 12, 2014 article, "Washington Post's Slimy Assault on Gary Webb," that "many extraordinary claims, such as assertions in 2002–03 that Iraq was hiding arsenals of WMDs, were published as flat-fact without 'extraordinary proof' or any real evidence at all, including by Leen's colleagues at the Washington Post."

Parry noted that different sets of rules govern American journalism and that journalists need extraordinary proof if a story puts the US government or an ally in a negative light, but pretty much anything goes when criticizing an enemy. Parry claimed Leen was wrong in another way because there was "extraordinary proof" establishing that the Contras were implicated in drug trafficking and that the Reagan administration was, at best, looking the other way.

Geneva Overholser, who served as the ombudsman for Leen's *Washington Post*, wrote that major media outlets, including the *Washington Post*, should have shown more passion "for sniffing out the flaws in the Mercury News' answer than for sniffing out a better answer themselves."[19]

Susan Bell of the *Independent/UK* newspaper wrote: "Webb's pieces were not dealing with nameless peasants slaughtered in some distant republic, but demonstrated a clear link between the CIA and the suppliers of the gangs delivering crack to the ghetto of Watts, in South Central Los Angeles." Not surprisingly there was very little pickup of the story by other independent news agencies and organizations, many of which the CIA controlled.

On July 23, 1998, the Justice Department released a report by its inspector general, Michael Bromwich. The Bromwich report claimed that the Reagan-Bush administration was aware of cocaine traffickers in the Contra movement and did nothing to stop the criminal activity. The report also alleged a pattern of discarded leads and witnesses, sabotaged investigations, instances of the CIA working with drug traffickers, and the discouragement of DEA investigations into Contra-cocaine shipments.[20]

On October 8, 1998, CIA inspector general Hitz published Volume Two of his internal investigation. The report described how the Reagan-Bush administration had protected more than fifty Contras and other drug traffickers and by so doing thwarted federal investigations into drug crimes.[21]

Hitz published evidence that drug trafficking and money laundering had made its way into Reagan/s National Security Council, where Oliver North oversaw the operations of the Contras. According to the report, the Contra war took precedence over law enforcement. To that end the internal investigation revealed that the CIA routinely withheld evidence of Contra crimes from the Justice Department, Congress, and even the analytical division of the CIA itself. This is another example of "the ends justify the means" and "anything goes." How many of our covert activities have, as the report noted, "taken precedence over law enforcement"? Does this happen in a democracy?

Further, the report confirmed Webb's claims regarding the origins and the relationship of Contra fund-raising and drug trafficking. More importantly, the internal CIA report documented a cover-up of evidence, which had led to false intelligence assessments. Why did the nation's major media outlets ignore Webb's findings, which have proven not only true, but much worse than even Webb imagined? Why also did the media, for the most part, give the subcommittee report scant attention? Did our nation's intelligence services and the economic elite have our top media outlets under control?

James Aucoin, a communications professor who specializes in the history of investigative reporting, wrote: "In the case of Gary Webb's charges against the CIA and the Contras, the major dailies came after him. Media institutions are now part of the establishment and they have a lot invested in that establishment."[22]

On May 7, 1998, Representative Maxine Waters revealed a memorandum of understanding between the CIA and the Justice Department from 1982, which was entered into the Congressional Record. This memorandum legally freed the CIA from reporting drug smuggling by CIA assets, a provision that covered the Nicaraguan Contras and the Afghan rebels.[23]

The Contra-cocaine connection was not the CIA's only involvement in drug trafficking. Alfred McCoy devoted a whole book to the subject, *The Politics of Heroin: CIA Complicity in the Global Drug Trade.* This book, as far as I know, is the first book to make a strong case of CIA and US government complicity in the worldwide drug trade. McCoy concludes that "American diplomats and secret agents have been involved in the narcotics traffic at three levels: (1) coincidental complicity by allying with groups actively engaged in the drug traffic; (2) abetting the traffic by covering up for known heroin traffickers and condoning their involvement; (3) and active engagement in the transport of opium and heroin."[24]

Ryan Grim, Washington Bureau chief for the *Huffington Post*, wrote on November 10, 2014, that "foreign critics are quick to blame the global drug trade and its attendant problems on the voracious demand of American drug users. Stop snorting so much coke, they tell us, and our farmers will stop growing coca. American drug warriors, meanwhile, treat the trade as a foreign threat that needs to be eradicated in root countries and stopped at the border. Stop growing so much coca, and we'll stop snorting it."

But both sides miss—or ignore—a crucial fact: for decades and for a variety of reasons, the United States has had some connection to the global supply chain, protecting and even funding drug-running organizations, Grim noted. The government has denied it for just as long. And American media, Webb discovered the hard way, can tie itself in knots trying to avoid discussing the issue.

I find it very odd that so little outrage has been generated in our so-called free press by revelations from Webb and others about government involvement in drug trafficking. The upcoming section on our malleable media might provide some answers to why the American press basically ignored Webb's findings.

Was the Reagan administration's "war on drugs" a diversionary propaganda tactic to make it appear there was an aggressive war-on-drugs campaign underway when, in reality, the Reagan administration may have been complicit in the introduction of drugs into the United_States? If so, it wouldn't be the first time our government has been complicit or looked the other way in the drug trade (I give specific examples in later chapters). Not only have we worked with drug kingpins; we have also worked closely and secretly with organized crime. Block and bridge propaganda is usually the cornerstone of such super-secret operations.

Block and bridge, as I have noted, allows you to manage a problem by blocking an original issue (such as allowing coke into this country) and redirecting it to another issue (the war on drugs) so that the redirected issue becomes of more interest than the original issue.

Propagandists for Reagan might have also employed the circuit breaker technique, which involves diverting attention from a primary source or problem (such as government direct involvement in the Contra-cocaine incident) by revealing information on secondary and less-sensitive theses (such as the administration's passive involvement).

In other words, a "we simply looked the other way" positioning is much less damaging and diverts attention from active involvement. Looking the other way involves standing down, which is part of the false-flag technique.

Still another propaganda technique that might have been used is the red herring. This involves presenting issues or data that, while compelling, are irrelevant to the argument at hand, and then claiming that it validates the argument. An example would be major media's attempts to discredit Webb and his reporting, rather than pursuing the primary issue (our complicity in allowing drugs into the inner cities). As noted earlier, the *Washington Post*'s own ombudsman stated that her newspaper had spent more time on looking for flaws in Webb's reporting than looking for a better answer.

• • •

Did the press ignore and/or mock these reports because of an unwillingness to confront their government sources with unpleasant questions? Were some of the reporters, editors, and publishers among the four hundred journalists Carl Bernstein identified as having CIA ties through Operation Mockingbird? Operation Mockingbird was a secret campaign begun in the early fifties by the CIA to recruit leading American journalists to help present CIA propaganda.

Is this the same kind of reporting that has allowed our government to subvert, bomb, and invade countries whenever it chooses, with little protest?

Poppy Bush exercised tight control over media coverage of Desert Storm. George Bush did the same in the Iraq War. They both, as we will show in detail, may have used disinformation to convince us we were undertaking just invasions. They also created some of the best propaganda in history.

Nancy Snow, author of an excellent book, *Information War,* said the younger Bush became an effective "commander-in-chief of propaganda" because of his ability to frame the war on terrorism in vivid and simplistic either/or terms ("you are either for us or against us").[25]

Snow also pointed out that the 9/11 attacks were packaged as our generation's Pearl Harbor and the US invasions and occupations of Afghanistan and Iraq as operations defending democracy, liberty, and freedom, all of which evoke positive emotional reactions in the majority of people. This leaves little wiggle room for someone to be against a war, because if you're against a war, it means you don't support freedom, liberty, or democracy

President Bush quickly succeeded in defining the parameters of our national dialogue in the war on terrorism when he said, "Either you are against us or you are with us." He wasn't just talking to terrorist "parasites." He was also speaking to the American people.

As Alfred McClung Lee noted, "The propagandist strives for simplicity and vividness, coupled with speed and broad impact. He stimulates popular emotional drives; in so doing he must for the most part bypass factual discussion and debate of any sort."[26]

Both Bushes and their handlers (propagandists) were excellent at keeping things simple and framing issues to appeal to the propaganda sweet spot—our emotions.

Both Bushes were also adept at controlling the media. *Newsweek's* Gulf War reporter, Bob Sipschen, wrote in the *Los Angeles Times* March 1991 that "Desert Storm was really two wars: Allies against the Iraqis and the military against the press. I had more guns pointed at me by Americans and Saudis who were into controlling the press than in all my years of actual combat."[27]

Note that the *Newsweek* correspondent said the Americans and the Saudis were controlling the press. We will go into detail in another chapter about the long-standing US-Saudi collusion, not just on propaganda, but on just about everything involving the Middle East.

Carl Bernstein, who broke the Watergate story, wrote a cover story in the October 20, 1977, issue of *Rolling Stone* magazine, in which he identified more than four hundred American journalists who secretly carried out CIA assignments from 1945 through 1970. What Bernstein discovered from CIA documents themselves is that the best way to put propaganda into the news is from the inside. Bernstein started his article by noting, "In 1953, Joseph Alsop, then one of America's leading syndicated columnists, went to the Philippines to cover an election. He did not go because he was asked to do so by his syndicate. He did not go because he was asked to do so by the newspapers that printed his column. He went at the request of the CIA."[28]

Besides Alsop, other media luminaries who cooperated with the CIA, according to Bernstein, were the president of CBS, William Paley, Henry Luce of *Time*, Arthur Hays Sulzberger of the *New York Times*, and James Copley of the *Copley News Service*. The most valued CIA assets were the *New York Times*, CBS, and *Time, Inc.* "The *New York Times* alone provided cover to the CIA for at least ten operatives between 1950 and 1966," Bernstein wrote.

Bernstein found that those journalists who played along with the CIA by signing secrecy agreements were most likely to succeed in their careers because the CIA connection gave them access to the best stories. "The journalists and their CIA handlers often shared the same educational background and the same ideal that both were serving the national-security interests of the United States," Bernstein said.

Among the many examples Bernstein gives of the intelligence community/media revolving door are: (1) the former CIA director Richard Helms (mid-1960s to early 1970s) was once a *UPI* wire service correspondent. (2) William Casey, the CIA director under Ronald Reagan, was once chief counsel and a board member at Capital Cities Communications, which absorbed *ABC News* in Reagan's second term. (3) Two prominent journalists, Edward R. Murrow and Carl Rowan, served as directors of the US Information Agency under Kennedy, while the *NBC Nightly News* reporter John Chancellor was director of the government international propaganda radio service Voice of America under L. B. Johnson. (4) The first deputy director of the NSA, Joseph H. Ream, had previously worked as executive vice president of *CBS* and, after NSA, he returned to *CBS* without disclosing his association with the super-secretive agency.

Washington Post owner Philip Graham was a military intelligence officer in World War II and later became close friends with CIA figures like Frank Wisner, Allen Dulles, Desmond Fitzgerald, and Richard Helms.

The key point that came out of Bernstein's extensive research of CIA files and interviews with CIA officials was that intelligence agencies and the media have had and do have close working relationships. Obviously, from the example I gave earlier of the *Los Angeles Times* reporter who worked closely with the CIA, these relationships continue to this day.

After World War II, most Americans believed the new medium of television would give them a variety of viewpoints and an objective look at the news. Yet from their very inception, all three TV networks have been guided by men who were products of and beholden to America's intelligence agencies and to the economic elite to which most of them belonged.

Many of the men who ran ABC, CBS, and NBC, as well as those sitting on their boards of directors, had CIA ties. William Paley, the head of CBS, served in the psychological warfare branch of the Office of War Information. Capital Cities owner William Casey became the director of the CIA under Ronald Reagan.

Television networks were also riddled with CIA assets. A key CIA contact was Sig Mickelson, the president of CBS News from 1954 to 1961. Later he went on to become president of Radio Free Europe and Radio Liberty, two major outlets of CIA propaganda.

If you recall, I noted earlier that I did some public relations work for Radio Free Europe and, at the time, had no idea it was founded by and funded by the CIA. It was a front for the CIA's propaganda, as was Radio Liberty. The CIA's relationship with the radio stations began to break down in 1967, when *Ramparts* magazine published an exposé claiming that the CIA was channeling funds to civilian organizations, such as the National Student Union. Further investigation into the CIA's funding activities revealed its connection to both Radio Free Europe and Radio Liberty. The 1967 *Ramparts* exposé revealed that, in addition to infiltrating American media, the Central Intelligence Agency had been secretly funding and managing a wide range of citizen front groups intended to counter so-called Communist influence.

Hugh Wilford, in his book *The Mighty Wurlitzer: How the CIA Played America*, gave a detailed account of the CIA's front network from its beginnings in the 1940s. "Mighty Wurlitzer" was the metaphor CIA agent Frank Wisner, as I noted in the last chapter, employed to describe the CIA's front organizations, which, Wisner said, were "capable of playing any propaganda tune we desired."[29]

Senator Frank Church's investigations through the Select Committee to Study Governmental Operations with Respect to Intelligence Activities revealed details of Operation Mockingbird in a congressional report in 1976. It noted:

> The CIA currently maintains a network of several hundred foreign individuals around the world who provide intelligence for the CIA and at times attempt to influence opinion through the use of covert propaganda. These individuals provide the CIA with direct access to a large number of newspapers and periodicals, scores of press services and news agencies, radio and television stations, commercial book publishers, and other foreign media outlets.[30]

Operation Mockingbird and the Bernstein revelations later showed that US intelligence agencies also conducted covert propaganda in the United States through close relations with US media.

Michael Hasty noted in a February 5, 2004, *Online Journal* article, "Secret Admirers: The Bushes and the Washington Post," that Philip Graham continued to have close contact with his fellow upper-class intelligence veterans in the newly formed CIA and "actively promoted the CIA's goals in his newspaper. The incestuous relationship between the Post and the intelligence community even extended to its hiring practices."[31]

According to Hasty, Bernstein quoted this from a CIA official: "It was widely known that Phil Graham was somebody you could get help from. Graham has been identified by some investigators as the main contact in Project Mockingbird, the CIA program to infiltrate domestic American media."

Hasty also pointed out that "in her autobiography, Katherine Graham described how her husband worked overtime at the Post during the Bay of Pigs operation to protect the reputations of his friends from Yale who had organized the ill-fated venture."

What is interesting about Hasty's investigation is that it shows how top media, financial, and government elites move in the same circles. For example, in an article published by the media watchdog group Fairness and Accuracy in Reporting (FAIR), titled "Washington Post Promotes Agendas of Power Elite," writer Doug Henwood traced the *Washington Post*'s establishment connections to Eugene Meyer, who took control of the *Post* in 1933. [32]

Meyer transferred ownership to his daughter Katharine and her husband, Philip Graham, after World War II, when Meyer was appointed by President Truman to serve as the first president of the World Bank. "Meyer had been 'a Wall Street banker, director of President Wilson's War Finance Corporation, a governor of the Federal Reserve System, and director of the Reconstruction Finance Corporation," Henwood pointed out.

Henwood also wrote another FAIR article, "Washington Post Owner Katherine Graham Advocates Secrecy in Press and Government." Graham has been identified by some investigators as the main contact in Project Mockingbird, the CIA program to infiltrate domestic American media.

Media have become much more malleable since Project Mockingbird first started. Paul Craig Roberts, former assistant secretary of the treasury under President Reagan and a former editor of the *Wall Street Journal*, *Business Week*, and other publications, wrote in 2006 that:

The uniformity of the US media has become much more complete since the days of the Cold War. During the 1990s, the US government permitted an unconscionable concentration of print and broadcast media that terminated the independence of the media. Today the US media is owned by five giant companies.

More importantly, the values of the conglomerates reside in the broadcast licenses, which are granted by the government, and the corporations are run by corporate executives, not by journalists, whose eyes are on advertising revenues and the avoidance of controversy that might produce boycotts or upset advertisers and subscribers.[33]

A very important graduate of Operation Mockingbird, the CIA's secret program to create a malleable media, was General Charles Douglas (C. D.) Jackson. General Jackson was not only a top US general, but he also was a top executive and publisher with *Time*, *Life*, and *Fortune* magazines, the three largest magazines in the country. In addition, he was a spook. During World War II, he served in the Office of Strategic Services, the forerunner of the CIA.[34]

Like many in the economic power elite, he was an Ivy League graduate (Princeton, 1924). In 1931 he joined *Time* magazine and in 1940 was president of the Council for Democracy. During his wartime OSS service, he became deputy chief of the Psychological Warfare Division, where he learned about covert propaganda. After the war he became managing director of Time-Life International from 1945 to 1949. He then became publisher of *Fortune*. From 1951-52 he served as president of the Anticommunist Free Europe Committee.

He was also a speech writer for Dwight Eisenhower's 1952 presidential campaign. Next, he was assigned to be President Eisenhower's liaison between the newly created CIA and the Pentagon. From February 1953 to March 1954, Jackson served as adviser to the president on psychological warfare. During 1953 and 1954, C. D. Jackson helped establish the Bilderberg Group and ensured American participation. He attended meetings of the elitist group in 1957, 1958, and 1960.

Jackson was a major backer and board member of Radio Free Europe. He later served in a position at the United Nations. From 1958 to 1960, he served as a speechwriter and White House manager. In 1960 he became publisher of *Life* magazine.

Jackson, like many others, is an example of someone involved in the top echelons of our military establishment, the media, big business, our intelligence services, and covert propaganda. The revolving door among these top supporters and members of the economic power elite is no accident.

Very few people know of Jackson, but he was one of the most powerful people in America for many years. He was someone who seamlessly moved between overt and covert activities, but most of the time he worked behind the scenes and was invisible to the American people. How many Jacksons are there today?

How many of the news stories that we follow daily are reported by or influenced by propagandists or intelligence operatives? How many legitimate-sounding media outlets are, in truth, intelligence agency fronts? The relationships Bernstein and others have unveiled not only affect what is written or spoken by certain members of the media; they can also impact what is not written or said.

Our nation's intelligence agencies' ability to use and cooperate with media on propaganda matters makes major media's claim of objectivity and a free press hypocritical. This is not to imply that every article you read and most of what you see or hear is compiled by journalists working with or for the CIA or another intelligence agency.

Most journalists are hardworking ethical people who believe in objectivity and have no idea their employer might have CIA ties or is cooperating with intelligence agencies or that the person sitting next to him or her in the newsroom might be an intelligence agent.

How many *New York Times* reporters, for example, knew in the fifties that Arthur Sulzberger, publisher of the *New York Times*, prevented his Central America reporter Sydney Gruson from even covering the CIA's

1954 overthrow of the democratically elected government of Guatemala at the direct request of Sulzberger's good friend Allen Dulles?

Dulles was not only CIA director when he told his publisher-friend not to cover the story; he also owned stock in and was on the board of Guatemala-based United Fruit. Protecting the assets of United Fruit was one of the primary reasons for the CIA-led coup. Numerous others in the Eisenhower administration were also connected to United Fruit, as I will discuss later.

This type of collusion among government, big business, and major media has been going on for nearly a century. It's the foundation of the mind manipulation campaign.

Do we truly have a free press in the country, or is that just a façade? The above examples are just a sample of how our media is influenced and manipulated by propagandists and covert operatives. CIA director Dulles telling his *New York Times* publisher-friend not to cover the CIA coup in Guatemala is another example.

Recently the *Washington Post* refused to run the initial Snowden revelations. There are hundreds of other examples of collusion among the elite of business, media, and government. Such collusions are partly because the owners and top executives of media, business, and government run in the same circles, have often attended the same elite schools, and frequently have the same socioeconomic outlooks. They usually hire managers with the same viewpoints.

In addition, what is critical is not what media choose to cover, but what they don't cover and their penchant for printing information from government without digging beneath the surface and asking hard questions. A perfect example of this acquiescence to government is nearly 100 percent of American media accepting at face value George Bush's claim that Iraq had weapons of mass destruction. Noam Chomsky and Edward Herman have explained that this commonality creates conformity of viewpoints and a self-censorship that protects the interests of big business, the government, and the military by advocating for the status quo. They note that in a democratic political order, there is always the danger that independent thought might be translated into political action, so it is important to eliminate independent thought at its base. They maintain as long as you have the proper boundaries and good propaganda, you will have maintenance of the status quo.[35]

• • •

Operation Mockingbird was a secret program to infiltrate American media. Another domestic program, possibly one of the most antidemocratic operations ever, was called Operation CHAOS.[36]

Operation CHAOS, which was also known as MHCHAOS, was a domestic espionage project conducted by the CIA beginning in 1967 on orders from President Johnson and, later, from Nixon. The operation was launched by CIA director Richard Helms. There were several key projects in this operation. Project MERIMAC, for example, involved CIA agents infiltrating domestic antiwar and radical political groups. Project RESISTANCE worked with college officials, campus security, and local police to identify antiwar activists and political dissidents. These so-called dissidents included countercultural groups even if they had no connection to the Vietnam War protests, such as groups and individuals active in the women's liberation movement (e.g., Women Strike for Peace).

A major campaign was conducted against *Ramparts* magazine, which scooped the mainstream media on numerous stories related to covert operations.

In twenty years, from 1947 to 1967, the CIA had moved from forswearing internal security functions to engaging in numerous domestic operations.

Not only did the CIA ignore US law by getting involved in domestic espionage; it also was a primary participant in the Interdivisional Information Unit. IDIU was made up of a myriad of covert intelligence agencies. Each shared a common goal: spying on American citizens. Operation Hydra, which was part of Operation CHAOS, contained files on 7,200 Americans and had a computer index on three hundred thousand civilians and approximately one thousand groups.[37]

In a national emergency, how many of those three hundred thousand Americans would be in danger of incarceration or worse, even though the vast majority was likely law-abiding citizens who simply believed in exercising their First Amendment rights?

Mark Zepezauer, author of *The CIA's Greatest Hits*, noted: "From 1959 to at least 1974, the CIA used its domestic organizations to spy on thousands of US citizens whose only crime was disagreeing with their government's policies. This picked up speed when J. Edgar Hoover told President Johnson that nobody would be protesting his Vietnam War policies unless they were directed to do so by some foreign powers.[38]

In response, the CIA vastly expanded its campus surveillance program, stepped up liaisons with local police departments, and trained special intelligence units in major cities to carry out black bag jobs (break-ins, wiretaps, etc.) against US "radicals."

Zepezauer also referenced the Huston Plan, which, as I pointed out earlier, was a program devised during the Nixon administration to round up dissenters and send them to detention camps in Western states if domestic dissent got out of control. He noted that this plan called for "wiretapping, break-ins, mail-opening, no-knock searches and 'selective assassinations.'" Bureaucratic infighting tabled the plan, but much of it was implemented in other forms, not only by the CIA but also by the FBI and the Secret Service.

Zepezauer also pointed out that after a period of "reform," much of Operation CHAOS's work was privatized so that right-wing groups and "former" CIA agents now provide the bulk of the CIA's domestic intelligence.

How many of these supposedly closed programs are still in operation under different names or disguises? How many similar programs are being conducted by private contractors in order to give the CIA plausible deniability?

Long gone are the days of journalists like Finley Peter Dunne, who once said that the role of journalists is to "Comfort the afflicted and afflict the comfortable."

Based on what Bernstein and others have uncovered in recent years, it may be more accurate to say today's media do just the opposite. They comfort the comfortable.

CHAPTER 7

The Most Powerful Propaganda Message Ever Delivered

IN THE FIRST CHAPTER, I pointed out that the initial salvo of the Cold War was the oil-for-security pact President Roosevelt signed with the king of Saudi Arabia in 1945. That pact followed a visit by American officials to the archconservative kingdom, during which an American diplomat said, "The oil in this region is the greatest single prize in all history."

There was a second salvo unleashed in the Cold War—dropping nuclear bombs on Japan. I only brought it up briefly earlier because I wanted to wait until the reader had some background information on covert propaganda in order to better understand the significance of dropping the atomic bombs. Without this background information, some would likely dismiss the second salvo as a conspiracy theory, no matter how much evidence I provided. Thank you to those who have had the fortitude to stick with me. I believe you now have at least a basic understanding of covert propaganda.

The United States dropped nuclear bombs on the cities of Hiroshima and Nagasaki, Japan, six months after the Saudi pact. The decision to drop the bombs appears to have been made largely for propaganda purposes, that is, to kick-start the Cold War. The Cold War, as I have noted, was a smokescreen and a block and bridge to make it appear the primary issue was a battle of ideologies when, in reality, the real battle was a race to build empire and to gain access to and control of oil.

If the Cold War had been an ideological battle, as we have been taught, then we should have had good relations by now with Russia after the collapse of communism. Good relations haven't happened because both countries are still fighting the propaganda war.

It's a war that we have won so far. No country has ever matched our propaganda expertise, although numerous countries are starting to catch up and are winning some propaganda skirmishes. The strongest propaganda message ever delivered was sent to both Russia and the entire world in August 1945.

By August the Soviet Union had amassed hundreds of thousands of troops along the Japanese border and was within days of invading. The Soviets had just finished playing the major role in Germany's defeat, had already fought many more battles than the United States, and had lost nearly 30 million people in the war, compared to approximately four hundred thousand for the United States.

The Soviets were ready for one last battle to end the war, but it wasn't to be. Truman beat them to the punch. Truman decided that there was one last thing he needed to do to secure sole US victory in the war and, most importantly, to send a strong propaganda message to the Soviet Union and to the world. The message was simple, but powerful: don't mess with us; we have the bomb, and we will not hesitate to use it. The two bombs, dropped three days apart, killed some two hundred thousand people, mostly women and children.

That's a big price to pay in human lives to deliver a message, but as I have shown throughout this book, many involved in covert activities believe we are fighting a "just war" and that "anything goes." Bombing an enemy during war is usually not a propaganda action. But it is when a powerful weapon like a nuclear bomb is used to send a message. Deploying or even threatening to deploy a nuclear weapon is the ultimate propaganda message for arousing the emotion of fear. Fear is one of the strongest human emotions and is one of the most common targets of propaganda. Fear often sucks us and nations into submission. It worked in Japan. It worked with Russia (remember the Cuban missile crisis?). It works now. Scare people enough and they will support just about any agenda.

Most Americans have been taught since grade school that the bombs were dropped to "save lives" because hundreds of thousands more would have died if the war continued. That is partially true, but even the staunchest defenders of Truman's action admit that we had anti-Soviet motives and that a bonus was to scare the Soviet Union. Those anti-Soviet motives, because of their propaganda value, overrode any other reason and were the key to the US decision making. The dropping of the nuclear bombs appears to be the ultimate in disinformation propaganda.

The US Strategic Bombing Survey Group, assigned by President Truman himself to study the 1945 air attacks on Japan, produced a report in July 1946 that concluded:

> Based on a detailed investigation of all the facts and supported by the testimony of the surviving Japanese leaders involved, it is the Survey's opinion that certainly prior to 31 December 1945 and in all probability prior to 1 November 1945, Japan would have surrendered even if the atomic bombs had not been dropped, even if Russia had not entered the war, and even if no invasion had been planned or contemplated.[1]

Weeks before the first bomb was dropped, Japan sent a telegram to the Soviet Union expressing the desire to surrender and end the war. Truman, according to the Survey Group report, had read the telegram and wrote in his diary about it being "the telegram from Jap Emperor asking for peace."

The United States Strategic Bombing Survey also stated in its official report: "Hiroshima and Nagasaki were chosen as targets because of their concentration of activities and population."

The July 21, 2005, edition of the British *New Scientist* magazine had a bombshell story in which it noted that two respected US historians had uncovered strong evidence that the US decision to drop atomic bombs on Hiroshima and Nagasaki was "meant to kick-start the Cold War against the Soviet Union, Washington's war-time ally, rather than end the Second World War."[2]

The two historians who discovered the evidence that disputes the official version of history were Peter Kuznick, director of the Nuclear Studies Institute at the American University in Washington, and Mark Selden, a historian from Cornell University in New York. Kuznick and Selden studied the diplomatic archives of the United States, Japan, and the Union of Soviet Socialist Republics. They found that three days before Hiroshima, Truman agreed at a meeting that Japan was "looking for peace."

Truman's senior generals and political advisers told him there was no need to use the A-bomb. But the bombs were dropped anyway, according to Kuznick. "Impressing Russia was more important than ending the war in Japan," said Selden. The desire to send a strong message to Russia was so pressing that President Truman was willing to commit what Kuznick said in the *New Scientist* article was "not just a war crime, it was a crime against humanity."

Truman was much more trigger-happy than his military advisers. Not only did most top US military leaders think the bombings were unnecessary and unjustified; many were morally offended by what they regarded as the unnecessary destruction of Japanese cities and what were essentially noncombatant populations.

General Leslie Groves, director of the Manhattan Project that made the bomb, testified: "There wasn't any illusion on my part that Russia was our enemy, and that the project was conducted on that basis."[3]

Truman's top military adviser, Chief of Staff William D. Leahy, a five-star admiral, said:

The use of this barbarous weapon at Hiroshima and Nagasaki was of no material assistance in our war against Japan. The Japanese were already defeated and ready to surrender. In being the first to use it, we adopted an ethical standard common to the barbarians of the Dark Ages. I was not taught to make war in that fashion, and wars cannot be won by destroying women and children.[4]

Commander of Allied Forces General Dwight D. Eisenhower reported his reaction when told by secretary of war Henry L. Stimson that the atomic bomb would be used:

> During his recitation of the relevant facts, I had been conscious of a feeling of depression and so I voiced to him my grave misgivings, first on the basis of my belief that Japan was already defeated and that dropping the bomb was completely unnecessary, and secondly because I thought that our country should avoid shocking world opinion by the use of a weapon whose employment was, I thought, no longer mandatory as a measure to save American lives. It was my belief that Japan was, at that very moment, seeking some way to surrender with a minimum loss of "face." The Secretary was deeply perturbed by my attitude.[5]

Eisenhower later said in a *Newsweek* interview in November 1963 that "the Japanese were ready to surrender and it wasn't necessary to hit them with that awful thing."[6]

Norman Cousins, consultant to General Douglas MacArthur during the American occupation of Japan, noted: "When I asked General MacArthur about the decision to drop the bomb, I was surprised to learn he had not even been consulted. What, I asked, would his advice have been? He replied that he saw no military justification for the dropping of the bomb. The war might have ended weeks earlier, he said, if the United States had agreed, as it later did anyway, to the retention of the institution of the emperor."[7]

That comment about General MacArthur not being consulted about use of the bombs is telling. It further reinforces that the bombings were a propaganda/political act and not a military decision. Lewis Strauss, special assistant to the secretary of the navy, recalled a recommendation he gave to secretary of the navy James Forrestal before the atomic bombing of Hiroshima: "I proposed to Secretary Forrestal that the weapon should be demonstrated before it was used. Primarily it was because it was clear to a number of people, myself among them, that the war was very nearly over. The Japanese were nearly ready to capitulate. My proposal to the Secretary was that the weapon should be demonstrated over some area accessible to Japanese observers and where its effects would be dramatic. Secretary Forrestal agreed wholeheartedly with the recommendation."[8]

Just in case those military leaders aren't credible enough, here are a few more. Admiral Chester W. Nimitz, commander in chief of the Pacific Fleet, stated, "The Japanese had, in fact, already sued for peace. The atomic bomb played no decisive part, from a purely military standpoint, in the defeat of Japan." General Curtis LeMay, the Army Air Force leader, said shortly after the bombings that "the war would have been over in two weeks. The atomic bomb had nothing to do with the end of the war at all." General Sir Hastings Ismay, chief of staff to the British minister of defense, told Prime Minister Churchill that "when Russia came into the war against Japan the Japanese would probably wish to get out on almost any terms short of the dethronement of the Emperor." On hearing the atomic test was successful, Ismay's private reaction was one of "revulsion."[9]

General George C. Marshall is on record as repeatedly saying that it was not a military decision, but rather a political one. Documents reveal that Marshall believed long before the weapons were deployed that "these weapons might first be used against straight military objectives such as a large naval installation and, if no complete result was derived from the effect of that, he thought we ought to designate a number of large manufacturing areas from which the people would be warned to leave—telling the Japanese that we intend to destroy such centers."[10]

This statement by Marshall raises the question: If the dropping of the bombs was simply to let the world know that we possessed powerful nuclear weapons, why didn't we drop them offshore or at a military target? Why did we deliberately destroy two cities and kill nearly a quarter of a million people, mostly women and children? All evidence points to a simple answer: Truman wanted to claim total victory for World War II and to let the Soviets know in no uncertain terms that we were the undisputed world leaders.

Neither Hiroshima nor Nagasaki was deemed militarily vital by US planners. (This is one of the reasons neither had been heavily bombed up to this point in the war.) Moreover, targeting was aimed explicitly on non-military facilities surrounded by workers' homes. Several months earlier, in March, the United States firebombed Tokyo using conventional bombers. By then we had made the decision to target civilians.

"Where earlier raids (before March) targeted aircraft factories and military facilities, the Tokyo firebombing was aimed largely at civilians, in places such as Tokyo's downtown Shitamachi area, where people lived in traditional wood and paper homes at densities sometimes exceeding 100,000 people per square mile," noted a March 9, 2015, *Associated Press* story. The article quoted a historian who said the area was chosen "because it was easy to burn."[11]

The Tokyo bombing campaign set a military precedent for targeting civilian areas that continued with the dropping of the atomic bombs and persisted into the Korean and Vietnam wars and beyond.

Many years later President Richard Nixon recalled that "[General Douglas] MacArthur once spoke to me very eloquently about it, pacing the floor of his apartment in the Waldorf. He thought it a tragedy that the Bomb was ever exploded. MacArthur believed that the same restrictions ought to apply to atomic weapons as to conventional weapons, that the military objective should always be limited damage to noncombatants. MacArthur, you see, was a soldier. He believed in using force only against military targets, and that is why the nuclear thing turned him off."[12]

Washington's Blog also quoted an article in *History.com*, which pointed out that a number of historians have suggested that one of the objectives of dropping the bombs was to demonstrate the new weapon of mass destruction to the Soviet Union. The article said that by August 1945, relations between the Soviet Union and the United States had deteriorated badly. "Truman and many of his advisers hoped that the U.S. atomic monopoly might offer diplomatic leverage with the Soviets. In this fashion, the dropping of the atomic bomb on Japan can be seen as the first shot of the Cold War."[13]

Gar Alperovitz, University of Maryland professor of political economy, former legislative director in the US House of Representatives and the US Senate, and special assistant in the Department of State, wrote in an August 2011 article in *Counterpunch* that: "Though most Americans are unaware of the fact, increasing numbers of historians now recognize the United States did not need to use the atomic bomb to end the war against Japan in 1945." Alperovitz further noted that "Pulitzer Prize–winning historian Martin Sherwin pointed out that a significant factor in using the bombs was to 'Impress the Soviets during the early diplomatic sparring that ultimately became the Cold War.'"[14]

• • •

During the war and for many years afterward, American propaganda demonized the Japanese as subhuman. This propaganda made it easier for the US government to round up Japanese-Americans and throw them into internment camps. This demonization propaganda campaign also made it easier for the American public to stomach the use of nuclear weapons and the napalming of Tokyo.

Admiral William F. Halsey told a news conference in 1944 that "the only good Jap is a Jap who's been dead for six months." This is classic demonization propaganda.[15]

We have used demonization propaganda throughout our history. We used it extensively during the labor unrest in the latter part of the 1800s to demonize striking workers, such as during the Ludlow Massacre in Ludlow, Colorado, in which state military gunned down and killed women and children with machine guns at a tent colony of striking mine workers (the excuse was that Communists were stirring up trouble).

We used demonization propaganda during World War I to demonize Germans as beasts and Huns through wartime atrocity stories designed to create hysteria (these scare stories were created by propagandists). We used it throughout the Cold War to demonize anyone associated with collectivism. We used demonization in Vietnam to justify killing "anything that moves" at MyLai and elsewhere.

We demonized Iraq soldiers who, "like barbarians," threw babies out of their incubators and left them to die on the hospital floor (a lie); and we have used the demonization technique throughout the Middle East war to depict Muslims as subhuman savages and barbarians.[16]

In summary, Truman, US propagandists, and covert operators met secretly in Washington and callously ordered the two most violent acts in history. They rejected military advice not to use the bombs on civilian targets. They also rejected alternatives, such as bombing military targets or demonstrating the power of the bomb offshore. They apparently wanted to inflict the most extreme human carnage possible, just as we had done in Tokyo with napalm.

"These terrible acts were intended to warn the leaders of the Soviet Union that their cities would suffer the same fate if the USSR attempted to stand in the way of Washington's plans," noted an August 2005 article in *Green Leaf Weekly*. Nuclear scientist Leo Szilard recounted to his biographers that Truman's secretary of state, James Byrnes, told him before the Hiroshima attack that "Russia might be more manageable if impressed by American military might."[17]

In other words, the bombs were a message, a message that Russia and the world heard loud and clear. Evidence of how effective the bombs were as a propaganda tool to scare the Soviets can be seen in the US and Russia standoff during the Cuban missile crisis, which brought us very close to a nuclear confrontation. We had nuclear-armed aircraft in the air.

Right or wrong, the fact that we had already dropped two nuclear bombs scared the hell out of the Soviets, which was apparently the intent all along of dropping the bombs. Former Ohio congressman Dennis Kucinich noted on August 7, 2014: "Our problem isn't simply our nuclear past, but is our present addiction to nuclear weapons which threaten humanity's future. The United States has historically positioned its nuclear arsenal for the purposes of deterrence, yet under President Obama's administration they are for brandishing. In today's security environment, the United States now reserves the right to use nuclear weapons against any country (first strike policy). Lest anyone forget that nuclear is a big business, the United States is the leader in the global nuclear energy market," Kucinich observed. "Nuclear energy technology is one of our biggest exports."[18]

Put away all the political and propaganda pieties and everything always seems to follow the dollar trail, that is, the interests of big business and the economic power elite. Their interests trump everything. Just as a commanding officer at My Lai, Vietnam, told his troops to "kill anything that moves" (including women and children), anything goes to protect the interests of the economic elite because the interests of the elite, the elite believe, are our interests.

One of the most vociferous critics of the atomic bombings was David Lawrence, founder and editor of *U.S. News & World Report*. On November 23, 1945, Lawrence wrote in an editorial:

> The truth is we are guilty. Our conscience as a nation must trouble us. We must confess our sin. We have used a horrible weapon to asphyxiate and cremate more than 100,000 men, women and children (it was later determined to be double that figure) in a sort of super-lethal gas chamber—and all this in a war already won or which spokesmen for our Air Force (and all military branches) tell us we could have readily won without the atomic bomb. We ought, therefore, to apologize in unequivocal terms to the whole world for our misuse of the atomic bomb.[19]

For anyone who might think Lawrence was a bleeding-heart liberal, he was an avowed conservative, a successful businessman, and someone who knew eleven presidents intimately.

Not one single American president or leader has ever apologized for dropping the bombs. President Obama apparently considered apologizing on his visit to Japan in 2009, but the plan was dropped. George Bush, while campaigning for the office of the president, promised that he would never apologize for the Hiroshima and Nagasaki bombings. "I don't care what the facts are. You heard that right. I will never apologize."[20]

Bush may not care about the facts, but the US Nuclear Regulatory Commission historian J. Samuel Walker does. He has studied the history of research on the bombings as much as, if not more than, anyone. As historian Doug Long has noted, Walker has emphatically stated: "The consensus among scholars is that the bomb was not needed to avoid an invasion of Japan and to end the war within a relatively short time. It is clear that alternatives to the bomb existed and that Truman and his advisors knew it."[21]

The vast majority of Americans then and now have supported the bombing of Hiroshima and Nagasaki not because they are immoral or heartless, but because they have been fed an unrelenting barrage of propaganda. And good covert propaganda gets people to take a stance like President Bush, who said, "I don't care what the facts are."

Facts don't matter to propagandists. It's all about manipulating our emotions and scaring us into submission. No one is better than American covert propagandists at getting their own citizens and most of the world to not cross certain lines in the sand for fear of consequences. They are also adept at getting us to accept an "anything goes" mentality, including the use of atomic bombs, even though this "means-justify-the-ends" mentality of the economic power elite and their propagandists is not designed to benefit the average American, but to protect the elite's financial interests, which, as I have shown, they ardently believe are our interests.

The economic power elite truly believe their interests are our interests and that whatever benefits them helps the rest of us. This elitist trickle-down outlook has largely gone unchallenged. The elite know they own us and control our destiny. Their propagandists know it. Unfortunately, I don't believe the average person knows it. Hopefully my book will at least get a few people to understand how a small group of extremely wealthy people have stolen our country. We, the people, need to reclaim it.

CHAPTER 8

A Beautiful "BOD":
The Engineering of Dissent

IN 1953 AN AMERICAN GENERAL went to Iran, contacted some "friends" in Tehran, and informed them it was time to replace the democratically elected and popular prime minister, Mohammed Mosaddegh, with the corrupt and dictatorial Shah of Iran.[1]

Mosaddegh had done two things that rubbed us the wrong way. One, he was liberal and initiated a few progressive social programs similar to American Social Security. Most importantly, Mosaddegh incurred the ire of the Western economic elite by nationalizing the oil holdings of the Anglo-Iranian Oil Company, a British consortium.

The Anglo-Iranian Oil Company was considered to be a strategic Middle East power base for the elite's banking, oil, and defense interests. These interests are known within the top circles of the economic elite by the acronym BOD (banking, oil, and defense industries). We've had an almost paranoid desire to do anything necessary to protect our BOD interests in the Middle East. This is the reason that we, with help from the British, orchestrated the overthrow of the democratically elected prime minister of Iran.

As I noted in the first chapter, the Iran coup followed three major events that have shaped the Middle East and world history: the American delegation's visit in 1944 to Saudi Arabia, where they discovered the "greatest single prize in all of history"; the 1945 US and Saudi oil-for-security pact; and the decision by the Truman administration to use atomic bombs to kick-start the Cold War and beat the Soviets in the race for control of the Middle East.

With those three events as the backdrop, the United States was hell-bent on gaining access to and control of Iranian oil. The only thing standing in our way was a very popular, democratically elected leader who had promised liberal reforms to improve the lives of the Iranian people. He had to go. We wanted Iranian and Mideast oil. We didn't care what the Iranian people thought or, for that matter, what the rest of the world thought. The message was straightforward: we had the bombs and weren't afraid to use them. The primary reason for our conspiring to overthrow Iran's elected government was to ensure Western control of Iran's petroleum resources. Another reason was to prevent the Soviet Union and anyone else from competing for Iranian and Middle East oil.

Actually the coup was a piece of cake because we used "invisible" operatives to pull it off. We unleashed our covert operatives and fronts on the Iranian people and slammed them with a barrage of engineering of dissent propaganda that was so effective they didn't know what hit them. We didn't even have to send in troops.

We were so successful that we would use the same covert engineering of dissent to overthrow a democratically elected leader in Guatemala a year later. We also used it for decades to stir up radical dissent in Soviet Muslim countries. Has that come back to bite us?

Middle East historian Ervand Abrahamian has stated that Iran's oil was the central focus of the 1953 Iranian coup though "much of the discourse at the time was linked to the Cold War. If Mosaddegh had succeeded in nationalizing the British oil industry in Iran, that would have set an example and was seen at that time by the Americans as a threat to U.S. oil interests throughout the world," Abrahamian wrote.[2]

Abrahamian has noted that Truman's secretary of state Dean Acheson said that "the 'Communist threat' was a smokescreen." This comment is from one of the key architects of our Cold War Red Scare campaign. With this kind of confession from an insider, you would think that it would get wide press coverage and that history books would be rewritten to reflect the smokescreen. Neither happened.[3]

In 2000 James Risen of the *New York Times* obtained a previously secret CIA version of the Iran coup. He summarized its contents as follows: "In early August (1953), the CIA stepped up the pressure. Iranian operatives pretending to be Communists threatened Muslim leaders with savage punishment if they opposed Mossadegh, seeking to stir anti-Communist sentiment in the religious community. In addition, the secret history (of the CIA) says that the house of at least one prominent Muslim was bombed by CIA agents posing as Communists. It does not say whether anyone was hurt in this attack."[4]

Risen said the CIA document described anticommunism as a "rhetorical device." He also pointed out that the agency had begun ramping up its propaganda campaign. As an example he noted that the owner of a major US newspaper received a $45,000 personal loan "in the belief that this would make his organ (his newspaper) amenable to our purposes."

The CIA also used Fascists and Nazis to help in their campaign to overthrow Mosaddegh. Political science professor Masoud Kazemzadeh of Sam Houston University wrote that several "Iranian Fascists and Nazi sympathizers played prominent roles in the coup. General Fazlollah Zahedi, who had been arrested and imprisoned by the British during World War II for his attempt to establish a pro-Nazi government, was made prime minister on 19 August 1953. The CIA gave Zahedi about $100,000 before the coup and an additional $5 million the day after the coup to help consolidate support for the coup,"

Kazemzadeh stated. Kazemzadeh also said Bahram Shahrokh, a trainee of Joseph Goebbels and Berlin Radio's Persian-language program announcer during the Nazi rule, became director of propaganda. The US government gave Zahedi a further $28 million a month later, and then another $40 million was given in 1954 after the Iran government signed an oil consortium deal.[5]

The reader should not be shocked about us getting in bed with Nazis. We have been doing it for many decades. I will point out later in the book how Carl Byoir in the thirties used the anti-Communist scare to convince many American businesspeople to embrace fascism or at least to look the other way because, Byoir said, Hitler (his client) and fascism were going to wipe communism off the face of the earth. I have also noted that the CIA secretly hired hundreds of Nazis shortly after World War II to help in the US Red Scare campaign. Some of these German American Nazis were involved in the CIA campaign to overthrow Mosaddegh. Numerous Nazis were also discovered in the seventies to have had prominent positions in the reelection campaign of President H. W. Bush. Bush's father was a Nazi sympathizer for many years. I will go into more detail about each of these Nazi connections later.

• • •

When Mosaddegh refused to step down, the CIA sent millions of dollars to buy off Mossadegh's supporters and to finance street demonstrations and a coup. This is a classic example of what I have called the engineering of dissent propaganda technique. We have used it for over a century to topple regimes and to discredit and disrupt domestic dissident groups, including domestic labor, civil rights, antiwar protestors, and recently, the Occupy Wall Street movement and protests against police using excessive force on people of color.

Mosaddegh was replaced in a coup by the Shah, a corrupt and brutal dictator who had previously ascended to Iran's highest office through a British coup.

The CIA-sponsored coup, called Operation Ajax, put the Shah back in power in what the CIA itself called an American operation from beginning to end.[6] This was one of many US-backed coups to take place around the world since World War II to unseat governments not to our liking, even when the leaders have been popularly elected. A partial list besides Mossadegh in 1953 includes Arbenz in Guatemala in 1954, Allende in Chile in 1973, Aristide in Haiti twice, Chavez in Venezuela briefly in 2002, Zelaya in Honduras in 2009, Morsi in Egypt in 2013, and Yanukovych in Ukraine in 2014.

In August 2013, sixty years after the coup, the CIA acknowledged it was involved in both the planning and the execution of the coup, including "the bribing of Iranian politicians, security and army high-ranking officials, as well as pro-coup propaganda." The CIA also said the coup was carried out "under CIA direction" and "as an act of U.S. foreign policy, conceived and approved at the highest levels of government."[7]

Eisenhower biographer Stephen Ambrose wrote: "Before going into the operation, Ajax had to have the approval of the President. Eisenhower participated in none of the meetings that set up Ajax; he received only oral reports on the plan; and he did not discuss it with his Cabinet or the NSC. Establishing a pattern he would hold to throughout his Presidency, he kept his distance and left no documents behind that could implicate the President in any projected coup."[8]

The CIA's "pro-coup propaganda" noted above was likely designed to give Eisenhower plausible deniability. By not discussing the coup with his inner circle and by leaving no documents behind, there is no link to him. This gives him deniability and is a propaganda technique that has been used over and over by presidents and other top officials.

I will give many examples. Plausible deniability is an ingenious and insidious propaganda tool that has allowed many top officials to lie, or worse, with little chance of getting caught.

President Teddy Roosevelt's grandson, Kermit Roosevelt Jr., wasn't quite as discreet as Eisenhower. He was a top CIA operative who directed Mosaddegh's overthrow and arranged for the Shah to take over. The Shah ruled Iran with an iron fist during the fifties, sixties, and seventies, thanks to US help.

General Norman Schwarzkopf, whose son led President Bush's Desert Storm on Saddam Hussein in 1991, trained the Shah's national police force, the dreaded Gendarmerie. That was done openly, but the CIA under Allen Dulles and Richard Helms helped the Shah set up and train a secret Iranian police force, the dreaded SAVAK.

Helms later became CIA director under Nixon, and after Nixon left office because of Watergate, Helms became US ambassador to Iran. The

Dulles name crops up in many places where there is a coup or a clandestine anti-Communist activity, as you will see shortly. Richard Helms went from being a UPI correspondent to joining the CIA and working with Allen Dulles to help overthrow Mosaddegh, to helping the Shah establish a secret police force, to becoming CIA director under Nixon, to becoming US ambassador to Iran after Nixon resigned. In 1979 the people rebelled against the Shah's rule and American interference in the affairs of Iran and overthrew him. The Shah fled to the United States, where the Rockefellers and Helms convinced Carter to admit him for medical treatment. This infuriated Iranians. They took over the US Embassy in Tehran and seized fifty-two American hostages. The hostage siege lasted for over a year.

The resulting tensions between the two countries persist to this day, largely because of the coup and our support for decades of a despotic leader. Bringing him to the United States just added insult to injury, to use an old cliché.

$$\bullet \ \bullet \ \bullet$$

Fresh off their success in overthrowing the democratically elected president of Iran a year earlier, the Cold War CIA warriors and American clandestine propagandists felt emboldened to do whatever it took to get rid of another democratically elected leader, this time closer to home, in Guatemala. As in Iran they succeeded by using the engineering of dissent propaganda technique (and others). The keystone of this dissent propaganda in Guatemala, as in Iran, was sending in provocateurs to destabilize a democratically elected government.

Edward Bernays, the father of modern propaganda and a person I have mentioned often, worked with the CIA in its engineering of dissent propaganda in Guatemala. How did Bernays get involved? His client was Guatemala-based United Fruit.

Bernays and the CIA conducted a massive propaganda campaign against Guatemala's liberal leader, Jacobo Arbenz. Bernays's propaganda onslaught paved the way for a 1954 CIA-led coup, which was appropriately called Operation Success. It was a success from the CIA's standpoint because Guatemala was the second country in two years in which a CIA-led coup had overthrown a democratically elected leader. It was a success for Bernays because his client, a banana company, reaped a bountiful harvest.

Would we help overthrow the elected leader of a small Central American country to protect the interests of a banana company? This was not just any banana company, as you will see. First, some background.

Arbenz was liberal and had threatened to make some reforms to better his constituents, as had Mossadegh in Iran. As part of his land reforms, Arbenz wanted to give back a few thousand acres of idle land to his people that a prior Guatemala dictator had basically given to United Fruit in a ninety-nine-year, eight-hundred-thousand-acre, tax-free land lease.

United Fruit didn't like the idea of giving any of Guatemala's land back to its people, even though the banana company controlled 42 percent of the country's land. United Fruit has had a long history of domination over often-corrupt governments in numerous Central American countries. The fruit company was not accustomed to working with a democratic-oriented leader like Arbenz. United Fruit has been accused of exploiting cheap labor in Central American countries (hence the name "banana republics") to provide its Chiquita-brand bananas sold into the US market.

The 1954 coup forced Arbenz from power and led to a succession of juntas in his place. In 1999, classified details of the CIA's involvement in the ouster of the Guatemalan leader revealed that the CIA, among other things, equipped anti-Arbenz rebels and paramilitary troops, supplied aircraft for the rebel army, set up propaganda outlets, and bribed Arbenz's military commanders into surrendering while the US Navy blockaded the Guatemalan coast. The CIA even pressured American media not to report the story.

Why were we so intent on protecting the interests of United Fruit? Besides Bernays's ties with United Fruit, Secretary of State John Foster Dulles was once a lawyer for a large Wall Street firm that represented United Fruit. Not only did Dulles have United Fruit as a client before becoming secretary of state; he was a former president of United Fruit and a stockholder while in office as secretary of state, as was his brother, CIA director Allen Dulles. Both were on United Fruit's payroll for thirty-eight years. This was one of the most blatant conflicts of interest in our history, but nothing was done about it because both Dulles brothers were staunch supporters and protectors for the interests of the economic elite.

Not only were our CIA director and secretary of state both major shareholders and on the payroll of United Fruit; the head of the National Security Council, General Cutler, had previously served as chairman of the board for United Fruit.

A prior CIA director, Walter Smith, was also on United Fruit's board. Our UN ambassador, Henry Cabot Lodge, was a big stockholder. It gets even better. The personal secretary to Eisenhower, Ann Whitman, was the wife of United Fruit's PR director. Larry Tye, author of *The Father of Spin: Edward L. Bernays & The Birth of PR,* writes that Bernays's papers "make clear how the United States viewed its Latin neighbors as ripe for economic exploitation and political manipulation and how the propaganda war Bernays waged in Guatemala set the pattern for future U.S.-led campaigns in Cuba and, much later, Vietnam."[9]

"The CIA devised a massive propaganda campaign in Guatemala to convince the populace of the invincibility of the forces seeking to take control of the country. Furthermore, CIA agents also conducted an intense psychological battle against the supporters of Arbenz, ranging from phone warnings in the middle of the night to death threats," according to the Cold War Museum. org.[10]

The CIA used propaganda in the form of political rumor, air-dropped pamphlets, poster campaigns, and radio, as it had done in Iran. It also used psychological warfare techniques, such as character assassination. For example, it would place signs on the homes of Arbenz's supporters that read: "A Communist Lives Here." The CIA and its operatives would also deliver false death notices to President Arbenz and his Cabinet.[11]

The engineering of dissent coups in Iran and Guatemala set the stage for numerous covert coups our country has engineered. Probably the most important coup was stirring up radical Islam in Soviet Muslim countries.

It was successful in that it helped accomplish our goal to bring down communism and the Soviet Union. But it has also had blowback. We are now faced with fighting the same radical Islamics we helped create.

In the Pulitzer Prize-winning book *Ghost Wars: The Secret History of the CIA, Afghanistan and Bin Laden, from the Soviet Invasion to September 10, 2001,* author Steve Coll takes a look at the CIA's activities in Afghanistan from the Russian invasion to after the 9/11 attacks. Coll gives a detailed account of how the CIA and Pakistan intelligence operatives (both of which were given funding by Saudi Arabia) built Mujahideen training camps on the Afghanistan and Pakistan border to train militant fighters from Arab countries to attack the Soviets. Coll says this decision would have long-lasting effects on the region.[12]

● ● ●

Engineering of dissent propaganda is not reserved just to help topple foreign governments we don't like. It has been used domestically to disrupt, divide, diminish, discredit, demonize, and destroy the civil rights movement, the anti-Vietnam war movement, and any attempts to organize progressive labor movements or social/economic movements, such as the 2013 Occupy Wall Street protests. This is not conspiracy theory. It's in black and white in FBI files and from other government sources.

For example, the 1976 Church Committee Senate Investigation of the FBI's COINTELPRO unveiled FBI records that show the FBI was actively spying on Americans without cause. The Church Committee also revealed that the FBI often used provocateurs throughout the fifties, sixties, and seventies to instigate violent acts for the express purpose of later blaming the acts on civil rights, antiwar, and other dissenters.[13]

The records show the FBI had been opening files on people who simply wrote letters to the editor objecting to the war in Vietnam. The papers also showed the FBI was encouraging agents to infiltrate schools and churches in the black community and using secret informants to turn people against each other.

Hoover was a master at the engineering of dissent. However, our government at all levels has secretly condoned dissent propaganda and practiced it for nearly a century. It still goes on here and abroad, and unfortunately, we seem to have trouble recognizing it.

False-flag propaganda is a key part of the engineering of dissent. As noted earlier, a false-flag is a manufactured incident that is used by one entity to put blame on another. It often involves a government attacking its own people, then blaming others in order to justify going to war against the people it blames. One person involved in Operation Gladio in Italy testified that the purpose of the manufactured violence there was to scare the public so much that they would want the government to protect them and provide better security.

Besides the false-flag/engineering of dissent incidents by the FBI and those noted earlier in Italy, Iran, Kuwait (babies on the hospital floor), and Guatemala, here are a few more possible false-flags (there are many more):

* In 2001, one week after 9/11, letters containing anthrax spores were mailed to some news outlets and the offices of two senators. Five people were killed. The White House almost immediately blamed Al Qaeda and Iraq. Subsequent investigations showed Al Qaeda and Iraq were not involved.

* President Johnson used the Gulf of Tonkin incident to get Congress to pass legislation giving him the legal go-ahead to deploy conventional US forces anywhere in Southeast Asia. The manufactured incident involved the claim that three North Vietnamese navy torpedo boats confronted the USS *Maddox* in the Gulf of Tonkin. It was later learned that there was no North Vietnamese engagement.

* In 2007 it was discovered that so-called radical leftists who carried rocks to a peaceful protest in Quebec were actually undercover Quebec police officers.

* In the sixties, declassified documents revealed a plan approved by the Joint Chiefs of Staff, in which we would blow up

American planes and engage in terrorist acts here at home so we could blame the incidents on Cubans. This would be used to justify an invasion of Cuba. ABC did a report on this on *World News Tonight* with Peter Jennings.

  * Another Cuban incident is one of the best examples of a false-flag, but it actually never happened; however, it was planned and approved at the highest levels of US government and came close to being implemented. It's called Operation Northwood. This was a proposed plot, uncovered with the release of classified documents in 1997, to justify an invasion of Cuba. It was designed by the Department of Defense. Among its proposals was to shoot down a passenger plane, sink a navy ship, and even stage attacks on Miami. The plan went up the chain of command to Kennedy. He refused to sign it. He was assassinated less than a year later.

Fresh off false-flag and coup successes in Iran and Guatemala, the United States tried to install "their man" as heads of state in places such as the Congo, the Dominican Republic, South Vietnam, Brazil, Chile, and, of course, Cuba. An excellent account of our attempts to bring about regime change in Cuba and the terrorism we unleashed to do so can be found in *Voices from the Other Side: An Oral History of Terrorism Against Cuba,* by Keith Bolender.[14]

In an introduction to the book, linguist Noam Chomsky wrote, "Since the early 1960s, few other countries have endured more acts of terrorism against civilian targets than Cuba, and the U.S. has had its hand in much of it. This book gives a voice to the victims.

"Keith Bolender brings to bear the enormous impact that terrorism has had on Cuba's civilian population, with over 1,000 documented incidents resulting in more than 3,000 deaths and 2,000 injuries," Chomsky wrote.

"*Voices from the Other Side* includes first-person interviews with more than 75 Cuban citizens who have been victims of these terrorist acts, or have had family members or close friends die from the attacks," Chomsky added.

It's a testament to the strong will of the Cuban people and its government to have been able to withstand almost unrelenting acts of what Chomsky called "terrorism against Cuba" by the United States, including a decades-long embargo that has hurt the average person, not the leaders of the country. Cuba is one of the few examples in recent history of a people being able to resist the United States' steady barrage of economic warfare, invasions, attempted coups, and frequent use of the engineering of dissent propaganda in an attempt to stir up and exploit dissent. The engineering of dissent propaganda didn't work as well in Cuba as it has in our country and in numerous other countries. Despite repeated failures to oust the Castro regime, we kept trying. We unleashed a steady barrage of engineering of dissent operations, most of which were backed up by the propaganda techniques of layering and plausible deniability.

Besides the failed Bay of Pigs operation, there were at least eight assassination attempts on Fidel Castro. Some strange bedfellows were involved. A few weeks before the November 1960 presidential election (Nixon vs. Kennedy), singer Frank Sinatra introduced Judith Exner to John Kennedy on the eve of the New Hampshire primary. A few weeks later, Sinatra introduced Judith Exner to Chicago Mafia boss Sam Giancana. Kennedy had an affair with Exner for two years while president. Kennedy also allegedly slept with some 12 other women while in the White House, as I will detail later. Exner became involved, as William Safire put it, in a "dual affair with the nation's most powerful mobster and the nation's most powerful political leader."[15]

Giancana was busy with more than his love life; he was hired to form assassination teams to go after Fidel Castro. The man who retained him was Robert Maheu, a businessman and former FBI and CIA operative. He was also Howard Hughes's right-hand man. Hughes, at the time, was the country's richest man. In testimony before the Church Committee on Intelligence in 1975, Maheu confirmed his role in the assassination plot against Castro. He made an interesting comment during his testimony. He said that he thought the United States "was involved in a just war."[16]

This belief of being in a just war against communism was a rationale held by many in clandestine government agencies, organized crime, and the economic elite and its business/financial interests. The primary strategy in this just war was to pacify the American people by arousing anticommunist hysteria and by manipulating their emotions, primarily the emotion of fear. Giancana put his Los Angeles lieutenant, Johnny Roselli, in charge of the Castro hit squads.

On June 24 and September 22, 1975, Roselli testified before the Church Select Committee on Intelligence about CIA plans to kill Castro. Roselli had hinted that his assignment was aimed at Kennedy as well as Castro.[17]

Roselli's hints about Kennedy sparked the committee's interest. Roselli was called to appear again before the committee on April 23, 1976, to testify not about Castro, but about a conspiracy to kill President Kennedy. Three months after his April testimony, the committee recalled Roselli for more testimony. There was a problem. No one could locate Roselli to serve him another subpoena. His body was found in August floating in a 55-gallon drum in a bay near Miami, Florida. Roselli's partner and boss, Sam Giancana, was found shot to death in the basement of his Chicago home before he was scheduled to testify.[18]

Is it just coincidence that the two chieftains of organized crime that were working with the CIA, FBI, Maheu (Hughes), and members of the economic elite on numerous projects were killed just before and after giving congressional testimony?

The Howard Hughes organization was represented for forty-three years by the PR/propaganda firm I worked for, Carl Byoir & Associates.

● ● ●

Carl Byoir was well acquainted with Cuba since he had earlier run two newspapers there, had befriended some casino-owning mobsters, and had handled public relations for Cuban right-wing dictator Gerardo Machado. Information about the Castro assassination attempts took many years to uncover, largely because the information was hidden by layering and plausible deniability. Some, but not all, of the details were uncovered when secret CIA documents were declassified under the Freedom of Information Act.

Who knows what Roselli and Giancana took to the grave with them involving the connection between organized crime, the economic elite, the CIA, and others in government? The first layer of the propaganda layering in the kill-Castro plan was mobster Roselli. He was the first one who would be held accountable. The second layer was his boss, Giancana. The third layer was the one who organized the plot, Robert Maheu. Next was the Hughes organization, which hired Maheu. The fifth layer was the CIA. The final layer was the president of the United States. He was so far removed from the operatives that he had near-unapproachable plausible deniability.

Obviously the first two layers were the ones most exposed, which is why the two members of organized crime were called to testify and possibly why they were killed. It would have taken a lot of work and evidence to get to the final layer, which is why the propaganda technique of layering is so successful in providing deniability.

After the failed attempt to assassinate Castro using the Mafia, the CIA tried again. This time a CIA-recruited group actually invaded the country in the Bay of Pigs fiasco, but was repelled.

Shortly after the Bay of Pigs failure, President Kennedy fired CIA director Allen Dulles. As I noted above, Dulles was involved directly in the overthrow of the president of Guatemala and was an arch anti-Communist and close to Hoover, Hughes, and other extreme right-wingers. Kennedy vowed to crush the CIA "into a thousand pieces and scatter it to the winds." He never had a chance to fulfill his promise.[19]

Supreme Court Justice William O. Douglas, in recalling a discussion he had with Kennedy shortly before his assassination, said: "This episode (Bay of Pigs) scared him. He had experienced the extreme power that these groups had, these various insidious influences of the CIA and the Pentagon, on civilian policy, and I think it raised in his own mind the specter: Can Jack Kennedy, president of the United States, ever be strong enough to really rule these two powerful agencies? I think it had a profound effect; it shook him up!"[20]

JFK had fired Allen Dulles and was in the process of founding a panel to investigate the CIA when he was killed. He also put a damper on the breadth and scope of the CIA and limited its ability to act under National Security Memorandum 55. Kennedy and his brother, Robert, were also after organized crime.

As noted earlier, linguist and MIT professor Noam Chomsky has often been critical of what he has called America's long and shameful history of terrorism against Cuba. Chomsky pointed out in his review of Keith Bolander's book that American terrorist attacks against Cuba have gone on for more than thirty years. He said that these attacks were amplified by the economic sanctions.[21]

In October 2014, the United Nations voted 188 to 2 (United States and Israel) to endorse the United States ending its economic sanctions against Cuba. It was the twenty-third time UN nations voted to end the sanctions.

Why would the United States thumb its nose at international law and the wishes of 99 percent of UN countries by continuing its fifty-year-plus economic warfare against the Cuban people? In 2015 the Obama administration was taking steps to improve relations with Cuba, but the sanctions remain as of this writing. Cuba, obviously, has never been a military threat to the United States. It's certainly not an economic threat. Could our treatment of Cuba have been related in any way to our concern that a vibrant, Socialist country so close to our border would serve as a model for other countries?

Cuba isn't the only country the United States has used economic warfare and economic sanctions against. In the spring of 2015, for example, the Obama administration announced sanctions against Venezuela, which President Obama said poses "an extraordinary threat to the security of the U.S." (MSNBC, March 9, 2015 – "Obama Declares Venezuela a National Security Threat.")

He didn't say what that threat was. Venezuela is a tiny country with a small military. How is it a threat? Could the threat be that they have a left-leaning, democratically elected president who is trying to improve the plight of the poor? Or could it be that Venezuela has large oil reserves?

Ironically, most of our so-called enemies for many decades have been countries with oil reserves, countries that border access routes to oil, and/or countries that don't bow to the demands and dictates of the United States. These countries and/or their leaders are usually demonized, disrupted, and often destroyed through economic warfare/sanctions and/or covertly engineered coups. It's in our DNA. We've done it over and over throughout the world. I give many examples.

In addition to violent coups to overthrow leftist leaders, we often do everything we can to subvert and destroy the economy of left-leaning governments (such as sanctions) and then use the economic failure we have caused as an example that communism doesn't work.

What would Cuba's economy be like today if the United States had not done everything in its power to destroy it? Cuba likely would have a much stronger economy and a thriving populace, which is exactly what the economic elite didn't what to happen. Before leaving Cuba and the Kennedy era, I want to introduce another propaganda technique called the "propaganda of silence."

• • •

One of the Byoir firm's primary roles in its propaganda work for Howard Hughes was to keep the press away so Hughes could operate his many business and political ventures in secrecy. I will go into detail about Hughes and this propaganda technique in a later chapter.

The Kennedy administration also used this technique to hide Kennedy's many affairs. Several members of the press confronted him on rumors about his sexual wanderings, but Kennedy always denied them.

One of the most interesting liaisons was, as noted earlier in this chapter, with Judith Campbell Exner. Here is how the *New York Post* described the two-year affair in a 2013 article: [22]

Frank Sinatra was the one who introduced JFK to his conquest Judith Campbell Exner, a California girl and ex of Sinatra's who would go on to become the mistress of mob boss Sam Giancana. The President met Exner in 1960 at the Sands Hotel in Las Vegas, where Sinatra was performing.

According to investigative reporter Seymour Hersh, Exner ferried envelopes from JFK to the mob, including alleged payoffs or instructions for vote buying in elections and plans to kill Fidel Castro.

"Jack never in a million years thought he was doing anything that would hurt me, but that's the way he conducted himself; the Kennedys have their own set of rules," Exner said. "Jack was reckless, so reckless." Exner also claimed she aborted JFK's child.[23]

Here are some of the women Kennedy was alleged to have had sex with besides Exner: actress Marlene Dietrich, actress Marilyn Monroe, nineteen-year-old White House intern Mimi Alford, actress Angie Dickinson, German prostitute Ellen Rometsch, socialite Mary Pinchot Meyer, stripper Blaze Starr, his wife's press secretary Pamela Turnure, Swedish socialite Gunilla Von Post, actress Gene Tierney, and White House secretaries Priscilla Wear and Jill Cowen.[24]

• • •

We are told in our history books that the United States won the Cold War because it won the battle of ideologies (capitalism over communism). I believe we won the Cold War because of superior propaganda and superior clandestine intelligence services, often with the help of Nazi propagandists.

The post–World War II US government was led by maniacal anticommunists, many of whom served during the war in the Office of Strategic Services, which became the CIA after the war.

Among the OSS graduates were Richard Helms, who was CIA director from 1966 to 1973; E. Howard Hunt, convicted Watergate conspirator and CIA officer from 1949 to 1970; and Edward Hunter, who, as I noted earlier, was involved in Operation Mockingbird and played the key role in covert propaganda, such as implanting the concept of brainwashing into the mass mind. Another member of the anti-Communist club was Howard Hughes, who was the richest man in the world during the fifties. Hughes's right-hand man, Robert Maheu, was Hughes's intermediary with the intelligence community.

These five arch-defenders of capitalism were not only in a revolving door relationship with the military-industrial complex, but they also got in bed with ex-Nazis and with Middle East Islamic extremists.

Would 9/11 have happened and would we have been mired down in the Middle East if Roosevelt had not signed the oil-for-security pact with the king of Saudi Arabia, if we had not engineered a coup to overthrow the democratically elected president of Iran, and if we had not used engineering of dissent propaganda to stir up radical Muslims in Soviet Muslim countries?

As I noted earlier, US intelligence services actually encouraged Saudi efforts to spread the extremist Wahhabi form of Islam to stir up large Muslim communities in Soviet-controlled countries. Why? To help defeat communism and to gain control of the large underdeveloped oil reserves.

These US-trained radical Islamics were not the average Muslim. Most Muslims were moderate and insular. The Wahhabis were the extreme wing of Islam, the ones who were behind 9/11. Did our lust for oil and our anticommunist mania contribute to 9/11?

In February 1945 Roosevelt met with Abdul Aziz on board the USS *Quincy* in the Suez Canal, and they signed one of the most important agreements in history. This agreement was the trade-off of oil for security. The agreement was reached and continues despite the fact that despotic and nondemocratic rulers of the royal family control all aspects of the country. But democracy is not so important to the elite when Saudi rulers control a lot of the world's oil.

The United States has served as protector of the Saudi royal family for decades, assuring its survival against any domestic or foreign threat despite its authoritarian and antidemocratic foundations.

Numerous defense and infrastructure contractors have made vast fortunes supplying the Saudis with military weapons and helping them develop their infrastructure. Among the beneficiaries of a strong relationship with the Saudis have been Texas firms such as Bechtel and Brown and Root, which was later bought by Halliburton, the world's largest defense contractor, whose CEO for many years was former US vice president and defense secretary Dick Cheney.

Prince Bandar, grandson to the late Saudi King Aziz, trained to be a fighter pilot in Texas and became the Saudi ambassador to the United States in 1983, a post he held while Poppy Bush was VP. Bandar remained in that post for twenty-two years. He was very close to the Bush family. George W. even nicknamed him "Bandar Bush."

The United States made a secret deal with the Saudi royal family to also develop its intelligence service. The Saudis, in return, provided funding for American propaganda and covert operations all over the world.

The US- and Saudi-trained radical Islamics were the extreme wing of Islam, as were the ones who were behind 9/11. Much of the political and business activities of both Bush presidencies were directly and indirectly subsidized, secretly, by the Saudis. The Saudis also provided funding to train radical Muslim fighters in Pakistan to fight against the Soviets in Afghanistan.

Why would we continually fund, support, and work with radical Muslims for many decades? Because the financial interests of the economic elite are more important than any ideology or religious system. One member of an official US delegation visiting Saudi Arabia in 1944 noted, "The oil in this region is the greatest single prize in all history."[25] Could that one statement summarize the real reason for the Red Scare campaign, the Cold War, our Middle East involvement, and other overseas entanglements?

As part of the trade-off of oil for security, the United States trained and equipped Saudi armed forces and police. The Eisenhower Doctrine of 1957 led to a deepening of commitment to the Saudis. Kennedy ordered US troops into the kingdom during the Yemen Civil War. Saudi Arabia remains today the leading recipient of US arms and military services, far exceeding even Israel. Much of its goes to the Saudi police force, SANG, whose primary role is to protect the royal family.

A navy commander with close ties to the Bush family told a Texas court that the Justice Department had blackballed him professionally and financially because he refused to keep quiet about his knowledge of a conspiracy to launder Middle Eastern money to the accounts of American businesses and politicians.[26]

• • •

Not only did the Bush presidents have close ties with Saudis; the Bush family was also close to Nazis. They weren't the only ones. I will show in more detail later how Carl Byoir represented Nazi Germany interests in the United States during the thirties. The Nazis hired Byoir primarily to convince American business leaders and members of the economic elite that fascism was a better alternative than communism and that Hitler would wipe communism off the face of the earth.

Former president H. W. Bush's father, Prescott, is believed by many to have been a supporter of fascism and to have had close ties to Nazi, Germany, through his connections with Union Banking, where he was a director of the banking conglomerate. The US government seized all shares he held under the Trading with the Enemy Act. The government claimed that a large part of Bush's empire helped the German war effort.

About the time word leaked out about Prescott Bush's involvement with Union Banking and his Nazi connections, Prescott Bush unleashed a propaganda technique known as "the straw man." The straw man technique is a way to shift focus from a primary issue to a secondary issue by using crafty diversions and multilayered distractions so potentially important facts can slip into the netherworld of confusion and deniability. Bush's straw man was shifting focus from his Nazi connections to patriotism. To do this, Bush volunteered to be chairman of United Service Organizations, which raised funds for troops overseas. Wrapped snugly in patriotism and the flag, Bush went around the country in the forties to raise money to help increase the morale of US troops. Not surprisingly the press ignored his Nazi ties and concentrated on his dedication to the troops.

A few years later, President Nixon used the same technique. In 1952 while he was campaigning for vice president, a revelation that he had diverted $18,000 in campaign funds for his personal use just about derailed the campaign. But Nixon had an ace up his sleeve (the famous "Checkers speech").

Instead of directly addressing the funds charge, Nixon's propagandists advised him to speak on national television of another "gift." This gift was a cute dog given to him and his family by a supporter. He noted in a nationally televised speech that his six-year-old daughter, Tricia, was wildly in love with her new four-legged friend, which she named Checkers. He said regardless of what anyone said about accepting gifts, his family was going to keep it.

This was an ingenious use of straw-man propaganda. Nixon's critics never criticized him for accepting the dog as a gift, but he was able to shift the focus to a heartwarming story that distracted the public from the original issue. He made his critics look heartless and nit-picking. Nixon received an outpouring of public support. The Republican ticket won by a landslide.

Although I have no proof of it, it's likely that Nixon's propagandists decided to recommend Nixon unleash the straw-man technique based on what they knew about its success for Prescott Bush, who, by the way, went on to win a Senate seat. Like Nixon, Bush was able to shift focus from his Nazi-ties to his support of the troops.

Prescott Bush wasn't the only member of the economic elite with Nazi ties. Investigative reporter Christopher Simpson says in his book *Blowback* that after World War II, Nazis were given CIA subsidies to establish a foothold in the United States. As part of this covert support, many Nazis were given top positions in the Republican Party.[27]

Calling upon a wealth of documents little known or never before made public, Simpson has unveiled some startling facts about the extent to which our government officials got in bed with Nazis immediately after the war and how this cozy relationship has had a long-range blowback effect. His book received the National Jewish Book Award for Holocaust.

Simpson documents the fact that these Nazis did not come to America as individuals, but as part of organized groups with Fascist political agendas. These Fascists moved to America and joined the far right of the Republican Party, according to Simpson. Simpson shows how the State Department and the CIA put high-ranking Nazis on the intelligence payroll "for their expertise in propaganda and psychological warfare."

Americans hiring Nazi propagandists is the height of irony because, as I will show later, Hitler and his propaganda chief, Joseph Goebbels, claim they learned most of their propaganda expertise from us, specifically from President Wilson's propaganda committee, on which Carl Byoir served.

Could it be that our covert propaganda activities were so secretive and sensitive after World War II that we believed hiring Nazi propagandists was safer than training and using our own citizens? Did the economic power elite feel they could trust Nazis more than Americans to handle secret, behind-closed-doors covert propaganda? Were Nazi political views more adaptive to the "no rules" anything-goes mentality of postwar propagandists and intelligence operatives, most of whom were staunchly conservative OSS graduates? OSS was headed by Wild Bill Donovan, whose political views were archconservative and close to fascism. He recruited like-minded agents, who became the core of the CIA.

Possibly because of its strong connections with American intelligence, our major media gave scant coverage to Simpson's revelations about our government's strong connections with Nazis. Two months before the

November 1988 presidential election, a small newspaper, *Washington Jewish Week*, disclosed that a coalition for the H. W. Bush campaign included a number of Nazis and anti-Semites. The article prompted six leaders of Bush's coalition to resign.

Simpson pointed out that in 1983 Ronald Reagan presented a Medal of Freedom, the country's highest civilian honor, to CIA consultant James Burnham. Burnham was a psychological warfare consultant who promoted something called "liberationism." Just before the 1952 election, the CIA worked up a multimillion-dollar public relations campaign aimed at selling Americans on expanding Cold War activities in Europe.

Part of the guiding theory (given the name "liberationism") was the idea that certain Nazi leaders from World War II should be brought in as "freedom fighters" against the Union of Soviet Socialist Republics.[28] Reagan said that Burnham's ideas on liberation "profoundly affected the way America views itself and the world," adding, "I owe [Burnham] a personal debt, because throughout the years of traveling on the mashed-potato circuit I have quoted [him] widely."

At a May 9, 1984, press conference, Simon Wiesenthal, human rights activist and Nazi hunter, said that "Nazi criminals were the principal beneficiaries of the Cold War." The Cold War mentality, hyped by Reinhard Gehlen and other Nazis, became the shelter for tens of thousands of Nazi war criminals' reason for being, Wiesenthal stated.[29]

A public relations man, Harold Keith Thompson, was principal US point man for the postwar Nazi support network known as "die Spinne," or the Spider. Thompson, who was born and grew up in New Jersey, was independently wealthy. He was a Yale graduate.

He became interested in fascism as a teen and campaigned during the thirties against US involvement against Hitler. He was a member of the German American Bund and later became an agent of the Nazi, Germany, Security Service (SS), the sister organization of the Gestapo. Why was an upper-class American never prosecuted for openly supporting fascism before and during the war, even to the extent of joining the enemy?

In the late forties and early fifties, Thompson continued working as the chief North American representative for the German Secret Service. Martin A. Lee, in *The Beast Reawakens*, says that during both the Reagan and Bush years, the Republican Party's ethnic outreach arm recruited Nazis. Lee writes that the wealthy Thompson gave generously to Republican candidates, such as Senator Jesse Helms and would-be senator Oliver North. Thompson's money gained him membership in the GOP's Presidential Legion of Merit.[30]

Thompson received numerous thank-you letters from the Republican National Committee. Those letters are now in the Hoover Institution Special Collections Library at Stanford University in Palo Alto, California, which I accessed while living in Palo Alto.

CHAPTER 9

Dead Babies and Other Propaganda Examples

"Happiness is the perpetual possession of being well deceived," wrote Jonathan Swift.[1]

If this is true, then Americans should be the happiest people on the planet because we have been deceived for many years by people we've never met, seen, or heard of. Everything from our lifestyles to our political and moral views has been secretly engineered using psychological, motivational, and communications tools as part of a well-orchestrated, secret mass mind manipulation program.

As noted earlier, the purpose of this mass persuasion program has been to establish acceptable parameters or, put another way, to draw lines in the sand that most Americans learn instinctively not to cross. These parameters have helped define who we are, as individuals and as a country.

For example, my wife belongs to a garden club that meets once a month. Before each meeting the thirty or so members stand and recite the Pledge of Allegiance. Nothing wrong with a little patriotism. However, I'm not sure what patriotism has to do with gardening.

There are two key propaganda techniques embedded in the pledge: "I pledge allegiance to the Flag of the United States of America, and to the Republic for which it stands, one Nation under God, indivisible, with liberty and justice for all."

The first propaganda technique is "appeal to authority," which involves connecting a message to a high authority. There's no higher authority to most people than God. The second technique is "association," or connecting an idea, belief, cause, or action to a credible idea, belief, cause, or action. In this case the association is connecting liberty and justice with the United States and nationalism/patriotism.

We often recite the pledge without even thinking what the words mean. Probably less than 1 percent of those reciting the pledge know that it was written by a socialist, Francis Bellamy. He didn't have a reference to God in the original pledge. It was added during the fifties by Congress during the height of the Red-Scare propaganda campaign. That congressional action was, in itself, an act of propaganda because it sent a clear message that we're a God-fearing nation, whereas the Soviet Union is a godless state. God is on our side.

It's no accident that presidents often say "God Bless America" as they leave the podium after a major speech. Their speechwriters know instinctively to use that phrase not for religious reasons, but because all presidents have to have some connection to God if they want to get elected or stay in office. It's also no accident that "God Bless America" is often sung during the seventh-inning stretch of baseball games, along with "Take Me Out to the Ball Game."

I'm not criticizing patriotism or religion. In fact, one or the other or both are encouraged in most countries, primarily because nationalism and religion are ideal tools for drawing very clear lines in the sand we learn not to cross. Let's assume someone in my wife's garden club didn't feel comfortable reciting the pledge and remained seated. She would have likely put herself in a very awkward position and would probably be stereotyped as unpatriotic or worse. The primary significance of the pledge is that it sets a line in the sand we instinctively know not to cross. This line in the sand is a propaganda technique known as "engineering of consent."[2]

A key subset of the engineering of consent is another propaganda tool called "conformity" or "consensus" propaganda. As Nancy Snow, author of *Information War*, said: "Un-American" is a favorite name-calling device to stain the reputation of someone who disagrees with official policies and positions. "It conjures up old red-baiting techniques that stifle free speech and dissent on public issues. It creates a chilling effect on people to stop testing the waters of our democratic right to question the motives of our government."[3]

The use of name-calling devices is the propaganda technique of emotionally laden words. This technique is often combined with other propaganda techniques, such as demonization and conformity propaganda. Most of the time, conformity propaganda is subtle and indirect, but it can sometimes be very direct and overt. Patriotism and nationalism are two key ways to instill conformity. For example, according to an *Associated Press* story on September 24, 2014, a Denver-area school board in the state's second-largest school district proposed history education for high school students that would focus on topics "that promote citizenship, patriotism and respect for authority." The school board proposal called for instructional materials that present positive aspects of the nation and its heritage. It would establish a committee to regularly review texts and course plans, starting with Advanced Placement history, to make sure materials "promote citizenship, patriotism, essentials and benefits of the free-market system, respect for authority and respect for individual rights" and don't "encourage or condone civil disorder, social strife or disregard of the law."

What does promoting patriotism and "the benefits of the free-market system" have to do with a history class? It appears the school board is asking not only for conformity and unquestioning loyalty to the state and the nation, but also to big business.

There was quite an uproar in the liberal press across the country about this patriotism proposal but, in reality, this kind of patriotic conformity (engineering of consent) propaganda has been part of school curricula for many decades. If we're bombarded with conformity propaganda long enough, we often end up practicing self-censorship without even knowing it.

I myself have been propagandized by self-censorship. I practiced self-censorship by putting off writing this book. I could have written it thirty years ago, but I had a family to raise and I didn't want to take a chance of reprisals by revealing information that some circles might not want in the public domain.

The engineering of consent propaganda technique was first described by Edward Bernays in the twenties, but what I call the engineering of dissent was used long before that. Organized and officially sanctioned mass persuasion began during World War I. We were so good at it that Adolf Hitler and his propaganda minister later thanked us for teaching them how to manipulate the mass mind.

"The 20th century has been characterized by three developments of great political importance: the growth of democracy, the growth of corporate power, and the growth of corporate propaganda as a means of protecting corporate power," noted Edward Herman and Noam Chomsky in *Manufacturing Consent: the Political Economy of the Mass Media.*[4]

As a journalist I was taught that my primary job as a reporter was to get the facts. What I wasn't taught was that the facts themselves are sometimes not as important as the truth about or behind the facts.

I developed a personal filter for analyzing so-called facts. I call it the SAM test. I use the acronym "SAM" on just about everything I read, see, or hear. "S" stands for "source." Who or what is the source? "A" stands for "agenda." What is their agenda? And "M" stands for "money." Follow the money trail.

Even if you ask all of these SAM questions and get what appear to be satisfactory answers, several propaganda techniques—including layering, diversion, and plausible deniability—could make it very difficult to determine the source (or a layer of sources), the agenda, and the money trail. But, and here is the kicker: thought control can be accomplished, and often is, by not using facts as the ammunition. Our emotions, not our rationality, are often the primary target of thought control. The bottom line, however, is that we have been manipulated using sophisticated mind manipulation techniques.

One of the key covert propaganda techniques is disinformation. Disinformation, as noted in the first chapter, is a lie. It shouldn't be confused with misinformation, which is an inaccurate statement that is not deliberately false. But disinformation is designed to deceive. Many believe, and there is strong evidence, that President Johnson lied about the Gulf of Tonkin and numerous primary issues related to the Vietnam War (per the Pentagon Papers), that Nixon lied about Watergate, that Clinton lied about having sex with an intern, and that the George W. Bush administration lied about weapons of mass destruction.

These are just a few examples of possible disinformation. There are many more. We teach our children to be honest, but allow our government to lie. Nonetheless, from a pure propaganda standpoint, the following "babies left to die on the hospital floor" disinformation tops them all.

• • •

On October 10, 1990, a teenager who only provided her first name, Nayirah, gave tear-jerking testimony before a congressional caucus that Iraqi soldiers invaded a Kuwaiti hospital and threw premature and newborn babies on the floor to die as they stole hospital incubators. The testimony was widely publicized and was cited numerous times by US senators and President Bush in their rationale to back Kuwait in the Gulf War. In 1992 it was revealed that the teenager was the daughter of the Kuwaiti ambassador to the United States.

It was also later learned that the entire testimony was a hoax designed to garner American support for the Gulf War. Just about every media outlet in the United States fell for the babies-on-the-floor testimony. That is largely because journalists are not trained in clandestine propaganda. Even if they were, they would have had to do a lot of digging to get to the source of the story and the truth. I have been in the propaganda business for many years. I fell for it.[5]

What is fascinating about the entire hoax is that it employed seven propaganda techniques. These are disinformation, emotionally laden words, demonization, association, the third-party front, layering, and plausible deniability. I have an entire chapter later on these and other propaganda techniques. Here is a brief description of the propaganda tools used in this hoax:

The emotionally laden words technique involved the "babies-in-incubators" angle. Everyone loves babies. Everyone feels sorry for premature babies that must be kept in incubators to survive. Tears swelled in the eyes of the girl giving the testimony and likely from millions of Americans watching on TV. It was wrenching, emotional testimony from a seemingly sweet, innocent-looking young lady. But she was lying.

The "demonization" technique involved making the hospital-invading Iraqi soldiers monsters for committing such an atrocity. What type of barbarians would throw babies out of incubators and leave them to die on a hospital floor?

The association technique connected these Iraqi "barbarians" with the Iraqi nation itself and with Saddam Hussein, their leader.

The "third-party front" technique involved the creation of the Citizens for a Free Kuwait. It was housed at the Washington office of a large PR firm. The PR firm was hired to conduct a national campaign to raise awareness in the United States about the dangers posed by Saddam Hussein to Kuwait.

Before launching its campaign, the PR firm conducted a study to determine the best way to win support for strong action by the United States. This study revealed that the best strategy to influence public opinion would be to emphasize atrocities.[6]

Another propaganda technique is "layering." This is one of the best examples of layering in our history. It's the primary reason that the press and the public were hoodwinked and fell for the story. It took years for the truth to come out. That's because there were at least six layers one had to go through before you could find out the true source or purpose of the plot.

The first layer was the fifteen-year-old girl, Nayirah. She was the obvious and most visible source of the information. But to get information from her, you had to go through several other layers, including the caucus that set up the hearings, the PR firm that thought of the caucus idea, and her family. But she was not part of just *any* family. She was Kuwaiti royalty.

Her family was another layer. It was not revealed during the testimony that she was the daughter of the Kuwait ambassador to the United States. Subsequent investigations revealed that she was not even in Kuwait when the alleged incident happened. And the family has refused repeated requests for years to comment on their daughter's testimony.

We do know Nayirah's testimony was scripted. The PR firm provided witnesses, wrote testimony, and coached the witnesses for accuracy. The PR firm is another layer.

Few, if any, news outlets reported the PR firm's involvement in the caper. A good reporter could have easily found out which organization was responsible for establishing the caucus and putting the entire event together but, as far as I know, no one bothered to ask the question.

As John Stauber and Sheldon Rampton noted in their book *Toxic Sludge Is Good for You*: "The man running the PR firm's Washington office was Craig Fuller, one of Bush's closest friends and inside political advisors. The news media never bothered to examine his role until after the war had ended, but if America's editors had read the PR trade press, they might have noticed this announcement, published in 'O'Dwyer's PR Services' before the fighting began."[7] Stauber and Rampton noted that Fuller, chief of staff to Bush when he was vice president, had been on the Kuwaiti account at Hill & Knowlton since the first day.

Is the media's lack of investigation into this hoax while it was going on another example of the CIA's Operation Mockingbird, which, as we have noted with several examples, was designed to manage the nation's media?

Still another layer was the Congressional Human Rights Caucus, which was set up as a front. Its façade was to investigate human atrocities in Kuwait. Its real purpose was to garner public support for invading Iraq.

The hearing was set up as a caucus and not a committee because you can't be charged with contempt of Congress when giving false testimony before a caucus, but you can for false testimony before a congressional committee. How does a PR firm set up a major congressional hearing and have it defined as a "caucus"? The trick is to get a congressman on your side and have him do it, which is what Tom Lantos, a California Democrat, did.

During the three months between her testimony and the start of the war, the story of babies torn from their incubators was repeated over and over again. President Bush told the story. It was recited as fact in congressional testimony, on TV, in newspapers and magazines, on radio talk shows, and at the UN Security Council.

Future investigations (even one by the Kuwaitis) revealed that her testimony, which Bush used numerous times to justify Desert Storm, was a lie. Another layer was the government of Kuwait. They were the money source (possibly with help from Saudi Arabia).

The final layers were the president and the CIA. But they were protected by all these other people and groups you had to go through before you got to the initial source. But even if you got to the original source, you would have to deal with the propaganda technique of plausible deniability. The committee established plausible deniability. They were set up as a caucus, not a committee. The Saudi royal family had plausible deniability. They couldn't be forced to testify because they appeared before a congressional caucus. In addition, the girl and her parents have refused to ever comment on the incident. The CIA had plausible deniability because they operate in secret and don't legally have to comment. And the president had plausible deniability. He was careful to say publicly that he got his information from press reports and that he was just repeating what the nation's press had written. Plausible deniability allows you to get something done in such a way that you can plausibly claim you had nothing to do with it.

Plausible deniability is often used by senior officials in a formal or informal chain of command to deny knowledge of and/or responsibility for any damnable actions committed by the lower ranks because they can claim their lack of knowledge confirms they were not a participant. In the case that illegal or otherwise disreputable and unpopular activities become public, high-ranking officials can deny any awareness of such acts in order to insulate themselves and shift blame to the agents who carried out the acts, confident that their doubters will be unable to prove otherwise. The lack of evidence to the contrary makes the denial so plausible that it's credible.

The question that still hasn't been answered fully is who funded the committee that, in turn, funded the PR firm? It appears on the surface to have been the Kuwait government, but did the CIA and/or Saudi Arabia contribute? We will probably never know. That is the whole idea of clandestine propaganda. How many other disinformation campaigns have been conducted covertly that have never seen the light of day?

Disinformation as a propaganda technique has been used frequently since World War I. Attorney General Mitchell Palmer, Carl Byoir, and a young J. Edgar Hoover set up a special Justice Department Publicity Bureau shortly after World War I to disseminate news articles about a Russian plot to invade the US and overthrow the US government. It was a lie, pure disinformation. But the media gave it big play, and it kick-started the Red Scare propaganda campaign to create a fear that there was a Communist under every bed.[8]

Now that I have given several examples of disinformation, I need to point out that most effective propaganda doesn't rely on lies. The babies-on-the-floor caper was an exception. Propagandists long ago began de-emphasizing lies and deceit (except as a last resort). Much more effective than lies are partial truths and truth out of context. These are really hard to spot.

In short, a good propagandist does everything possible to avoid lying. When a propagandist lies, he or she sets a trap for having to produce proof. No proof is needed when you simply mask your intentions. Even Joseph Goebbels, Hitler's chief propagandist, was quick to state facts. The propagandist prefers to hide facts rather than lie when the release of factual information becomes dangerous. Saying nothing, or silence, hides facts and can help modify context. Using favorable facts and then distorting them can also manipulate context.

When propagandists present a fact, they often position the fact in such a way that you can't understand the context or draw rational conclusions. For example, we often see news accounts announcing that production is up, say, 20 percent, and the standard of living is up, say, 15 percent. Those statistics mean little without stating the base year or figures from past years. On the occasions that lies are employed, propagandists prefer to use the "big lie," that is, to lie in depth. As Hitler noted in *Mein Kampf*, "In the very magnitude of a lie is held a good amount of credibility. The primitive simplicity of the mind of the masses is more easily misled by a great than by a tiny lie; they are accustomed to telling insignificant lies themselves and so they can detect them. But they generally fail to detect a truly gigantic distortion."[9]

Hitler, who learned his propaganda expertise from us, knew that disinformation or lies are much more effective if they are "big lies" and not small ones. The Kuwaiti lie was a big lie and multilayered. If it had been a small lie, people would have likely detected it.

Another big lie was revealed in the Pentagon Papers, which was a Department of Defense history of the Vietnam War covering 1945 to 1967. The papers were discovered and released by Daniel Ellsberg and brought to public attention in 1971. A 1996 article in the *New York Times* said that the Pentagon Papers had demonstrated, among other things, that the Johnson Administration "systematically lied, not only to the public, but also to Congress."[10]

For his disclosure of the Pentagon Papers, Ellsberg was initially charged with conspiracy, espionage, and theft of government property, but the charges were later dropped after prosecutors investigating the Watergate scandal soon discovered that the staff members in the Nixon White House had ordered the so-called White House plumbers to engage in unlawful efforts to discredit Ellsberg. Discrediting someone involves numerous propaganda techniques, such as demonization.

• • •

For decades "communism" and "socialism" were by far the most demonized and emotionally laden words in the English language. One key emotionally laden word of recent years has been "terrorism" and words associated with it, such as "savagery." The Canadian prime minister used both of these words in the same speech before Parliament to describe an apparently mentally ill person who shot and killed a Canadian police guard in October 2014. PM Steve Harper told Parliament the day after the shooting: "(The shooting) will strengthen our resolve and redouble our efforts to work with our allies around the world and fight against the terrorist organizations that brutalize those in other countries with the hope of bringing their savagery to our shores. They will have no safe haven."[11]

A few hours after the prime minister used these emotionally laden words (terrorist, brutalize, and savagery), a *New York Times* story noted there was no terrorist conspiracy and only one disturbed shooter. Journalist Glenn Greenwald, who broke the Snowden NSA spying story, wrote an article in *The Intercept*, in which he noted that: "The right-wing Canadian government wasted no time in seizing on the incident to promote its fear-mongering agenda over terrorism, which includes pending legislation to vest its intelligence agency, CSIS, with more spying and secrecy powers in the name of fighting ISIS."[12]

Did the prime minister play on people's emotions and fears because he wanted to get surveillance legislation passed?

Another example of the propaganda value of emotionally laden words was when the US Senate voted November 18, 2014, against a bill that would reform NSA's mass surveillance. Even though the reform bill would not have stopped mass surveillance or even put a dent in NSA's surveillance, the bill to debate the issue was still defeated by the conservative majority. When the bill came to the floor, some members of the Senate stood up to scream "9/11" and "terrorism," as they often do.

Just as "terrorism" has become a popular emotionally laden word, so has the word "militant." People killed in drone strikes are often called "militants," when in reality we usually have no idea if those killed were militants or even how many were actually killed. One reason we can't get accurate body counts is that many of the strikes are carried out by people sitting at computer terminals in Nevada, directing the drones like some video game. Greenwald's *Intercept* has reported that targeting decisions can even be made on the basis of nothing more than metadata analysis and tracking of SIM cards in mobile phones.

Another reason we have no idea how many militants have been killed is because George Bush and his CIA head, General Michael Hayden, implemented "signature strikes" (another government/military euphemism). Signature strikes authorize us to shoot at military-aged males associated with suspicious activity even if their identities are unknown.

Signature strikes are "not a concept known to international humanitarian law," according to Christof Heyns, the UN special rapporteur on extrajudicial or arbitrary executions. The proper standard for attacking a person under the laws of war, he said, is whether the person has a "continuous combat function" or is "directly participating in hostilities."

"If a signature strike rests on targeting without sufficient information to make the necessary determination, it is clearly unlawful," wrote Steve Coll in the *New Yorker* magazine. [13]

Coll noted that a joint 2012 report from the law schools of Stanford University and NYU, "Living Under the Drones," documented that not only can drones cause injuries and death; they can also cause psychological damage by just flying over communities. He pointed out that drones sometimes hover twenty-four hours a day over some communities in Pakistan and strike without any warning. Imagine the fear this causes. This pattern "terrorizes" the population.

Coll and others have pointed out that drones have a tremendous psychological effect even if they don't attack. Not knowing when or if the drones will strike not only has a psychological impact; it also sends a strong propaganda message: stay within the boundaries we've set.

"Drones may kill relatively few, but they terrify many more," Malik Jalal, a tribal leader in North Waziristan, told Coll. "They turned the people into psychiatric patients."

What is ironic is that our drone actions in Yemen, Pakistan, and other countries meet our own definition of terrorism. The US Joint Chiefs of Staff annual Counterterrorism Report for 2014 defined "terrorism" this way: "Terrorism is the unlawful use of violence or threat of violence, often motivated by religious, political, or other ideological beliefs, to instil fear and coerce governments or societies in pursuit of goals that are usually political."

The UN special rapporteur has even said some US drone attacks may constitute war crimes. "Given their intended effects, both physical and psychological, on entire populations, there is a very compelling case to make that continual, sustained drone warfare in places such as Pakistan and Yemen meet the UN's formal definition of 'terrorism' found in its latest strategy document," Greenwald said.[14]

The observant reader will note that drone attacks and surveillance have one element in common: they arouse the emotion of fear. Even if there are no surveillance or drone attacks, just the chance that they might happen is enough to get the majority of people to conform. The observant reader might also recall that we dropped two nuclear bombs to send a propaganda message of fear. Drones also create fear and, thus, send a strong propaganda message.

In a December 20, 2014, article in *Reader Supported News*, William Boardman makes it clear that the US use of torture during the so-called war on terror is not something new. He noted that: "Torture has long been a chronic, low level vein of criminality by U.S. government operatives, with bipartisan collusion at least since the beginning of the Cold War. Not just the CIA, but its fronts, private contractors, and proxies have used torture since the forties."

He pointed out that torture (and murder) was endemic in our massacres against Indians in the nineteenth century and in the Philippines (1899–1913), where Mark Twain described the American troops as "our uniformed assassins."

Boardman also said American torture was common in Laos, Cambodia, Iraq, Guatemala, and Iran and in the CIA's Phoenix Program in Vietnam, which combined torture and assassination in a years-long terror campaign against the Viet Cong.[15]

• • •

False-flag propaganda is a subset of the engineering of dissent that has been used for decades to disrupt, discredit, demonize, and sometimes destroy enemies, usually leftists or "terrorists." A false-flag is a manufactured "incident" designed to arouse passions and to stimulate a desired response. False-flags are sometimes applied to events that governments are aware of and could stop, but choose to let happen anyway, which is called "standing down."[16]

Did the Reagan Administration know about the CIA importing drugs into the United States, but choose to do nothing? If so, that is a perfect example of standing down. We have already noted that the war on drugs may have been a classic case of block and bridge propaganda designed to use the war on drugs as a diversion to allow tons of narcotics into our country. In short, it could have been both a block and bridge and a false-flag/standing down. Another example I gave earlier of a standing down false-flag could be Operation Gladio.

Operation Gladio was one of the most secretive and repugnant covert operations in world history, yet US media have given it little coverage. Operation Gladio was a false-flag terrorist operation allegedly set up by intelligence operatives of several countries after World War II to hinder and halt all Soviet and Socialist influence or inroads in Western Europe, particularly in Italy, where Socialists were gaining in popularity.

On August 2, 1980, a bomb exploded at the Bologna, Italy, train station. It killed eighty-five people and wounded over two hundred, including numerous women and children. The massacre was blamed on Italian leftists, who the US and Italian governments feared were gaining popular support and could possibly win an upcoming election. Largely because the voting public associated the bombing with leftists, the leftists lost the election. Years later it was learned that right-wing and Fascist elements were responsible for the bombing.

Did our staunchly anti-Communist covert operatives know about the bombing beforehand and stand down? Could they have worked with NATO and Italian intelligence in using the right-wing perpetuators as agent provocateurs? If so, it would not be the first time we planned, implemented, or looked the other way in acts of terrorism as part of our engineering-of-dissent propaganda campaigns (such as in Iran and Guatemala, to name a couple examples).

Acts of terrorism that can be blamed on an adversary are a very effective propaganda technique to influence public opinion by manipulating the emotion of fear. What better way to discredit a person, group, or state than to link them with terrorist atrocities?

For example, the United States claimed in December 2014 that a cyber-attack on Sony Corporation was conducted by North Korean government hackers angry that Sony was releasing a motion picture called *The Interview*, a satirical comedy revolving around a plot to murder Korean leader Kim Jong-Un.

Marc Rogers, director of security operation for DER CON, the world's largest hack conference, and the top security researcher for the world's leading mobile security company, Cloudflare, wrote an article in in which he claimed that the FBI's and the administration's news announcements and evidence were not based on knowledge of hacking technology. He basically said the FBI hacking rationale had no scientific basis and there was not "remotely plausible evidence that the attack was orchestrated by North Korea."[17] Rogers punched technical holes in the FBI's malware evidence and showed numerous ways that the FBI was wrong.

Greenwald, in a January 1, 2015, *Intercept* article, also had suspicions about the government's North Korea announcement. Greenwald noted that President Obama, in a December 19 press conference, announced: "We can confirm that North Korea engaged in this attack. We will respond. We cannot have a society in which some dictator some place can start imposing censorship here in the United States."[18]

Greenwald pointed out that numerous cyber experts echoed the same doubts as Rogers. Cyber expert Bruce Schneie, according to Greenwald, said he was "deeply sceptical of the FBI's announcement on Friday that North Korea was behind last month's Sony hack. The agency's evidence is tenuous, and I have a hard time believing it."

Yet none of this expert skepticism made its way into countless media accounts of the Sony hack. One could not read about this incident in major US media without concluding that North Korea was responsible for the hacking. Mainstream media, as it often does, took what the government said at face value.

"Time and again, many journalists mindlessly regurgitated the U.S. Government's accusation against North Korea without a shred of doubt, blindly assuming it to be true, and then discussing, often demanding, strong retaliation," Greenwald stated.

Treating government assertions as truth and rarely questioning or digging into what's behind government proclamations is the mark of a malleable media, a media that I show throughout this book serves the interest of the economic power elite first and foremost.

"It's pretty tasteless for the United States, a country complicit in so many assassinations of foreign leaders, to make a comedy movie about assassinating a foreign leader," wrote Ken Klippenstein and Paul Gottinger in a *Reader Supported News* article January 2, 2015, titled "The Interview Is Propaganda Masquerading as Comedy."[19]

The authors wrote: "Though Hollywood's lack of tact wasn't much surprise, it was shocking to learn that the State Department signed-off on the film. If, say, the Venezuelan government formally approved a film about the assassination of Barack Obama, one suspects Washington would accuse them of quite a bit more than poor taste."

On January 2, 2015, President Obama announced economic sanctions against North Korea for the alleged hacking incident. In his announcement he still did not present proof.

A couple weeks later, after increasing media doubt about the credibility of the accusations, the Obama administration on January 19, 2015, shifted focus and claimed that they knew about the North Korean hacking because the United States had first hacked North Korea. Is that another block and bridge?

It really doesn't matter from a propaganda standpoint whether the FBI was right or wrong or whether or not North Korea was actually involved. The important thing is that the FBI and the government were able to widely disseminate another scare story that received widespread news coverage, coverage that did not include any hint of the objectivity that major American media often praises itself for. Whether it was a block and bridge, false-flag, or actual North Korean plot, the bizarre hacking caper was just one more in a long list of scare stories that arouse the emotion of fear. Our media post-9/11 has been filled with scare stories.

Loch K. Johnson, a professor at the University of Georgia and a former Church Committee investigator who helped investigate CIA after Watergate, said that the Senate Committee did its work in the seventies "in a semi-benign period of international affairs" compared to today's environment. "There wasn't the same kind of fear in the air (as today)," Johnson told the *New York Times* Mark Mazzetti.[20]

As pointed out earlier in this chapter, drone attacks, because they induce fear, are a perfect propaganda tool, particularly when they circle a village for several weeks before striking. Such a tactic is obviously designed to send a message of fear to the entire population. Just knowing that drones are overhead (or could be) is often enough to pacify a population. It is a form of engineering of consent, which tells us to conform or face the consequences. Obama's policy of letting the CIA make the final decision and conduct drone strikes gives him plausible deniability.

The CIA shifted from capturing and interrogating terrorism suspects to targeting them with armed drones beginning in June 2004 in Pakistan. The agency's first drone strike, ironically, was launched shortly after CIA's secret prisons and abuse of prisoners were first revealed.

Why is the American public fearful? Fear doesn't just happen. Someone or something has to make you afraid. That is usually done through the media and often through well-planned and thought-out covert propaganda campaigns.

A *CBS News* poll taken in December 2014, shortly after the Senate Intelligence Committee's torture report was released, revealed that 49 percent of Americans believe that brutal interrogation methods (torture) are sometimes justified. No wonder nearly half of Americans support torture. We're afraid.

In the months leading up to the release of the torture report, media were full of scare stories, ranging from the North Korean plot to the savagery and brutality of ISIS beheadings. Were any of these false-flag incidents? Did they involve agent provocateurs deliberately stirring up dissent or horrendous acts as they have done so often throughout our history? How much disinformation was involved?

It would take hundreds of pages to chronicle government disinformation propaganda. In addition to the ones already pointed out, a few others include the death of professional football player-turned-hero soldier Pat Tillman and the capture of Jessica Lynch.

Tillman was exalted by the press as a true American hero and patriot after he turned down a multimillion-dollar contract and volunteered to fight in Iraq and Afghanistan after 9/11. The government concocted a story that made Tillman a hero who died in a blaze of glory. The army initially claimed that Tillman and his unit were attacked in an apparent ambush on a road outside of a village. An intensive investigation eventually revealed he was accidentally killed by friendly fire. Yet the military spun the incident to make it appear Tillman was a hero who died fighting the enemy.

Jessica Lynch's story of being captured by the Iraqis and later rescued by US Special Forces has also come under attack as disinformation. It appears to be a brazen example of news management by government propagandists. Lynch was presented as a nineteen-year-old hero soldier whose squad was ambushed after making a wrong turn in Iraq. She was supposedly taken prisoner while seriously wounded by gunfire and taken to an Iraqi hospital, where she was said to have been abused by Iraqi guards for a week before being "rescued" by a team of US Army Rangers and Navy Seals in a daring, made-for-TV raid. Lynch, however, didn't remember anything, and eyewitnesses said the Iraqi guards had left a day before the rescue. She also apparently didn't have the bullet wounds she was said to have had.

One of the most blatant examples of disinformation was the claim that Saddam possessed nuclear weapons and biotoxins. The American public fell for these lies hook, line and sinker. Remember the Orange Alerts that were staged because of this disinformation?

Subsets of disinformation are staged events and cover-ups.

One of the most glaring staged events was the toppling of the statue of Saddam in the Baghdad square. Hundreds of Iraqis (brought in to cheer their newfound liberation and freedom) applauded as a huge crane tore down the large Saddam statue. It was all staged.[21]

Several examples of cover-ups include the torture of prisoners at Abu Ghraib (and at other sites) and the My Lai incident in Vietnam. Both of these cover-ups were exposed by journalist Seymour Hersh.

Hersh also exposed a potentially huge disinformation campaign with a May 2015 article in the *London Review of Books*, "The Killing of Osama bin Laden." Hersh gave evidence that the government version of what happened with the death of Osama bin Laden involved a lot of disinformation about the events before and the day of Osama's death.

After Hersh's exposé appeared, mainstream journalists began an unrelenting attack on Hersh himself and largely ignored the validity of what he reported. If you recall, similar attacks were waged against journalist Gary Webb, who exposed the Contra-cocaine scandal.

Government propagandists have become so adept at disinformation, staging events, and managing news that the American public continually falls for propaganda spinning. We fall for these lies partly because they're usually presented by media in a convincing fashion and because we've been conditioned since childhood to trust what our government says. We also fall for disinformation because covert operatives have had decades to master propaganda techniques that are very difficult to detect.

CHAPTER 10

War on Drugs and Jim Crow

IN THE FOLLOWING CHAPTERS, I will make a strong case that propaganda is one of the primary weapons that has propelled the United States to world dominance. However, America's misuse of propaganda, including conducting a "just" propaganda war against its own people, may be backfiring.

Overt, open propaganda, such as advertising and public relations, is typically not a primary weapon in mass mind manipulation, but covert propaganda usually is, particularly when combined with surveillance and new communications technologies, such as social media, smartphones, and the Internet. The dichotomy is that these and other new technologies are allowing other countries to catch up and to counter our clandestine propaganda.

Some might be inclined to defend the mind manipulation campaign because they believe it's necessary to protect us from "terrorism" (a much propagandized word). Mind manipulation programs began nearly a century before Bush's war on terror, which, as I will show, is a master stroke of propaganda genius. However, Bush used propaganda techniques that have been used for decades. Even his use of the word "terror" is not new.

Senator Robert La Follette of Wisconsin used it when he described President Wilson's Committee on Public Information as "creating a State of Terror" in a 1917 Senate speech. He said, "It appears to be the purpose of those conducting the propaganda campaign to throw the country into a state of terror, to coerce public opinion, to stifle criticism, and to suppress discussion of the great issues involved in this war."[1]

Others might say we need mind manipulation for national security reasons and to protect us from enemies. The problem is we have always had "enemies"; and when we didn't, we have a history of inventing them. And, as I noted earlier, one of the participants in the mind manipulation program said we, the American people, are often considered "the enemy."

Denial of and rationalization for mind manipulation are exactly what the economic elite want. Denial of propaganda's existence or its impact reinforces one of the elite's key goals: to make us so propagandized that we don't even know we're propagandized.

How can the average American level the playing field of mass persuasion when those controlling the communications are, in effect, ghosts?

Even in-depth reporting from award-winning investigative reporters such as Gary Webb hasn't been able to crack the veil of secrecy that our invisible government hides under (often with media protection). Unfortunately, those who get too close to the truth, as Webb may have, become a top-priority enemy. Enemies of the invisible government like Webb have little if any defense because they don't know who, if anyone, is after them.

While the Contra-cocaine scandal is important, concentrating too much on a single issue like Webb did can cause us to not see the forest for the trees. The Nicaragua drug scandal is not an aberration or an isolated event. Our government has known of and participated in numerous drug-related operations and experiments for decades. It is a matter of record. Investigative reporters like Webb have provided a great service for democracy by demonstrating that things aren't always as they appear. However, although the Contra-drug scandal is a critical issue, it's just a tree in the forest.

Clandestine propagandists are experts at preventing even the best investigative reporters from seeing the forest for the trees. In other words, the big picture is very difficult to detect. It's much easier to spot the trees in the forest than the forest itself. Just the reality of sensory overload, the overwhelming amount of information we are bombarded with daily, makes it difficult to step back and see the big picture. Propaganda techniques like diversion, misdirection, obfuscation, third-party fronts, block and bridge, layering, and red herrings make it even more difficult.

I belong to the University Club of Winter Park, Florida. One of our members for many decades was Tom Polgar, a career CIA veteran who died in 2014. The *New York Times* rarely does obituaries on CIA agents, but Tom received a long obituary, even though he was a Florida and not a New York resident. Tom had a long career of CIA service all over the globe.

He joined the agency in 1947. He was one of the first agents. He was in charge of CIA activities in Vietnam and was one of the last Americans to get on the helicopter that evacuated Americans off the roof of Saigon's American embassy.

Tom was a nice guy. He believed he and his cohorts provided a service to their country. He also was fairly open-minded for a spook. He knew I had a background in journalism and propaganda, but I believe he also respected my strong belief in transparency and in a level economic playing field for everyone.

He never revealed to me any secrets (I wouldn't expect him to), but he knew I understood there was a big picture, a picture few of us have seen. Polgar also knew that I probably would not like the pictures our covert agencies paint and frame on consignment for the upper classes (and the CIA ultimately works for the interests of the economic elite).

What is the big picture for our invisible government? It is to do anything necessary to protect and promote the economic/financial interests of the economic power elite. The biggest perceived threats to those economic interests during the past century have been anything that smacks of collectivism, particularly socialism and communism, and anything that threatens the elite's primary commodity, which is oil.

Why would the US government secretly hire hundreds of top-level Nazis shortly after World War II and allow them to escape war crimes prosecution? For the same reason many American business leaders, at the urging of American propagandist Carl Byoir, supported fascism in the thirties and even attended a large pro-Nazi Madison Square Garden rally—because Hitler promised to wipe communism off the face of the earth.

That was the big picture and music to the ears of the economic power elite. Fascism might be evil, but at least it didn't threaten the assets of the economic elite. The United States has shown throughout the past century that it will let nothing get in the way of protecting and growing the financial interests of the elite, even if that means sacrificing democracy, people dying, people getting hooked on drugs, large numbers of poor and blacks being imprisoned, or getting in bed with Nazis and radical Muslims.

President Carter's national security adviser, Zbigniew Brzezinski, proudly admitted that "the unleashing of radical Islam played a crucial role in destabilizing the USSR (its Muslim countries) and ending communism as a dominant world force."[2]

You can't get much blunter than those words from one who was involved in the anti-Collectivist propaganda campaign. This was a historical confession, but it received little press coverage. Brzezinski knew the big picture: defeating anything that hints of collectivism.

The big picture in the Nicaragua drug scandal also involved doing anything necessary, no matter how immoral or unlawful, to remove a left-leaning Sandinista government. Ethics don't enter into the big picture.

Sure, there might be side effects, such as highly addictive drugs entering our country, but to those involved in the campaign, these were the side effects of a "just war."

• • •

Speaking of side effects, about the same time *Kill the Messenger* was released in the fall of 2014, Mark Levin released the documentary *Freeway: Crack in the System.* Levin's film not only explores the corruption in the drug war, but also calls into question the draconian jail sentences the US justice system has meted out to a mostly minority population.[3]

"I knew that these laws were a mistake when we were writing them," said Eric Sterling, according to Levin. Sterling was counsel to the US House Judiciary Committee in the 1980s and a key contributor to the passage of mandatory-minimum sentencing laws.

"There is no question that there are tens of thousands of black people in prison serving sentences that are decades excessive," Sterling says. "Their families have been destroyed." In 1980 there were roughly forty thousand drug offenders in US prisons, according to the Sentencing Project, a prison sentencing reform group. By 2011 the number of drug offenders serving prison sentences had ballooned to more than five hundred thousand, most of whom are not high-level operators and are without prior criminal records, Levin reported.

The irony is that the Contra-cocaine scandal happened in the eighties during the height of the so-called war on drugs. The eighties also saw the beginning of the militarization of local law enforcement, the tentacles of which are seen to this day, most recently in Ferguson, Missouri, in the fall of 2014 and in Baltimore during the spring of 2015.

According to the United Nations' mandate we signed, the war on drugs was intended to discourage the production, distribution, and consumption of psychoactive drugs. One thing is for sure. We certainly didn't discourage drug distribution. It's a matter of record that the Contra-cocaine scandal involved drug distribution in the United States and that we knew about it. The Global Commission on Drug Policy released a report on June 2, 2011, in which it stated that "The War on Drugs Has Failed."[4]

The Global Commission said emphatically in its report that the United States did not discourage drug distribution. If the United States looked the other way or condoned cocaine being introduced into the inner cities, then why did Reagan in 1985 hire a public relations staff, according to reporter Susan Grigsby, "to publicize the scourge of crack cocaine?"[5]

Was Reagan's war on drugs PR program a diversionary propaganda tactic to make it appear there was an aggressive war on drugs campaign underway when, in reality, the Reagan administration may have been complicit in the introduction of cocaine into the United States? It would not be the first time that our government has used a false-flag or the block and bridge propaganda technique to divert our attention. I have already given several examples of this technique and will give more.

For an administration that was either complicit or looked the other way in the introduction of cocaine into the United States, it certainly went on a propaganda offensive to make it appear the Reagan administration was fighting drugs. For example, the Reagan administration's public relations team heavily publicized the administration's so-called "zero tolerance" policy on illegal drugs. They also had a "Just Say No" propaganda slogan.

Could the war on drugs have been a false-flag or smokescreen to divert attention from a primary goal, such as militarizing police or using drug addiction as a means to pacify potential disrupters of the status quo, including the poor, minorities, and the disenfranchised? If we have the resources to send people to the moon, to explore vast reaches of space, to develop sophisticated technologies, and to fight endless wars, you would think we could at least make a little progress in reducing drug use.

I'm not saying there was a conspiracy to hook Americans on drugs, but if I were a member of the economic power elite, I could see the advantage of having militarized police and millions of potential troublemakers either in a drug stupor or behind bars. For one thing, they would not be radicalization fodder for a charismatic leader like Dr. Martin Luther King.

A drugged or jailed lower class is much more manageable than having sober radicals roaming the streets seeking jobs and demonstrating for economic justice. The elite likely would not want to see a repeat of the civil rights and the anti–Vietnam War movements, particularly if it was a large socioeconomic-based movement.

"The War on Drugs has seen our prison population explode over the past 30 years, from 300,000 to over 2 million, the majority being due to drug-related offenses," noted Susan Grigsby. Michelle Alexander calls the war on drugs part of *The New Jim Crow* in her book of the same name. Cornell West in the introduction to Alexander's excellent book wrote: "For too long, there has been no mass fight back against the multileveled assault on poor and vulnerable people; *The New Jim Crow* is a grand wake-up call in the midst of a long slumber of indifference to the poor and vulnerable," West said. [6]

"While the Age of Obama is a time of historic breakthroughs at the level of racial symbols and political surfaces," West said, "Michelle Alexander's magisterial work takes us beyond these breakthroughs to the systemic breakdown of black and poor communities devastated by mass unemployment, social neglect, economic abandonment, and intense police surveillance."

Alexander doesn't disparage our racial progress, but she does strongly criticize the use of state power to incarcerate poor blacks in the name of the war on drugs. I agree with West and Alexander that the poor and the vulnerable (such as the mentally ill) are a low priority for America's leadership (the economic elite).

Toward the end of her book, Alexander notes that American leadership has "never really cared" about the poor or the vulnerable. That, I believe, is because their primary care is market share and profit growth. Everything else is secondary. The elite react to perceived threats to their economic interests with the same tools they use to keep the general populace pacified: propaganda and surveillance. If those don't work, the full powers of a militarized police force are called into play.

Most individuals and groups are free to critique and even to organize and protest against perceived injustices as long as they don't cross certain lines in the sand. Those who do, do so at their own peril, particularly people of color, radical dissenters, and the poor and mentally ill. Remember, it wasn't that many years ago when lynching was used to keep what Southerners called "uppity Negros" in line.

Bill Moyer said on February 6, 2015, (*Moyer & Company*) that there were 4,743 recorded lynchings in the United States from 1882 to 1968 (throughout the country), plus a lot of racist-motivated bloodshed. This doesn't include lynchings that were not recorded.

Martin Luther King won the Nobel Peace Prize and will likely go down in history as one of the greatest Americans. Yet there is irrefutable evidence from FBI files that the FBI did everything it could to discredit, demonize, and destroy the civil rights leader.

The FBI's anti-King campaign increased significantly after he began speaking out on economic inequality. Speech after speech in King's later years was filled with warnings against the evils of economic injustice, not just against blacks, but against all races. When he was killed, King was in Memphis to support a garbage workers' demonstration for better wages and working conditions. In 1999 a Memphis jury found local, state, and federal government agencies guilty of a conspiracy to kill King.[7]

According to a November 14, 2014, article in *Yahoo News* and first published in the *New York Times*,[8] a handwritten letter was discovered in the National Archives in College Park, Maryland, which was sent by an anonymous FBI agent to the Reverend Martin Luther King Jr., threatening to expose the civil rights leader's womanizing unless he took the "one way out"—an apparent reference to suicide.

The letter "shines a disturbing light on the well-documented efforts of Hoover to discredit King," the article noted. The article said that one of Hoover's top deputies, William Sullivan, apparently wrote the letter. The final paragraph of that letter makes a strong, veiled threat: "There is only one thing left for you to do. You know what it is."

The anonymous letter was the result of the FBI's comprehensive surveillance and harassment strategy against King, which included bugging his hotel rooms, photographic surveillance, and physical observation of King's movements by FBI agents.

The agency also attempted to break up his marriage by sending selectively edited "personal moments he shared with friends and women" to his wife. If you recall, I noted earlier that the FBI's own documents revealed the FBI's numerous efforts to break up marriages and get people fired from their jobs because of their socioeconomic beliefs. Is this kind of covert activity by our top law enforcement agencies the hallmark of a democracy or a police state?

According to Nadia Kayyali, writing for the Electronic Frontier Association, the FBI's letter to King demonstrates exactly what lengths the intelligence community is willing to go to and what happens when they take the fruits of the surveillance they've done and unleash it on a target. "The implications of these types of strategies in the digital age are chilling," Kayyali wrote. "Imagine Facebook chats, porn viewing history, emails, and more made public to discredit a leader who threatens the status quo, or used to blackmail a reluctant target into becoming an FBI informant. These are not far-fetched observations. They are the reality of what happens when the surveillance state is allowed to grow out of control, and the full King letter, as well as current intelligence community practices illustrate that reality richly," she said. [9]

As Professor Beverly Gage, who discovered the FBI letter, asks: "Should intelligence agencies be able to sweep our email, read our texts, track our phone calls, locate us by GPS?" Much of the conversation swirls around the possibility that agencies like the NSA or the FBI will use such information not to serve national security, but to carry out personal and political vendettas, she said.[10]

Not only did our government agencies attempt to destroy one of the most respected men in history; they also spied on deaf, dumb, and blind humanitarian Helen Keller. How is it justified to spy on and attempt to discredit and demonize a deaf, dumb, and blind person?

For the same reason, King was harassed by the FBI and vilified in the media. Both had strong convictions concerning equality (racial and economic), and both believed that they should be able to express their beliefs openly in a democracy. John Denver believed the same thing. He thought he had a democratic right to attend an antiwar rally in 1971. He did, and ended up in FBI files.

In his later years, King believed that America needed a radical redistribution of economic and political power. He challenged America's economic class system and its racial caste.

Was the FBI's demonization of King and its continuous attempts to discredit him an aberration? Some have blamed the FBI's anti-King activities on Hoover's obvious dislike of King, but there is overwhelming evidence that there were many in top levels of government who loathed King, not because of his civil rights movement, but because of his support of economic equality and his anti–Vietnam War proclamations. These are the same reasons Helen Keller and John Denver were in FBI files. They, like King, believed in economic justice and were against war. Were their socioeconomic beliefs seen as a threat to the interests of the economic power elite? One thing is for certain: government covert agencies used a myriad of covert propaganda techniques to discredit and demonize King and, to a lesser degree, Keller and Denver.

· · ·

A truism with covert propaganda is that things aren't always as they appear. This will always be true as long as we have thousands of mass mind manipulators working in total secrecy so that we don't know who they are, where they work, what they do, or what their agenda is.

To make things even more shadowy, our covert agencies often destroy sensitive files before they ever see the light of day. Those that are seen are often heavily redacted. In fact, most of the MKULTRA records were destroyed in 1973 by the order of CIA director Richard Helms, according to the Senate's Church Committee, which wrote that his destroying the files "hampered" their investigative efforts. It was also the practice of MKULTRA to maintain as few records as possible.[11]

In 2014 the Senate Intelligence Committee only released about 10 percent of CIA files related to torture of prisoners. What was in the other 90 percent? Not all mass mind manipulation is covert and done in secret, but even some open and overt propaganda can be deceptive.

For example, President Obama announced on November 7, 2014, that he was sending an additional 1,500 American troops to Iraq after he had said over and over that we would not put American troops back on the ground in Iraq.

The announcement was made three days after the November 4 midterm elections and on a Friday, a day usually reserved in Washington for the release of bad or embarrassing news that officials hope won't still be fresh enough for Monday's newspapers and so will quietly sink. It was also announced after the election to avoid political discussion before the election. The growing size of the US contingent (to three thousand) was not the only news. The United States was also re-establishing a "command" in Iraq.

Juan Cole noted in a November 9, 2014, article in *Informed Comment* that: "If ISIS really is a dire threat to U.S. security, as administration officials maintain, then they should go to the U.S. public with the news that they are going to have to put thousands of U.S. forces on the ground in Iraq. So far they are trying to spin us, and to pretend that there are just some trainers and advisers.

"It is far more than that; U.S. special operations forces will be operating in Iraq brigades, likely in part to paint lasers on targets for U.S. warplanes to bomb. In an age of weasel words and Orwellian diction, it would be refreshing to hear Mr. Obama call this escalation what it is," Cole wrote.[12]

This is an example of overt media manipulation or, as Cole put it, "spin." The administration showed us a few of the trees in the forest, but not the big picture. The big picture is usually top secret, eyes only, or in other words, for a few select people. Sometimes there is a fine line between overt and covert propaganda.

On November 24, 2014, a Ferguson, Missouri, grand jury found that police officer Darren Wilson would not face charges for the killing of an unarmed black teenager, Michael Brown. Two hours before the grand jury decision was announced, the governor, mayor, and former police chief held a press conference. At the end the governor took questions from the press.

Just before the governor's aide informed the assembled that the governor had to leave and could only entertain one more question, a journalist for a Communist publication, *Revolution Newspaper*, interrupted the journalist that the governor had called on and demanded to ask the last question.

Who was this so-called Communist journalist? What was his background? What was the *Revolution Newspaper*? Why did the governor not seem very shocked at the interruption? Could he have known in advance this interruption was going to happen? I did a Google search of national media coverage on the press conference. I could not find a single media outlet that investigated this so-called Communist journalist or the *Revolution Newspaper*. Why do I bring this up?

Because both as a former journalist and one who has practiced and researched propaganda in depth, I know that our covert agencies have a long history of playing the communist scare tactic to arouse public passion. And I know from past investigative reporting that there aren't many Communists in the United States.

While a reporter for the Scottsdale (Arizona) *Daily Progress*, I investigated the Communist Party for a feature story in the late sixties. I contacted the national party and requested the name of an Arizona party member I could interview. They didn't have any Arizona members, so they gave me the phone number of a party member in New Mexico. After I talked with her, she gave me the name of someone in Arizona who wasn't a Communist, but was sympathetic to collectivist philosophy. His name was Pablo. He lived in a teepee on the outskirts of Phoenix. Pablo wasn't an Indian, but he was a fan of their culture, and since he eschewed material possessions, he lived simply in a teepee. Pablo was slightly eccentric and politically liberal, but hardly a threat to the security of the United States. He was in his seventies.

My interview took place at a time when the anti-Communist propaganda campaign was still in full swing and many feared there was a Communist under every bed. Yet my investigative reporting showed there was nothing near a Communist threat in this country. The Red Scare campaign was plain and simple a propaganda program to instill fear in the American public.

An example of likely Ferguson-related propaganda was a news story the same day as the no indictment announcement. It was headlined "FBI Says 76 Law Enforcement Officers Died in the Line of Duty in 2013—27 During Criminal Acts." "This information is proof positive of the dangers that all officers willingly face, day in and day out, to protect the rest of us," the FBI said.[13]

Why would the FBI release this report twelve hours or so before the no indictment was announced? Why would they use the words "proof positive"? Were they trying to diffuse anti–law enforcement sentiment by noting how police are putting their lives on the line to protect us?

Whether or not the FBI timed the release to coincide with the Ferguson turmoil is irrelevant. What is relevant is that the media didn't question the timing of the news release. Journalists should have also tried to find out if the so-called Communist who disrupted the press conference was a covert government provocateur. But the media, as I noted earlier, rarely ask the big questions except for a few mostly independent journalists like Glenn Greenwald, Gary Webb, and Robert Parry. This is not so much the fault of journalists at major media outlets, but of media management and owners who set the parameters of acceptable news coverage.

In addition journalists also face the difficulty of having to wade through the web of secrecy that covert agencies weave to deliberately keep the press (and us) from knowing the truth. Propaganda techniques like plausible deniability, layering, and disinformation often make a true agenda very difficult to detect, as does the act of secrecy itself. Some things are so secret that even presidents are out of the loop.

The CIA has a division that basically reports to no one. This provides plausible deniability and allows a leader or top operative simply to say, "I don't know," and be telling the truth even though he or she might have known in general terms about a covert project.

I'm confident that most Americans, once they become aware of the pervasiveness of secret mass mind manipulation, will support an environment in which it would be impossible for someone like Webb to be destroyed, directly or indirectly, simply for searching for the truth or for Rose Stokes to receive a ten-year prison sentence, as she did in 1918, for simply saying at an antiwar rally, "I am for the people, while the government is for the profiteers."[14]

CHAPTER 11

Language and Propaganda

THE MANIPULATION OF LANGUAGE IS the key to successful mind manipulation. As Disraeli observed, "With words we govern men."[1] Words are the linguistic and semantic tools propagandists use to manipulate our thoughts and behavior. Among these tools are generalizations, specializations, degradation, elevation, euphemisms, hyperbole, minced forms, value-laden words, and unintelligible words and phrases.

Generalization is often used to make a word that once had a narrow, specific meaning take on a broad, general meaning. This technique is often used to devalue a word or concept or to make a strong word a soft word. It can also be used to lessen the impact of a particular word or concept. The word "revolution," for example, originally meant the overthrow of one ruler or government by the governed. Now, through generalization, it has taken on a broad, general meaning to refer to any kind of radical change, from a revolutionary new car to a revolutionary new dress style. Through overuse and devaluation, the romanticism of the word "revolution" has lost its sting.

Generalization can involve a deliberate shift in meaning, or it can take place over a long period of time through inherent linguistic changes. Words, like everything else, are constantly changing. "Companion" once meant someone who shared bread with another. Now it refers to a much broader range of association. A "butcher" at one time meant someone who slew goats. Now, butchers prepare and cut meat from a lot of different animals. "Injury" once meant an injustice. Now it refers to any act that hurts.

"Liquor" once had one specific meaning: a liquid. Now it refers to a kind of alcoholic beverage.

Specialization is the opposite of generalization and occurs when a word that was once general takes on a specific meaning. "Girl" once meant a young person of either sex and, thus, had a general meaning. Now it has a specific meaning limited to one sex. Certain words conjure up different specialized meanings for different listeners. The American word "football" means a game of touchdowns and field goals to most Americans, but in many other parts of the world, the same word means "soccer." "Pipe" has a specialized meaning that is different to the plumber, smoker, and organist. "Gay" used to be a generalized word for happiness; now it is primarily applied to sexual preference.

Degradation is a linguistic technique in which a word that at one time stood for something good or pleasant has come to mean something bad or unpleasant. Degradation causes a word like "lust" to change from meaning simple pleasure to meaning intense sexual desire or a word like "lewd" to change its meaning from ignorant to indecent or unprincipled.

Elevation is the opposite of degradation. Under elevation a word that once meant something bad or neutral comes to mean something good. Elevation, for example, causes a word like "angel" to change its meaning from a mere messenger to a supernatural messenger of God and the word "martyr" to change its meaning from witness to someone willing to suffer or die for a cause. "Pretty" once meant sly and clever. It now means "beautiful."

Generalization, specialization, degradation, and elevation can be used by the propagandist separately or in various combinations to change the meaning of words and, even more importantly, context.

Generalization can be used with elevation, for example, to change the meaning of "sex." What do most people think about when they hear or see the word "sex"? Do they think of gender, male or female? Or do they think of pleasure, sensuality, or the act of intercourse itself? Most likely they think of the latter.

One hundred years ago, sex referred primarily to gender. It was also a rather unpleasant word, often associated with pain and sin. Today sex means pleasure more than sin. Decades of exposure in media to the pleasures of sex have obliterated the image of sex as sin.

No matter its meaning or context, sex to most people is an emotional word. Not that many decades ago, sex had a shock value, but most people have been inundated with so much media sexual themes that its shock strength has been dissipated. I will note later how Byoir client Howard Hughes caused a national uproar and likely started the sexual revolution when he gave viewers a peek (and a very small peek) of Jane Russell's cleavage in the thirties movie *The Outlaw*. Now people go to church showing as much cleavage. Strong, emotionally charged words soon lose their strength when used often enough in light, frivolous contexts.

Euphemisms have often been used in sexual contexts. Euphemisms are words or phrases that substitute pleasant expressions for unpleasant ones. It's a technique often used by propagandists to avoid the truth without actually lying. Instead of saying someone died, we say they "passed away." Instead of saying people in ghettos are starving, we say they are "suffering from malnutrition." Instead of saying we destroyed a neighborhood in Iraq, we say it suffered "collateral damage." Instead of saying we tortured prisoners, we say they underwent "enhanced interrogation." Instead of saying prisoners were kidnapped, we say they were retained under "extraordinary rendition." Instead of saying "mass surveillance," a move is underway by the government to use the phrase "bulk collection." It sounds a lot better.

Instead of saying suspects detained at Guantanamo were prisoners of war, a statement that would make us liable for breaking the Geneva Convention on war, the Bush administration classified them under a new rubric, "unlawful combatants." This allowed us to claim that we were not bound by the Geneva Convention.

Euphemisms sound better. They're less harsh than the direct words or phrases. During World War II, frontline replacements were changed to "reinforcements" because replacements implied death. In Vietnam, "protective reaction raid" was a euphemism for "destroying the enemy."

Euphemisms are particularly effective propaganda tools for obfuscating and hiding the complete truth. For example, the American Civil Liberties Union (ACLU) won a Freedom of Information Act lawsuit in 2014 requiring NSA to release hundreds of pages of reports detailing various ways in which its intelligence gathering violated US law over the past decade.

When released, the NSA pages were heavily redacted. Redaction is common procedure for our intelligence agencies. This allows the truly important stuff to never see the light of day.

Jesselyn Radack with the Government Accountability Project of the ACLU was quoted in a *Newsweek* article about the NSA report as saying, "There's been semantics games with the NSA not using regular definitions for words like 'collection' and 'analysis,' which makes it very difficult to find the documents we're looking for."[2]

What's interesting from a propaganda standpoint is how NSA and other covert agencies often use language manipulation to obfuscate or hide their activities and to make "it very difficult" for the American public to know what they are doing. Since NSA operates in secrecy, we have no idea if the information NSA provides in probes like this are truths, half-truths, lies, diversions, or maybe propaganda techniques like the block and bridge.

Hyperbole is a linguistic technique used in propaganda to exaggerate reality. It involves the use of adjectives such as best, better, grand, great, superb, fantastic, and many more. Labeling a particular automobile as "the best car on the American road" without concrete proof to back up this statement is a basic example of hyperbole. Propagandists frequently inject hyperbole into the cultural idiom in order to elevate certain words and ideas. If media say something is best or better or fantastically pleasurable long enough, people usually start to believe it.

Minced Forms are words that compromise and suggest, rather than state something. They approach the forbidden, but then shy away from it. Use of the slang word "darn" instead of "damn" is an obvious example of this linguistic technique. Minced forms are often combined with hyperbole and euphemisms to introduce new ideas.

Value-Laden Words are used to give legitimacy and credibility. They're much like euphemisms in that they make things sound better. "Tax incentive" gives legitimacy to (and sounds better than) "tax loophole." "Nonprofit" implies legitimacy to a self-interest organization.

Unintelligible Words and Phrases are often used to hide the truth. These are usually words or phrases that aren't intelligible except to special interests. They often require special translation. This technique is often used by closed, professional groups to keep the public from understanding their special interests. The legal and medical fields, for example, are filled with mumble-jumble language that few but experts can translate. Medical and legal documents frequently contain excessive abstractions and unneeded complexities whose purpose can only be to confuse the unwary.

Besides provoking deliberate confusion, government, medical, and legal jargon is often so long and complex that people tune out. This deliberate complexity is called obfuscation, which is a common propaganda technique.

The combination of obfuscation and the use of unintelligible words can be used to reinforce specialization and professionalism by limiting access to critical information to those who understand and can use the language and symbols of a particular discipline. The most successful professionals are often those who best understand and know how to manipulate the symbols of their exclusive language. This holds true in law, medicine, communications, economics, and many other disciplines. Deliberate language obfuscation protects self-interests.

• • •

Omissions and Lies are propaganda tools that have been used for centuries. Omissions are a common way to avoid the truth without actually telling a lie. Omissions are also an effective way to suppress selective facts so that other facts, when released, take on added importance. What you don't see in media is often more important than what you do see.

Omissions provide convenient escape hatches for thought manipulators. A good propagandist always has "outs" or contingencies available in order to cover his or her tracks if circumstances require such action. If you're asked if it's raining outside, it's not a lie to say it appears to be clearing up. You're not telling the whole truth, but you aren't lying, either. And you've left yourself with a way out if someone questions your circuitous answer. Both truth and lies are valuable propaganda tools. Which is used depends on which technique will be the most effective in obtaining the end result. Most propagandists prefer truth and omissions to lies, but they will use lies if it helps the cause.

Samm Baker, in his book *Permissible Lie,* noted long before Watergate and the corporate scandals of the seventies that a lie that helps the cause or helps build profits is considered a permissible lie. "Of course the lie must not be so blatant that it results in eventual damage to the company's profits,"[3] he said.

Robert Maheu, a Howard Hughes employee who was involved in the failed coup against Castro, told a congressional committee that he and other operatives consider themselves in a continuous and "just war." CIA agent Vince Marchetti said that many covert operatives consider us the enemy. Both Maheu and Marchetti were insiders and had no reason to lie about the unethical things they observed. If what they said reflects the mind-set of most covert operators, it could mean there's a continuous need for government to lie in order to save itself—from us![4]

Norman Moss noted in *The Pleasures of Deception* how William Randolph Hearst fabricated brutality and fighting in Cuba and, as a result of these fabrications, helped spark the Spanish-American War.[5]

Propagandists frequently cover up omissions and lies by telling the truth often enough to develop credibility. The cause is supreme in propaganda. Everything else is a variable, including the message, its form, its content, and the method in which it is presented. What counts are results beneficial to the cause. Compassion, honesty, and fair play are used only if they will help the cause more than lies, omissions, and diversions. This doesn't mean all propaganda is dishonest. It isn't. Lies are a last line of defense or, at times, offense. Propagandists for the economic power elite rarely have to resort to lying because the elite is so well-insulated from public scrutiny. Secrecy, however, can be considered a form of lying, especially in terms of omissions.

David Wise, author of *The Politics of Lying*, notes that "policy makers who consider it desirable to mask their decisions or their objectives, or who wish to mislead the public or withhold information, can do so easily as reaching for the nearest rubber stamp. In short, lying and secrecy are two sides of the same coin."[6]

Nietzsche once described history as the lie through which nations survive.

Poker, interestingly, is the only card game that is entirely American. It's also the only card game in which bluffing, a form of lying, plays a major part.

I've given numerous examples of lying (or disinformation) in earlier chapters. Effective disinformation depends on the understanding and implementation of numerous propaganda techniques. It also depends on an understanding of how meaning (semantics) and the structure of language (linguistics) affect how we see the world around us.

• • •

Meaning is determined by definition, structure, and context. Definition is a statement of meaning. This doesn't mean that definitions clarify meaning. There's a big difference between a statement of meaning and a clarification of meaning, a difference astute mind manipulators exploit.

Definition often confuses more than clarifies meaning. This is particularly true the more we try to define something. The more things are defined, the less descriptive definitions become, and the more difficulty we have in using them. For example, the field of law has become so filled with definitions that it is almost unintelligible. If you doubt this, try reading through a legal document or a mortgage or a user agreement.

Definitions contribute to the obfuscation of language because definitions aren't good descriptive tools. Sometimes a simple statement of meaning gets lost in the complexity of clarification. Our attempts to define things often make us more confused than ever.

Thought manipulators are much more interested in definition as a means to confuse meaning than as an instrument for stating meaning. They're more interested in the little mental pictures that pop up in our minds when we hear or read certain words than they are in the true definitions of words. Definitions don't mean anything to the propagandist. He or she is more interested in the verbal signals and the emotions that definitions evoke, such as fantasies and stereotypes. They know these verbal signals lock us into set ways of perceiving things. They know, as Ludwig Wittgenstein of Cambridge once said, "The limits of my language means the limits of my world."[7]

People often choose words and illustrations that reinforce comfortable associations rather than those that accurately describe things. This is particularly true in situations where we believe words "ought" to mean something, but we can't put our finger on a precise definition. Most of us know what "subconscious" ought to mean, but we can't give an exact definition. Most of us know what "love" should mean, but a precise definition is difficult.

Definitions aren't good for description, but they are very good for creating and maintaining ceremony. And ceremony is of vital importance in maintaining myths and symbols, especially as once-revered institutions begin to fade away. Definitions hide inconsistencies and contradiction. Definitions, often cloaked in ceremony, perpetuate symbols and myths. Thought manipulators exploit language to excite imagination and emotions and to stimulate interest much more than to provide information, facts, or dogma.

Linguists Neil Postman and Charles Weingartner have pointed out how "Most people have an emotional commitment to the ways in which we use language that often prevents us from exhibiting an appropriate objectivity and detachment."[8]

Thurman Arnold has noted that it becomes necessary for anyone who thinks objectively about human institutions to realize the traps that lie beneath words. Einstein recognized the limitations of language and how words can trap us because of our tendency to define things through mental pictures and images.

In one of the greatest contributions to science, Einstein began the use of mathematical symbols as scientific tools. Mathematical symbols don't conjure up mental pictures and, thus, are effective descriptive tools, especially in a discipline like physics, where word pictures can interfere with accurate description. For many years physics terminology was tied up in word pictures that couldn't accurately define the concepts of matter and energy. Early physicists had mental pictures of matter as small lumps of material, with the atom as the smallest unit. Time was seen as an ordered sequence. These mental images simply were inadequate to describe matter as a form of energy or time as a rhythm or dimension, not as an ordered sequence. Einstein made scientists realize that mental pictures inhibit scientific observations.

Words used to describe human institutions are usually so bogged down with mental imagery that they alter accurate perception. One of the most dangerous traps of language is found in "polar" words, or words that have no meaning by themselves. The words "up" and "down," for example, are polar words that have no meaning apart from each other. Up has no meaning if there is no down. The idea that the sky is up and the sun goes down confused astronomers for centuries. The sun, of course, doesn't go down and the sky isn't up, but the association of the polar words up and down with the sky and sun gave astronomers a completely distorted view of the universe.

"Justice" and "injustice" are polar words that have no meaning apart from each other. In order to establish justice, you have to understand injustice. And, of course, justice for one person might be injustice for another. Thus, polar words are more effective as motivators and stimulators than as descriptive tools.

Propagandists and politicians use polar words very loosely in public, but if they're smart, they don't believe them. That's why they often do one thing in private and just the opposite in public. That's why business leaders will talk passionately in public about free enterprise and then privately lobby for protection against competition. They know that words like "justice" and "injustice" and "freedom" and "repression" and "good" and "bad" can become trapped in their own definitions. What the good propagandist does is select a pair of polar words or dualities that can be played against each other; they apply a nice polar word to their cause and a less-pleasant polar word to the opposition. Thus, the good guy's actions are just, and the bad guys are unjust. Polar words are often given emotional attachments that deliberately prevent objectivity. Propagandists aren't the least bit interested in objectivity.

People often believe words are linked to things, so that if you forecast happiness and good times often enough, good times will occur. Blind faith in the "magic" of language leads to a self-delusion, whereby people often say what they believe others would like to hear rather than what needs to be said. We ignore people who tell us what we don't want to hear, and our value systems are reinforced by those who say what we want them to say.

Listen to conversations between people who don't know each other well. It will soon become obvious in many cases that they are using each other as sounding boards and little else. One talks about herself or himself; the other listens, and vice versa. The listening is usually a courtesy and little more. The listener is often thinking more about what to say next than truly listening to the other person. We often play verbal games with each other and have very little true verbal contact.

Columnist Sydney Harris has noted, "If you should listen, God help you, to 100 speakers before any political or business assembly, 99 of them at least will be telling the assembled faith what they would like to believe, not what they ought to hear.

"The egos are massaged, their prior convictions confirmed, their faith systems fortified by speakers who want to make them feel good. But this is not what most of us need. What we need is the truth, no matter how painful or distasteful. In fact, we should pay only those people who are willing to tell us things we do not like to hear; we have no need of the others. Until such a time, we are still children," Harris wrote.[9]

Thought molders bombard us with a cul-de-sac of code words and symbols that signal what we often "want" to hear. They often engineer these wants and present them in such a manner that we believe they are our desires, arrived at after careful consideration. For example, phrases like "doing your own thing," "getting in touch with yourself," and "relating" don't just happen, but are manufactured psychobabble.

Researchers have shown that people do not so much listen to what we say as to how we say it, so that the expression of a statement often carries a stronger charge than its content. It is often the secret language of our emotions and not the words themselves that people listen to.

Languages, like the communications channels that transmit language, often enslave us in their own processes so that we surrender ourselves to the limits of our language. And often, the limits of our language become the limits of our world.

Obviously, a definition of anything depends on who's doing the defining. In thought manipulation, definitions are verbal strategies to help achieve an objective. Those who create the message and control its distribution do the defining. Words are for the most part convenient symbols that mean only what those who are using them agree to make them mean. There must be a large amount of consistency in the response to linguistic signals; otherwise, communications would be impossible.

Thought manipulators control this consistency of response by manipulating verbal signals and the mental pictures that we associate with words. This manipulation of verbal signals, especially stereotypes, prejudices, and code words, creates a verbal intoxication whereby people often become captive of ideas and feelings they're scarcely aware of having picked up. Manipulation of these verbal signals closes our communicative space, just as high-speed media restrict our mental space through sensory overload.

The basic structure of words can affect meaning. One of the smallest and most important units of word structure is the phoneme. A phoneme is the distinctive sound of a word. Word sounds are often as important as meaning. In greeting people, for example, the tone of a salutation often means more than the literal interpretation. A flat and unenthusiastic "hi" means something entirely different than an enthusiastic "Hi!" Wilson Key has described speech as an assembly-line process involving impulses traveling along neuron conveyor belts to the brain.[10] The words we speak are several seconds behind or ahead of those already assembled and waiting to come off the production line. Word sounds are obviously auditory. We hear sounds. But we can also see sound. Cathode rays that cause sounds to take noticeable shape allow deaf people to use visible speech in learning silent reading.

In addition to structure and definition, meaning is affected by context. "Cold" to an Alaskan native means something entirely different than to a native of a tropical Caribbean island. The word "green" can mean a certain color, but it can also mean fruit that is not ripe. The propaganda technique of repetition can be used to cause one definition to take over for another definition. By continually associating green with not being ripe, it might be accurate to say, "Blackberries are red when they are green."

Words govern the way we see the world. Some people believe that words are fairly stable and don't change much or that words have fixed meanings. Meanings, however, do change. This change follows definite patterns that the astute propagandist can exploit, and as I noted with words like brainwashing, there are words that propagandists create out of thin air. Communications professionals who knowingly or unknowingly practice propaganda usually have one thing in common: they have a way with words, written or spoken, and they know how to use these words to manipulate our emotions.

As Muriel Barbery noted in *The Elegance of the Hedgehog*: "Humans live in a world where it's words and not deeds that have power, where the ultimate skill is mastery of language. This is a terrible thing because basically we're primates who've been programmed to eat, sleep, reproduce, conquer and make our territory safe, and the ones who are most gifted at that, the most animal types among us, always get screwed by the others, the fine talkers."[11]

• • •

Terrance Qualter, a leading propaganda researcher, has said, "It's impossible to understand the success of propaganda without also understanding how great a part of what men regard as knowledge is in fact no more than a collection of stereotypes."[12]

Propagandists learned long before social scientists and other researchers got in on the act that prejudices, symbols, and stereotypes play a key role in the decision-making process. Walter Lippmann used the term "stereotype" to describe the knowledge we think we have of things: the knowledge that is based on myths, dreams, and fantasies, as distinct from genuine factual knowledge. Lippmann knew that popular passions, religious, racial, or regional traditions, national pride, and other abstract feelings were often more real to people than actual reality.[13]

Lippmann, considered the father of modern American journalism, was also a writer of propaganda leaflets during World War I and worked closely with Carl Byoir and others on the CPI, the first official government propaganda agency. Nancy Snow noted in her book *Information War* that Lippmann "saw how easily people could fall for lies…Lippmann became so disillusioned by the public's inability to analyze policy that he wrote *The Phantom Public*, in which he basically claimed that the public had no role to play in addressing important questions of state because the media system created a pseudo reality of stereotypes and emotional impressions along with facts," Snow stated.[14]

The public is easily manipulated, Lippmann believed, because media create these stereotypes and emotional impressions and we don't have the necessary tools to counter their propaganda. It's not that the public is ignorant; it's because few people have been exposed to propaganda tools and techniques. This creates a situation where we are at the mercy of the manipulators, the media, and their messages.

Propagandists, particularly those who work for government clandestine services, have a big advantage over the most intelligent of us. They are invisible. We don't know who they are, where they work, or who they work for. We don't know their agenda.

One thing I know for sure. Propagandists have spent many years researching the latest psychological, social, and motivational techniques to manipulate and mold the mass mind. The most effective way to mold our thoughts with a propaganda message is to penetrate our perceptual system with stimuli that sidetrack and distort rationality and awareness. When we initially perceive something, we see it totally and immediately. However, only a small part of that total picture registers because of a built-in editing system that involves both the conscious and subconscious or subliminal levels of perception.

A good way to understand how this selective perception works is to imagine that you're looking through the viewfinder of an old camera that has both a telephoto and wide-angle lens. The depth of field you have with the telephoto lens is narrow, linear, and structured. It is tunnel vision. You see only a small part of the picture you would see with the wide-angle lens or without the camera: with the naked eye. The wider lens, however, gives you a large perception and a better view of the total picture. The wide-angle camera lens is like your subconscious or subliminal level of perception. The telephoto lens represents your conscious level of perception.

Wilson Key, author of *Subliminal Seduction*, noted that: "Subliminal perception is a subject that virtually no one wants to believe exists, and—if it does exist—they much less believe that it has any practical application. The techniques are in widespread use by media, advertising and public relations agencies, industrial and commercial corporations, and by the Federal government."[15]

My intention isn't to mimic Key's thesis that subliminal seduction is in widespread use, although he made a strong case for it in his book, but I agree with him that there are plenty of advertising and PR practitioners and business and government propagandists manipulating our perceptions.

How much of this manipulation is subliminal I don't know, but I know they have exploited our tendency toward "selective perception" so their messages will make an imprint on our senses. Another way to understand these different levels of perception is to pick out a single object from a cluttered background. Concentrate on one object; isolate it from everything else, and then suddenly shift your concentration to the entire picture. Try to see everything. The more you try to see, the more confused you become. Objects may pop in and out of your consciousness.

Try concentrating once more on the one object. Then look at the panorama. Pretty soon you'll become frustrated or extremely nervous as a struggle ensues between your different levels of perception. No matter how long you try this exercise, you'll eventually come back to the initial object. It's embedded in your conscious. Most of the extraneous objects, however, will move back and forth between the two levels of perception. This exercise shows how much easier it is to perceive a single entity than to try and perceive the total picture.

These perceptual examples are not meant to imply that manipulating our perceptual senses is only used in broadcast or visual media manipulation. They can also apply to numerous types of propaganda that aren't in media.

The obfuscation technique we discussed earlier works by overwhelming our senses by providing us with so many stimuli that we lose focus or interest. We noted in a previous chapter how even the high-speed nature of modern communications itself can cause overstimulation, which, in turn, can numb and desensitize us and cause us to lose focus.

Much of these extraneous stimuli we are bombarded with are stored in the subconscious. The subconscious serves as a storage vault for the uncomfortable, the unpleasant, and the complex.

Various propaganda techniques can often trigger whether or not we open that subconscious storage vault. The subconscious is also an editor, but its editing takes place on an internal level. It edits what the conscious sends down, and it decides whether or not something should be stored in its vault or sent back to the conscious level.

The subconscious often plays games with the conscious and even manipulates it by allowing only certain things to stick or register. There is continuous interplay, and even struggle, between these two levels of perception. This struggle takes place frequently with sex, for example. Someone may have an overwhelming desire for sex on the conscious level, so much so that it's frequently thought about even though subconsciously this person may have a fear of sex and not really want to engage at all. This subconscious fear may penetrate to the conscious level once the fantasized opportunity becomes a reality.

The conscious mind serves as an external editor of sorts for perception. It sends (represses) information to the subconscious that it can't reasonably handle. Our levels of perception are often narrowed and restricted by the manipulation of symbols, prejudices, and stereotypes. These instruments of persuasion are used to make us see only a limited part of the total picture, that is, enforced tunnel vision or just seeing the trees, but not the forest.

Symbol manipulation is often the most efficient means for an indirect and subtle manipulation because of our innate need to connect, associate, and identify and symbolize. Most of us aren't aware of this innate need, which propagandists began using during and after World War I thanks to strides in psychological and motivational research.

Ivan Pavlov planted the seed for symbol manipulation when he taught pioneer propagandists how people are creatures of "conditioned reflex" in how they relate to symbols.[16]

Alfred Korzybski and Alfred Whitehead built on the conditioned reflex theory by showing how language is related to symbolic logic.[17]

Researchers also taught propagandists how certain symbols trigger fears of failure, self-doubt, guilt, loneliness, oral gratification, and other inner tensions.

I worked on some public relations campaigns for a developer of greeting cards. Their early research discovered that card scenes that depicted loneliness sold particularly well when they had archetype symbols like the moon.

Gleem toothpaste was successfully positioned as a guilt symbol, "for those who can't brush after every meal." Sugar has long been positioned as a reward symbol. Marlboro sold "man-sized" flavor (which subconsciously had sexual overtones) in ads with macho fishermen, cowboys, and outdoorsmen, all of whom wore tattoos and other symbols of masculinity. Buick sold manly power and prestige when it sold us cars that would "make you feel like the man you are."

Motivational researcher Pierre Martineau noted that the symbolic meaning of ads "quite obviously cannot be expressed openly. The consumer would reject them quite violently. The difference between a topflight creative man and the hack is this ability to express powerful meanings indirectly."[18]

Although thought manipulation goes much deeper than efforts by advertisers to get us to buy their products, the advertising community often uses some of the same clandestine manipulation techniques propagandists use to influence attitudes and behavior.

Whether in advertising or other forms of overt propaganda, manipulation must be as indirect and subtle as possible to be most effective. A straightforward approach is usually quickly rejected because it is obviously self-serving.

One of Byoir's clients for many years and an account I worked some on was the Children's Television Workshop and the Public Broadcasting Service (PBS), producers of *Sesame Street*, which is one of the most popular children's television series in history. A whole generation of kids was brought up on *Sesame Street*, including my own.

One of the main characters was the Cookie Monster. This fun-loving, philosophical Muppet frequently voiced his love for sugar, which he associated with fun and good spirits. He is best known for his huge appetite and proclamations such as, "Me want cookie!" and "Me eat cookie!" Both Cookie Monster's mother and father shared his enormous appetite and craving for cookies. The Cookie Monster's song, "C is for Cookie," became one of the most popular songs from *Sesame Street*.

Besides representing the Children's Television Workshop and *Sesame Street*, we represented the Sugar Association, which was founded by large corporations with connections to the US sugar industry. The Sugar Association began in 1943. The role of the Sugar Association is to promote the consumption of sugar.[19]

Our job for the Sugar Association was to communicate "the healthy benefits" of sugar. Our sources were usually "scientific" reports from academic researchers. Scientists or experts who back up your claims are known as "third-party fronts." We also used the technique of "appeal to authority" by getting indirect endorsement of the benefits of sugar from academic researchers and other "experts." In addition to representing the sugar industry and *Sesame Street*, we conducted a nationwide campaign for a manufacturer of sugar-laden cereals to connect fitness with eating cereal. We used nationally known professional athletes as our appeal to authority.

The difference between effective propaganda and ineffective propaganda is rooted in this ability to express powerful messages and meanings indirectly. The publication *Christianity and Crisis* warned in the fifties about the threat to the quality of life due to an abundance of material goods and an expanding economy based on mass production and consumption of new goods: "We are being carried along by a process that is becoming an end in itself and which threatens to overwhelm us; there is a loss of a sense of proportion in living when we become so quickly dissatisfied with last year's models."[20]

We face a constant barrage of media messages that remind us that it is OK to constantly change models and replace products. No wonder we have one of the highest divorce rates in the world. Divorce is so common that trading him or her in for a new one is not much different than trading for a new car.

Those who promote newness and the symbols with which it is connected have us caught up in a whirlwind that enslaves us to the consumption process. This whirlwind is so much the substance of our lives that it is often difficult to get outside it long enough to look at it and ask where it all leads. The whirlwind we are caught in is not just about selling us products; it also targets thoughts and behavior.

Stereotype manipulation plays a key role in influencing our thoughts and behavior. Propagandists long ago learned that people will often go to great lengths to avoid thinking.

We often say during times of stress, "I don't want to think about it."

Stereotypes are often used to exploit our fear of separation from the majority by narrowing and restricting our levels of perception and by giving us only a limited part of the total picture. Stereotypes don't often deal in facts, but in emotions, beliefs, myths, visions of the future, justifications, and rationalizations. Myth is the most important form of stereotype. Because myths are intangible, they're easier to mold than fact.

Stereotypical beliefs are based on opinions, which, research has shown, are rarely based on fact. As we noted earlier, a lot of things we cherish as our own opinions or beliefs, arrived at by careful and independent thought, are often only conditioned, predictable responses to well-orchestrated and often camouflaged campaigns to control our thoughts and behavior.

You probably have never carefully thought about what an opinion actually is. Propagandists have. Philosopher Friedrich Nietzsche, as I also noted earlier, said opinion is thought largely based on vanity and hubris, not necessarily based on fact. People, he said, can't tell you the source of their opinions. They cannot even tell you the facts behind their opinions. People get very possessive about their opinions and often feel they own them like a piece of property, Nietzsche said.[21]

• • •

The true propaganda battlefield is not our critical awareness, but the fertile grounds of our innermost needs and desires. Propagandists exploit our tendency to feel first and to think second.

Have you ever interrupted a factual conversation with the statement "That's the way I feel about it"? If so, you've done what many of us do. You've felt first and thought second. That is largely how the Kuwaiti caper we talked about earlier was pulled off. It appealed to our emotions.

Propagandists have long known that many people don't want to think for themselves and are emotion-driven. That is largely why religion is such a powerful force. We want answers.

David Hapgood, author of *Screwing of the Average Man*, claims the average person "doesn't reach out and smash the roulette wheel that keeps on showing him up a loser because he is continuously kept off balance."[22]

The role of covert propaganda is to help keep us off-balance, to make us feel we are among the takers and not the taken so that we will passively accept our own screwing. Throughout history the exploited have passively let themselves be manipulated by their exploiters. In ancient Rome, small farmers fought so rich Romans could obtain slaves for the plantations that proved to be the ruin of small farming.

In the Old South, many plantation servants (called "house Negroes") supported slavery because they were given just enough to make them believe they were better off than the field slaves. Jewish prison trustees helped administer Nazi prison camps right up until they themselves were pushed into the gas chambers. Today some of the most vociferous sentiment against welfare comes from people just one step up the ladder from being on welfare themselves.

The Reagan and Bush administrations promoted a laissez-faire trickle-down capitalism. There is not much evidence that trickle-down works well except for those doing the trickling, but it works great in mass persuasion and mind manipulation.

Just as they did in the Old South on plantations, the economic elite, filled to capacity, push back their plates and say, "I can't eat any more caviar; give the rest to the servants." People are given just enough to make them believe they are among the takers and not the taken, to keep them off-balance. Propaganda plays a key role in convincing us to passively accept our own manipulation. For example, film, television, and print media are filled with lifestyles and role models that encourage us to identify with upper-middle class and upper-class values.

This "upward identification" propaganda technique encourages envy, rather than resentment. Envy is a safe way to channel socioeconomic and class frustrations. Celebrities and sports figures, with their grossly inflated incomes, have been particularly effective in keeping the average person's eyes turned upward, to make him or her feel there's a chance, if not for him or her, for his or her children "to make it big."

For example, in May 2015, Floyd Mayweather Jr. pocketed an estimated $180 million by defeating Manny Pacquiao in a welterweight championship fight. Pacquiao was expected to receive close to $100 million. Why was there no public ire over this obscene amount for an hour or so of two grown men hitting each other?

One reason may be that the numbers are so big that the average person can't relate to that much money. Another reason (and the one most likely) is that we have become propagandized not to be concerned, but to admire huge business, sports, and entertainment salaries. One thing is for sure. The boxers are laughing all the way to the bank. Mayweather, in fact, proudly showed reporters his nine-figure, $100 million check, which he received shortly after the bout. Boxing, interestingly, has been banned in some countries because of its violence. That's never been considered here. We love violence.

The fighters are excellent propaganda vehicles for upward identification. They have given a lot of people hope that they, too, might someday strike it rich and hit the jackpot. Ironically, the bout was fought in Las Vegas, whose very existence is based on selling people on the striking-it-rich myth.

Upward identification's primary goal is not to make a few individuals wealthy, but to create a climate that will protect the financial interests of the economic elite. Most of the members of this elite ruling class would consider a mere $100 million a drop in the bucket.

Upward identification (or what I call "trickle up" propaganda) is often combined with the propaganda technique of diversion to divert attention from the average person's economic status by creating the illusion that he or she has moved out of the have-not status and is among the takers, not the taken. One way to accomplish this is to give the average person just enough of the economic elite's leftovers to make him or her feel he or she has a piece of the action. I've been directly involved in this "piece of the action" strategy to make people think they are among the takers and not the taken.

CHAPTER 12

Getting Jailed for Your Beliefs

PROPAGANDA BEGAN WHEN THERE WAS a public, when there were people whose attitudes needed to be influenced to bring about a change of behavior. Julius Caesar's *Commentaries on the Gallic Wars* convinced the citizens of Rome that he would be a good leader and led to his seizure of the city. The early Catholic Church established the Society for the Propagation of the Faith to win people over to the Catholic cause. The priests of ancient Egypt, according to Bernays, were also experts at public opinion and persuasion.[1] Throughout history, all dictators have preferred to rule by persuasion (that's how Hitler started out). If persuasion doesn't work, dictators usually resort to repression.

Propaganda played a major role in the American Revolution. Contrary to how it's often portrayed, the revolution wasn't a spontaneous uprising. People had to be stirred up. Only a small minority of the people were politically active as Whigs and Tories (loyal to the Crown). Most people just wanted to be left alone to go about their everyday business. Most people didn't get very cranked up over issues as prosaic as molasses, Stamp Act, and tea taxes. The Stamp Act and tea taxes were small. The molasses tax only affected rum distillers. In short, most people could live with the higher taxes.

People such as Samuel Adams, a key colonial propagandist, realized that something more dramatic was needed to arouse public passions. The Boston Massacre fit this need to inflame passions.

Just as the American press helped push America into World War I by over sensationalizing the sinking of the *Lusitania*, so did the colonial press overplay the Boston Massacre with lurid accounts of how brutal British soldiers had shot several peaceful Americans.

Within hours of the shooting, Samuel Adams had sent messengers to all of the colonies with accounts of the "massacre." These accounts effectively turned victims into martyrs. The goal of numerous propaganda campaigns since then has been to create martyrs through the propaganda techniques of association and identification.

The Boston Tea party was the nation's first staged public relations event. The Sons of Liberty, dressed as Indians, threw 342 cases of tea into the Boston Harbor to dramatize colonial opposition to the tea tax, not to destroy the tea.

This event was carried throughout the colonies by the Committee of Correspondence, a letter-writing campaign Adams helped establish to arouse popular passions against the Crown. The colonial press in Boston, New York, Philadelphia, and Charleston, South Carolina, also served as vehicles for the anti-Crown movement. The press carried hundreds of highly dramatic and sensational stories of British repression and injustice. I've read a lot of newspapers from that period. The anti-Crown movement was a lot like the anti-Communist crusade a couple hundred years later.

Even the Constitution has its elements of propaganda. The Bill of Rights reflects public opinion of the times and was added primarily to create a favorable opinion about the new national government created by the Constitution.

The wedding of propaganda and politics began to emerge in the nineteenth century. Andrew Jackson employed a newspaperman, Amos Kendell, to study public opinion, suggest policy, and write articles and speeches. Kendell's primary responsibility was to package Jackson as a champion of the common man. The McKinley-Bryan presidential race of the 1890s featured a large variety of mass persuasion vehicles. The campaign had canned speeches, campaign slogans, parades, billboard messages, press kits, advertising, and free whiskey.

The latter part of the nineteenth century was the era of the "robber barons," or business leaders who manipulated the investment markets, raped the forests, rigged railroad rates, and cruelly exploited labor and consumers, all in the name of squeezing maximum profits during a period of rapid industrial growth. Commodore Vanderbilt, owner of the New York Central Railroad, spoke for many of the business elite with his famous "the public be damned." Such a statement is not very good public relations, but it was good newspaper copy for media that flourished on sensationalism and "yellow journalism." Stories about the robber barons allowed publishers to sell more newspapers and magazines, while at the same time they portrayed robber barons as corrupt individuals, not as commanders of corrupt institutions. Criticism of individuals has always been open game for our media, but rarely do media attack institutions with such intensity. Even when the media of that period did criticize big business, it was usually tempered or balanced with Horatio Alger stories of businessmen who had worked their way to the top through hard work, perseverance, and loyalty.

More prevalent than business success stories were media attempts to demonize and discredit anything (individuals, groups, or countries) that smacked of collectivism, be it socialism, communalism, or communism. During the latter part of the nineteenth century, the nation's press and other communications outlets were filled with ant-Collectivist propaganda that connected all things anti-Capitalist as "un-American."

Collectivism was repeatedly represented as the antithesis of everything we had been taught to cherish. It was positioned as antidemocracy, antifreedom, antireligion, and even antifamily. Once the association between collectivism and un-American was established in the group mind, a second key propaganda technique was launched: emotionally laden words. In short, this technique added another layer to the anti-Communist mind-set by demonizing all words connected to collectivism, particularly socialism and communism.

Professor Roswell Dwight Hitchcock of the Union Theological Seminary wrote in the late 1870s that "today there is not in our language, nor in any language, a more hateful word than communism."[2]

The word "communism" as the antithesis for everything we held dear was freely applied by the nation's media during the 1870s to labor negotiations and protests, to legislative proposals for cutting working hours to a ten-hour day, and to proposals for railroad regulation, farm reforms, and decent housing. Connecting a bogeyman word like "communism" to these other issues is a classic example of the propaganda techniques of association and emotionally laden words.

Ironically, most editors and reporters knew very little about communism. The average American knew even less, yet it didn't take long for "communism" to become one of the most emotionally laden and demonized words in history. The economic elite during the late nineteenth century had a good reason to propagandize the American public against anything that smacked of economic equality: the growing power of the American labor force. The elite's anti-Collectivist paranoia was growing during this period, not just because of the fear of socialism, but because there was a growing militancy among workers and farmers for unionization.

An 1873 recession added to a growing sense of economic inequality in the United States, as did high unemployment, poor working conditions, long work hours, and low pay. These conditions led to numerous demonstrations for unionizations and some sort of economic relief. Labor had suffered considerably from the post–Civil War recession of 1866–68 and, a few years later, a concerted campaign by large employers to wipe out the labor movement through force and other nebulous means, including widespread propaganda.

Between 1868 and 1873, fourteen new national unions were organized. One example is the National Labor Union (NLU), which led major strikes related to working hours. By the mid-1870s, farmers were active through the Granger movement.

Soon anyone associated with labor activities was a threat to public safety. Police action to break up things as simple as the unemployed marching for jobs was common during this period. In 1875 in Chicago, for example, police dispersed crowds of destitute, unemployed workers who were so desperate for jobs and money to feed their families that they marched to appeal to charitable groups.

In Fall River, Massachusetts, destitute, unemployed workers marched because they wanted bread for their starving children. As they approached the city council to present their concerns, they were met by hundreds of armed state militia.

On January 13, 1877 police brutally attacked seven thousand demonstrators at Tompkins Square in New York City. State officials, along with the press, charged repeatedly that the entire affair was the work of foreign "Communist" agents (even though there was not a Communist government anywhere at that time). Police began to routinely infiltrate labor groups with what we now call agent provocateurs, people hired to pose as group members so they could gain members' confidence in order to incite violence, which would give police a pretext for making arrests.[3]

Probably the most significant event during this period was the Molly Maguire affair, which took place in the coalfields of Eastern Pennsylvania. Horrendous working conditions in the coalfields owned by Philadelphia & Reading Railroad led miners, known as the Molly Maguires (or Mollies), to protest working conditions and low pay. The president of the railroad hired private Pinkerton detectives to infiltrate the miners and encourage them to protest. These detectives were the pioneer agent provocateurs and instigators of false-flag propaganda.[4]

On the basis of testimony by these private infiltrators, twenty-four alleged Mollies were convicted of murder and other crimes stemming from protests related to mining conditions. Years later, in 1947, documents were uncovered that showed agents for the coal owners had instigated some of the attacks on the miners and later blamed them on the Mollies to provide an excuse for smashing the Mollies. This was one of the first major examples of a false-flag engineering of dissent, which involves provoking and encouraging dissent in order to later repress it to send a message that dissent will not be tolerated.

As Joseph Rayback wrote, "The trial of the Mollies temporarily destroyed the last vestige of labor unionism in the coal area. More important, it gave the public the impression that miners in general were inclined to riot, sabotage, arson, pillage, assault, robbery, and even murder (to reach their goals). This impression became the foundation for the anti-labor attitude held by a large portion of the nation to the present day; thereafter, any union that tried to organize in the area would find itself soaked in the brew of Molly Maguireism."[5]

The Molly Maguire syndrome has been used throughout the past hundred-plus years as a major weapon of political repression and propaganda against organized labor. As noted above, this was the first time business leaders employed agent provocateurs and paid infiltrators to disrupt labor activities. It would not be the last.

Shortly after the Molly affair, businessmen throughout the country began using private police on a wide scale. The first head of what became the FBI was a private detective who specialized in helping corporate leaders in union busting. In the Molly Maguire affair, a private police force, hired by corporations, was even allowed to arrest the alleged offenders. The state provided the courtrooms and the hangmen.

Another major labor event happened a few months after the Mollies affair: a nationwide railroad strike in July 1877. The strike was started because of repeated wage cuts and poor working conditions. In city after city, striking rail workers received massive support from other workers outside the railroad industry. This labor solidarity brought out the "red menace" fear brigades. Corporate leaders, police, government officials, and the press began claiming "Communist influence."

The rail strikes, which were largely spontaneous, were finally broken by massive use of federal and state troops and citizen "militia." These citizen militias were often made up largely of businessmen who had a stake in protecting the interest of the railroad owners. As in the Molly Maguire affair, the strikes were exploited by the press to cement fear of socialism, subversion, and "foreign" influence. The public soon became more and more convinced that coal miners, railroad workers, and other union laborers were inherently criminal and that steps had to be taken to protect law and order.

The crushing of the 1877 strikes and the effects of the Depression devastated the labor movement. The linking of the disturbances to an international Communist conspiracy was successfully implanted in the American psyche. Many business leaders and other groups used the Red Scare to strengthen their own organizations. In 1878 Reverend Joseph Cooke proclaimed that the church was "The chief barrier against Communist inroads from the howling sea of an ignorant and unprincipled population."[6] (Note: I would change the word "ignorant" to a "propagandized" population.)

The National Commissioner of Education, John Eaton, urged public schools to train children to resist the evils of strikes. The National Education Association head in 1881 told the NEA convention that year that public schools should be enlisted "to eliminate the threat of communism."[7]

The anti-Collectivist movement grew stronger year by year. As the labor movement grew in strength and numbers, so did big business, government, law enforcement, and media attacks on collectivism.

The power elites of the time had no problem with exaggerating the red menace and using all means necessary to crush labor and communism. Any truly radical activities were quickly demonized and crushed. Police throughout the country began a reign of terror against labor and radical leaders.

In Chicago, police arrested hundreds of workers during a May 4, 1886, rally that became known as the Haymarket Affair. Police claimed to have found bombs all over the city during their massive roundup of labor protestors. It was later proved that the bombs did not exist. In sworn testimony, the chief of police revealed that a police captain in charge of the investigation wanted to keep things stirring. The chief added that the captain wanted bombs to be found everywhere to break-up radical groups so less radical labor groups could be formed"[8]

Labor leaders suspected, but never proved, that police set off the first bomb to have a reason to wipe out the local labor movement. It would not have been the first time, or the last, that law enforcement has broken the law to elicit a desired response. It might have been another example of the propaganda technique of "engineering of dissent," a way to provide an excuse to attack those you disagree with. It could have also been a false-flag or manufactured incident.

Police attacks on workers intensified. Seven workers were killed in East St. Louis by police. Six Milwaukee strikers were killed by militia. The Haymarket Affair, which was later celebrated worldwide as "May Day," gave the power elite the perfect opportunity to put into practice demonization. They demonized labor as radicals and even aliens. The Haymarket Affair gave the elite the opening it needed to crush the labor movement.

For months after the Haymarket Affair, the press was filled with news articles, cartoons, and editorials connecting labor and immigrants with violence. This is another example of the propaganda technique of association.

A stereotype was created of dissenters as ragged, unwashed, long-haired, wild-eyed fiends, armed for violence. These "hippies" of the 1880s conjured up the same images as beatniks and hippies created in the 1950s and 1960s. It appears that the hippie movement of the 1880s was a deliberate creation of a mass media bent on creating a negative image of dissenters.

The anti-labor hysteria of 1886 was followed by a wave of anti-labor legislation. Congress increased state militia appropriations for the first time since 1808. Although labor suffered setbacks that would take over a decade to overcome, there's considerable evidence that Chicago authorities and others sought to keep the radical menace alive in order to obtain leverage over dissenters.

Nonetheless, the effect of the Haymarket Affair was to drive American labor movements to the right, just as the protests of the 1960s and early 1970s turned many Americans, including protestors themselves, further to the right.

In other words, protests and demonstrations (and even wars) can actually be beneficial to the power elite by introducing an element of fear into breaking with the status quo. Persuading the average person to reject or not even consider radical associations has been one of the key goals of American propaganda since the 1870s. A similarity of techniques to accomplish this goal, such as the engineering of dissent, has cropped up again and again and can't be dismissed as aberrations or as natural defensive responses to a perceived threat.

The economic elite, fearful of a workers' revolution, began a massive campaign to diffuse the growing spirit of collectivism. These fears reached a zenith in the nationwide Pullman rail strike in 1894. The Pullman strike centered around Pullman's policy of reducing wages during the Depression while maintaining high rents on company housing. Injunctions, troops, and five thousand federal marshals were unleashed on strikers. Over seven hundred were arrested.

The attorney general who called in the troops and marshals, Richard Olney, was a former corporate attorney who served on the board of directors of one of the railroads that was struck. At the same time they were cracking down on progressive unions, local and national campaigns were launched to build support for more conservative unions.

In 1894 hungry unemployed hobos ("tramps") roamed the country to look for work and food. The unemployed army organized a march on Washington demanding jobs. They faced a massive display of troops. Many were arrested.

American Federation of Labor (AFL) president Samuel Gompers, who would later work with Carl Byoir on President Wilson's Committee on Public Information propaganda, became obsessed with a desire for union "respectability."

In 1894 Gompers fought hard to defeat the socialist platform of the AFL, which he had passively supported a year before. Gompers's philosophy was to sacrifice unskilled workers and consumer interests to win gains for skilled "respectable" workers. His philosophy was also the philosophy of the economic aristocracy, which during this period saw labor co-optation as important for preventing potential eruptions. Co-optation is a key part of the engineering of consent.

During this period a number of business and government leaders had even argued for a foreign war to divert attention from domestic labor and political unrest. They got such a war in 1898, the Spanish-American War.

Diversion is another propaganda technique. From the mid-1890s, a uniquely American approach to labor took place, that is, unions that agreed to work within the Capitalist framework were granted limited accommodations, while radical unions were harshly repressed.

The AFL made a deal with the National Civic Federation, a big-business group (forerunner to Business Roundtable, which Byoir would represent). The federation's goal was to crush the "common enemy," which was radical unions. At the turn of the century, big-business interests began to use the propaganda technique of association to connect radicalism with "foreign subversion."

Laws were passed making it a crime to have Anarchist beliefs. You didn't have to do anything to get arrested; you only had to have Anarchist beliefs. Until the anarchy laws were enacted, government involvement in political repression usually took place only when business and their private enforcers weren't able to handle disruptive situations by themselves.

The Anarchist laws set precedence for penalizing people for simply belonging to a group (guilt by association) and having "bad ideas." These laws became the basis for later legislation connected with "bad ideas," such as the criminal syndication laws of 1917–1920.

"Bad ideas" legislation was also passed in 1917 with the Espionage and Sedition Act. Similar bad ideas legislation was passed in 1917, 1918, 1920, 1940, 1950, and 1952. The 1940 Smith Act outlawed advocating or belonging to any group that advocated revolutionary change.

In Colorado, for example, business interests formed a statewide anti-union organization that had close ties to conservative Gov. James Peabody. This business group conducted massive anti-union propaganda campaigns using local newspapers to spread the message that unions were poison to our way of life.

At the request of the mining industry and sympathetic business groups, Gov. Peabody continually sent state militia into mining areas, where they arrested and deported hundreds.

They intensified their repression and propaganda, particularly the use of the engineering of dissent or the deliberate inciting of violence in order to discredit (by association) any and all radical dissent. In 1905 the governor of Idaho was killed by a bomb in Caldwell, Idaho. The state, at the urging of a powerful business lobby, hired James McPharland, a Pinkerton detective who was involved in crushing the Mollies. His job was to link the killing to the Industrial Workers of the World (IWW), also known as Wobblies. The man finally arrested turned out to be an agent provocateur.[9]

About this same time, government and business leaders began to work closely with "respectable" unions, such as the AFL to counter the perceived threat from the left. Included in this coalition were AFL president Gompers and United Mine Workers president John Mitchell. Both Gompers and Mitchell worked with the Committee on Public Information to help co-opt the labor movement during World War I.

Also during this period, an army private received three years in jail for publicly shaking hands while in uniform with Anarchist leader Emma Goldman. Even worse than Anarchists to the business elite were Socialists.

From 1900 to 1912, membership in the Socialist Party increased from 10,000 in 1900 to almost 120,000 in 1912. Particularly upsetting was the growing strength of socialism among native and rural Americans (this was before communism was established in Russia).

In just about every advanced country in the world, Socialist parties are treated with the same respect as mainstream political entities. Many Socialists are fairly conservative on social and economic matters. They're rarely involved in radical political activities, yet American business and government leaders have demonized those who believe in any form of collectivism.

Demonization is a key propaganda technique that has been used throughout our history.

The *San Diego Tribune* editorialized that "hanging is none too good for them (Socialists). They would be much better dead, for they're absolutely useless in the human economy. They are the waste matter of creation, and should be drained off into the sewer of oblivion, there to rot in cold obstruction like any other excrement."[10]

In January 1912 over twenty thousand woolen workers in Lawrence, Massachusetts, joined picket lines. After two days of peaceful marches, police and private detectives hired by the woolen industry charged the strikers in an attempt to break up a peaceful rally. A female striker was killed. The next day a militiaman killed a fifteen-year-old boy by stabbing him with his bayonet. Police charged two strike leaders with the slaying, even though they were in a motel three miles from the killing site. They were eventually found not guilty, but not until after spending ten months in jail.

During the trial it was revealed that provocateurs had been hired by the president of a Lawrence mill to stir up trouble and to incite violence that would implicate workers. This is another example of the engineering of dissent and a false-flag.

Another aspect of engineering of dissent used in Lawrence was legal warfare. The arrests of the union leaders, long detentions, and the use of the courts to break unions became a common practice for the next one hundred-plus years. Legal warfare was used frequently in attempts to discredit and break the civil rights and antiwar movements.

The repression against radical labor continued in April 1914, when Colorado militia attacked and burned a tent colony of UMW miners attempting to organize the coalfields of Ludlow, Colorado. Eleven children and two women were asphyxiated. Three strikers were also shot while unarmed and under guard. The incident became known as the Ludlow Massacre.

Dissension, whether peaceful or not, was not allowed during this period of our history if the dissenters had non mainstream socioeconomic and political beliefs. The line in the sand had been set.

CHAPTER 13

The Invisible Man in the Wilson Administration

CARL BYOIR WAS INVISIBLE. AT least that's the impression one gets poring over historical records from World War I to the fifties, when he died. Who was this mystery man of the elite, a man practically invisible to the American public, yet remarkably visible to the most powerful of his time, from presidents and foreign leaders to the business and economic elite?

Why would Byoir and the agency he founded provide propaganda services to two US presidents, the top echelons of American business and government, the right-wing Shah of Iran, Nazi Germany, a Cuban dictator, the very conservative Howard Hughes, the CIA-created Radio Free Europe, Lithuania, the New York Stock Exchange, *Sesame Street*, the Sugar Association, and Business Roundtable, to name just a few Byoir clients? How did this powerful and fascinating man avoid historical scrutiny? How was he able to have such an impact on modern history and yet remain so much in its background?

Could it be that the very nature of his job and the job of many top-level mass persuaders requires secrecy and staying out of public view? Or could it be that he and the other leaders of the mass persuasion campaign had a hand in selecting those who wrote the history of the World War I period and that these chroniclers knew to keep Byoir out of the limelight?

The Committee on Public Information (CPI) was created by executive order in April 1917. George Creel, a journalist from the *Rocky Mountain*

News in Denver, was named chairman. Byoir was one of the key propagandists on the committee.[1]

Although Creel received top billing publicly, privately he had less power than Byoir, whose behind-the-scenes work with media barons, industrialists, labor leaders, and government and military intelligence caused him to be, as Creel himself put it, "a committee into himself."

I can't emphasize enough how these connections Byoir made with the power elite of our country helped him later in building a public relations/propaganda empire, an empire whose spinning may have indirectly influenced the person you are today. Joining Creel and Byoir in top leadership positions were Bernays, John Price Jones, Vira Whitehouse, Ernest Poole, Maurice Lyons, and the secretaries of the war, army, and navy. Jones was the fund-raising expert. Bernays was the propaganda theorist. Byoir had been an executive for Randolph Hearst's magazines when recruited by Creel and President Wilson. Byoir may have contributed as much as anyone to World War I and to major national and international events in later years, but his name isn't even a footnote in history. A Google search will reveal a few tidbits, but there isn't much known about him considering his impact. About the only mention of him during the World War I era is in some obscure files tucked away in the National Archives in the Library of Congress.

Interestingly two thirds of the Committee on Public Information (CPI) files are "missing." They were supposedly "lost." (In later years Byoir's personal files and papers also disappeared, as have CIA files when they were requested by various investigators.) The one third of CPI files that now exist were also lost for nearly twenty years after the war and were only accidentally discovered in the later 1930s.[2]

That means historians who wrote about the Wilson war years, a critical time in our history, did not have all of the facts, and even if they did, they would have likely put a favorable slant on the CPI and government activities because Byoir and his CPI cohorts recruited many historians from academia and, instead of serving on active duty, these academics were allowed to fulfill their patriotic duty by working in the "education" section of the

CPI. Note: When a mass persuader uses the word "education," he is typically using it as a euphemism for "propaganda." The CPI was not in the education business. Its sole role was to propagandize the American public.

Reporting and recording an event accurately, as any journalist or historian knows, is difficult enough even when the most trustworthy and accurate sources are available for attribution. It's much more difficult when you're at the mercy of prejudiced insiders trained in the intricacies of mass persuasion, secrecy, deflection, diversion, and other means to hide or put a slanted spin on the information they control.

The most brilliant journalists and scholars can spend years seeking the truth without making progress if they're working within the wrong framework or if they're dealing with partial truths or untruths. As Donald Rumsfeld so astutely noted, "There are unknown unknowns." Many of the historians of that era, and possibly future eras, had no clue what the unknown unknowns were. They only recorded the known. How many unknown realities are hidden from the historical record? Most of the leading historians of that era were recruited by the CPI to serve in the propaganda campaign in exchange for avoiding active-duty military service. Thus, much of the history of the World War I era was written by historians working as government propagandists.

History is full of well-intended experts "barking up the wrong tree," to use a well-worn cliché. Keeping so-called experts barking up the wrong tree is a propaganda technique known as "diversion." It's one of the best propaganda tactics, particularly when historians are being fed information from ghost propagandists. Engineering of consent propaganda also played a crucial role in the history of the era and in America's overwhelming support for the first world war (after the CPI worked its magic).

Historian Robert Dahl found during this period "an astonishing unity of views in America on basic political and economic questions." The development of a unity of views on basic issues was, and is today, a major role of the engineering of consent.[3]

Consensus propaganda has allowed most of America's social, economic, and political policies to enjoy immunity from comprehensive public criticism, that is, criticism that breaks significantly with the status quo and outside the mainstream of accepted dissent.

Some will argue that we do have diversity of opinion, such as liberal vs. conservative, but that diversity is well within accepted bounds. It doesn't cross the line in the sand. One of the most frightening aspects of American political life has been the exclusion of socialism and communism from serious political debate, even though both are part of the political discussions and public debate in many other non-Collectivist countries.

As noted in the previous chapter, the anti-Collectivist propaganda movement began in the 1870's when the Red Scare (even though there were no Communist countries) was used to repeatedly crush labor movements. World War I did not stop the anti-labor propaganda.

For example, Robert W. Babson was director of industrial relations with the CPI. His primary job was to pacify the rank and file and labor leaders. As he wrote to Byoir, "I now have a following of 200,000 workers who know me and my work." The committee's effort to pacify and propagandize labor was often handled through organizations like the National Association of Manufacturers, now known as the National Manufacturers Association (NMA).[4]

The United States' long history of anti-Collectivist repression creates a self-censorship that inhibits many Americans from even thinking about alternative political solutions. Self-censorship creates political tunnel vision, which prevents us sometimes from solving major problems. The fear of being fired from a job, of being investigated by the FBI, of being deported, or of being hauled into court has been a very real fear for a lot of people and has led to this self-censorship. As Ralph Miliband has observed, "The fact that we accept without question the Capitalist context in which government operates is of absolute fundamental importance. This general commitment deeply colors the specific response and affects not only the solution envisioned for the particular problem perceived, but the mode of perception itself; indeed ideological commitment may and often does prevent perception at all, and makes impossible not only prescriptions for the disease, but its location."[5]

The key to democratic theory is the wide circulation of all viewpoints and ideas, no matter how untasteful they might be. Without a free exchange of ideologies, we're prevented from deciding for ourselves since we're denied access to alternatives. The suppression of unpopular ideas may prevent us from finding out vital information to correct mistakes or to consider new ways of solving previously unsolvable problems.

The consensus propaganda of Bernays and others has softened the outlines and flattened the crises of much of American history and has given us a history in which conflict is muted and issues of social and economic injustice are downplayed.

Consensus propaganda has been most effective when combined with political repression. Largely because of consensus propaganda, the extent of political repression in this country, going back to the post–Civil War era, has largely been obscured. By the time the CPI was established some fifty years after the Civil War, political repression was well established.

All that remained was for the CPI's pioneer propagandists to tie in the merging fields of public relations, motivational research, sociology, and psychology with previously developed methods of repression. The CPI and its offshoots were a particularly enlightening experience for writers, editors, publishers, and scholars. Instead of being on the outside looking in, they were now able to work side by side with the most powerful government and corporate leaders. Alliances made during this time of government service established a legacy of cooperation and resource sharing that is still going on today.

• • •

Bringing journalists, researchers, and educators into government was one of the most significant results of the CPI. This basically allowed CPI members to oversee and control the flow of information from journalists and educators to the American public.

A small number of propagandists were running everything. Politicians, military leaders, and corporate chieftains had worked together prior to the war, but not in conjunction with educators and journalists. Wilson, who gave the CPI free reign, was the first president to bring scores of journalists and educators into government. Wilson's academic background (he was president of Princeton University before entering politics), his penchant for publicity, and his belief in government run by a small cadre of intellectuals made his decision to create the nation's first official propaganda agency a rather easy and natural one.

Although well-known among the intellectual elite of the East for his speeches, books, and magazine articles, Wilson was relatively unknown nationally until he was introduced to some wealthy Democrats by George Harvey, president of Harper & Brothers Publishers and editor of *Harper's* magazine, one of the leading publications in the country. Harvey shared Wilson's elitist belief that the masses should follow the dictates of educated leaders. At the requests of his Democratic business friends, he began to promote Wilson as a national political leader. The first step in the Wilson buildup involved front-page coverage in Harvey's magazine. Harvey then rallied other media leaders to give Wilson some national exposure. Operating for Wilson behind the scenes were some wealthy Democrats, such as Thomas Chadbourne and Bernard Baruch.

Wilson's meteoric rise to national political prominence is strikingly similar to the events that led to Jimmy Carter's rise from relative obscurity to national prominence. Both men were national unknowns until selected by wealthy business leaders as good presidential candidates. Both had private meetings with a top media executive suggested by the business elite. These meetings were followed by front-page coverage in a national magazine.

Wilson was an ideal candidate for business and media barons to support. As president of Princeton, he had rubbed shoulders with both the economic and academic elite. He also had a special feel for publicity. He used speeches, books, and newspaper and magazine articles to convey his conviction that education should be for the elite, not the common person.

Wilson faced great pressure from American arm merchants, munitions' makers, a growing chemical industry, and the new electric power industry.

These special interest groups saw American involvement in the European fighting as the economic stimulus needed for their industries.

Wilson's greatest pressure, however, came from the nation's economic power elite. These elite power brokers had given huge loans to the Allied cause. American involvement, they believed, was necessary to protect these loans and to stimulate the domestic economic activity they believed the war would generate.

J. P. Morgan, for example, exerted tremendous pressure on Wilson. Morgan had put together a syndicate of the nation's leading banks in August 1914. This syndicate loaned $500 million to the French and British governments (a large amount at the time). An Allied victory was necessary to protect this investment.

At the same time that Morgan and John D. Rockefeller were urging Wilson to enter the European conflict, neutralists such as William Jennings Bryan and Senator Robert La Follette were pointing out that Wilson was leading the nation toward war in order to appease bankers and arms manufacturers. In response to this criticism, Wilson put propagandists like Byoir to work to discredit his detractors. Pacifists and neutralists were stereotyped as disloyal and unpatriotic. Wilson claimed, according to the June 16, 1916, *New York Times*, that there was "a disloyalty active in the United States that must be absolutely crushed."

• • •

It was Wilson's ire at his pacifist detractors that led him to create the nation's first official propaganda agency. The CPI, besides handling routine public relations functions, such as press liaison, speech writing, and the development of news materials favorable to Wilson's strong pro-war views, also handled Wilson's liaison with major bankers and industrialists with a stake in the war and advised Wilson on how to discredit his critics through the manipulation of public opinion. Committee members also created and executed a highly effective propaganda program to improve Wilson's image and to convince Americans to support the war effort.

CPI members became the generalists in a growing era of specialists. While most of us have been taught for decades that the way to get ahead is to become specialists, such as doctors, lawyers, engineers, scientists, and professors, the reality has been that the generalists have often been the ones running the show.

Generalists like Byoir and Bernays became the ones allowed by the economic elite to draw the big picture and to draw the lines in the sand we would learn not to cross. These early generalists knew that we were entering an era of high-speed technology, which, by its very nature, would turn most of us into specialists. Specialists, by their very nature, have to spend time, energy, and most of their attention on their specialties. They tend to know more and more about less and less. Most specialists don't have the time, inclination, or training to see the big picture.

Byoir called this separation between generalists like himself and specialists "mass fragmentation." He knew that the specialist and the intellectual elite would be the easiest to manipulate because they had to be focused on their specialty to keep up.

The foundation for this strategy of fragmentation, as I've noted, goes back to early-twentieth-century pioneer industrial psychologist Frederick Taylor. Taylor told owners they could best gain control over the workforce by dividing worker against worker through job specialization. This division of labor, he believed, would do away with past forms of labor collectivization, such as the work gang. Taylor saw labor collectivization in any form as a threat to owner control in a new era of high technology. As companies grew after the Civil War, owners' contact with workers was replaced by foremen. This indirect control caused unrest, and owners began searching for other means of control. Taylor gave them a structural answer: job specialization/fragmentation.[6]

CPI members heavily recruited many of the nation's leading scholars to join the public information effort as part of their patriotic duty. The scholars-turned-propagandists soon became enamored with their first taste of power in worldly affairs. They no longer looked at themselves as Ivory Tower intellectuals isolated from the uneducated masses, but as men of affairs. They began to think more like generalists. The group mind became their new classroom. While some scholars believed after the war that educators were used and exploited by the CPI (which is true), most educators relished being able to rub shoulders with the governing elite.

Guy Ford supervised the CPI's mass education program and its interface with the academic community. He had been a dean at the University of Minnesota before being recruited to do his patriotic stint as a scholar-propagandist. Because of Ford's influence in both academic and civic circles, Byoir named him to head the committee's division on civic and educational cooperation. Ford quickly became fascinated with the art of propaganda and mass manipulation. The propaganda techniques Ford learned from Byoir and Bernays stayed with him after the war. He maintained close contact with the journalists and the business and government leaders he had worked with during the war.

Ford could be considered a World War I-era Henry Kissinger. Or maybe it should be said that Kissinger was a modern-day Guy Ford. Both men went from academia to government service and back to academia. Both men, even after government service, were called on by their media friends for think tank-type news analysis, a practice that was unheard of before World War I. Ford, in fact, had a major postwar impact on both news and history. As a historian Ford became president of the American Historical Association. The AHA was also headed after the war by CPI-trained scholar-propagandists Carl Becker of Cornell and Andrew C. McLaughlin of the University of Chicago.[7]

It's no accident that many of the country's top historians served on Wilson's CPI. Wilson knew that he would obtain a more favorable place in history if that history was written by his own apologists. Byoir saw historian-scholars as valuable allies for perpetuating a postwar view of history that would serve the interests of the economic elite.

Even though the CPI altered the courses of both American journalism and education, few journalists or educators today know anything about how their supposedly objective disciplines were manipulated and used for propaganda purposes during World War I. Of course, that was the whole idea: to hide the true agenda from public view. Was it an accident that CPI files suddenly disappeared after the war?

The CPI established a connection and interchangeability among media, academia, and government that has never been broken. It made outsiders insiders. Muckrakers like Tarbel, Steffens, and Sinclair had criticized government and industry from the outside but, until the CPI was created, had never had a chance to observe the inner workings of government or to taste the power and prestige that journalists like Creel and Byoir showed them they could obtain by associating with government leaders and special interest business groups.

Pre–World War I muckrakers were primarily liberal reformers who followed the classic liberal tradition which, as historian John Sproat has noted, claimed to detest the "crude businessmen" who ran the large corporations in post–Civil War America. In reality, however, these early liberal reformers were elitist and more philosophically aligned with the interests of businessmen than the masses, according to Sproat in his book *The Best Men: Liberal Reformers in the Gilded Age*.[8] He says these reformers were open-minded on some issues, but were rigid in their economic viewpoints and were often distrustful of mass movements. When push came to shove, the liberal tradition gave way to businessmen because they stood for property.

In short, Sproat pointed out that in the end, liberal reformers readily and often put the rights of property above human rights. (Excuse me for editorializing, but elitism and property rights still seem to prevail over human rights.)

• • •

The World War I propaganda experience showed journalists, educators, and politicians how to work together for the first time on a mass scale. Initially the CPI served as a liaison between the press and various government departments. Its offices were open twenty-four hours a day, grinding out news releases, which were unheard of before the CPI started the practice.

Creel and Byoir soon organized more ambitious projects. Their task, they believed, was to sell the war to the American people and the CPI's idea of democracy to the world. Success at the grassroots level was one of the CPI's most notable achievements.

Not only did the CPI have a staff of press agents working out of a central office; it also had a decentralized propaganda network that extended into just about every factory, business, church, labor group, and even Indian reservation. Novelists, dramatists, musicians, actors, cartoonists, and motion-picture directors were all employed to spread patriotic enthusiasm.

Slogans such as "the war to end all wars," hang the Kaiser," and "make the world safe for democracy" penetrated the group mind, thanks to the CPI's grassroots propaganda campaign.

Carl Byoir and his agency would later conduct numerous of these bottom-up, grassroots campaigns, several of which I was involved in.

Also successful was a nationwide pro-draft program, which succeeded during a period of significant anti-conscription sentiment. Other successes included efforts to get people to make sacrifices for the war effort, such as planting victory gardens, having meatless and wheatless days, and a Liberty bond drive, which produced some $20 million for the war effort.

Probably the most successful domestic grassroots program involved the deployment of eighty thousand "Four Minute Men." The Four Minute Men were for all intents and purposes part-time propagandists who gave brief pro-war speeches at the local level. They were so named because of their brief talks. Research had shown, according to Bernays, that the average person only had an attention span of four minutes; hence, the Four Minute Men name. They invaded factories, offices, meeting halls, theaters, churches—anywhere a large group of people were gathered. Their charge was simply to deliver the CPI's pre-scripted propaganda line. There was to be no deviation from the script.

This army of mini-propagandists included sports figures, actors, novelists, playwrights, educators, and even ministers. They gave the widest possible circulation to Wilson's war aims. The CPI propagandists did not limit their propaganda to American soil. They conducted extensive propaganda and political warfare overseas, including numerous campaigns to encourage the German people to put down their arms. For example, CPI-developed propaganda bombs were dropped behind enemy lines to impress the German people of the hopelessness of their cause.

The War Trade Board and military intelligence worked closely with Byoir on his foreign propaganda programs. While head of the foreign section, Byoir met Thomas Masaryk, president of the Czechoslovak Republic. The East European country became a Byoir client after the war.

The CPI's foreign propaganda, as Hitler later noted, had a major effect on the German defeat, as much as Pershing or Baruch. Byoir played a key role in designing these foreign propaganda tools, which were aimed primarily at the German population. This success is another reason Hitler later hired Byoir to conduct Nazi propaganda in the United States.

The scope of CPI activities was described by Creel himself:

> Three thousand historians are at our call in the preparation of pamphlet matter; virtually every writer of prominence is giving time to work on the committee; the Division of Advertising enlists the energies of every great advertising expert in the United States; there are close to 80,000 speakers in the Four Minute Men; the war conference of the states are under our supervision; men and women of all nationalities go from coast to coast at our bidding; the famous artists of the United States are banded together for the production of our posters; the motion-picture industry has been mobilized and is giving us ungrudging support without thought of financial return; and in every capital there are men and women serving the CPI with courage and distinction.[9]

Historians James Mock and Cedric Larson noted that Creel and Byoir "assembled as brilliant and as talented a group of journalists, scholars, press agents, editors, artists, and other manipulators of the symbols of public opinion as America had ever seen united for a single purpose."[10] It was a gargantuan advertising agency, the historians noted, the like of which the country had never known, and the breathtaking scope of its activities was not to be equaled until the rise of the totalitarian dictatorships after the war (many of which patterned their propaganda after CPI techniques).

"George Creel, Carl Byoir, Edgar Sisson, Harry O'Higgins, Guy Ford, and their famous associates were literally PR counselors to the U.S. Government, carrying first to the citizens of this country and then to distant lands, the ideas which gave motive power to the stupendous undertaking of 1917–1918," Mock and Larson said.

While Mock and Larson were amazed at the CPI's gargantuan-like advertising and PR efforts to enlist support for the war, much more important for the future was the CPI's development of clandestine propaganda techniques, which were used throughout the remainder of the twentieth century (and to this day) in concert with political repression against labor and all forms of dissent. These techniques have largely been applied clandestinely to manipulate and mold the mass mind in order to create a consensus of opinion and a unity of views on the basic issues so that we know instinctively which lines in the sand not to cross and when not to step outside the box of acceptability.

Byoir and Bernays deliberately recruited journalists and business and government leaders, not only because they would help them propagandize the entire country, but because the CPI leaders knew the cozy relationships would come in handy in the future. And they did. The World War I propaganda was so successful, both at home and abroad, that CPI members felt they had discovered a new power of nature: a way to control the public. "In every town, in every factory, and on every farm, public opinion was mobilized and manipulated in support of policies believed necessary for success in the war."[11]

President Wilson was so pleased with the newly discovered power of propaganda that he took Creel, Bernays, and Byoir with him to the Versailles Peace Conference. Wilson was indebted to the pioneer American propagandists (as was Hitler) for their expertise in mastering new techniques for molding public opinion.

The business community was particularly interested in the committee's propaganda successes. The CPI had taught business leaders that new mass persuasion tools were now available to control labor and increase profits by manipulating public opinion.

• • •

During the 1930s various investigations delved into Wilson's true war motives. By the mid-thirties, many Americans had come to believe the war had been fought in vain. Why?

For one thing, all they had to do was to look across the Atlantic and see that the success of Wilson's "War to End All Wars" had been short-lived as they watched Nazis march through Europe. For another, business-oriented publications like *Fortune* magazine reported the results of extensive probes into charges of war profiteering. These investigations showed that many defense industries had, as charged by obstructionists, made exorbitant profits during the war and had engaged in other questionable activities.

Many Americans came to believe they had been duped into fighting by the Allies, maybe by "Wall Street" or maybe by the "Merchants of Death" (arms manufacturers), but certainly by propagandists. Americans became distrustful of Allied propaganda. Ironically, this American distrust of Allied propaganda helped Byoir spread German propaganda in the United States during the early thirties. I will discuss Byoir's work for Nazi Germany in the next chapter.

Byoir, a key architect of Allied propaganda during the first world war, was instrumental in orchestrating the chorus against Allied propaganda on behalf of his new client, Hitler, during the thirties.

People began to ask if the antiwar activists hadn't been right after all in warning that the European conflict was primarily a series of civil wars and boundary disputes, in which American involvement would do little more than provide economic pump priming for American industry.

A lot of Wilson's former supporters began to believe that maybe Wilson's primary war motive really was to protect the loans and other economic interests of his banking and industrial friends. A *Fortune* magazine exposé on war profiteering led to the creation of a House investigating committee, led by Gerald Nye of North Dakota.

The Nye Committee concluded that munitions makers had, indeed, reaped bountiful profits from the war and had avoided paying taxes on much of their excess profits. The committee report revealed how political connections helped many industrialists obtain lush contracts. It revealed how the armed forces allowed corporate corruption to go unchallenged.[12]

The Nye Committee also verified the charges of World War I pacifists, many of whom were jailed for their dissent, that American bankers and financiers had indeed been instrumental in America's involvement in the war. The revelations about America's true motives for entering the war revealed, in effect, that the American people had been lied to, at worst, and manipulated, at best, to support the war effort on behalf of business interests. These revelations from the Nye Committee came at a time of growing domestic unrest because of the Depression.

Franklin Roosevelt met with Byoir to discuss how potential public distrust of government and business could be diffused. Roosevelt was concerned that public cynicism from the Nye Committee reports and the Depression, plus growing labor unrest, might provide fertile ground for the growth of collectivist ideology.

Roosevelt knew Byoir was both a top propagandist and a staunch anti-Socialist. This was such an attractive combination that it caused Roosevelt to overlook the fact that Byoir had given public relations advice to Nazi, Germany. Another twist was that Byoir himself was Jewish.

The richest person in the world, Howard Hughes, would call on Byoir to bail him out of trouble at congressional hearings (similar to the Nye hearings) on war profiteering during World War II.

The first world war gave American propagandists the chance to get in bed with the media, business, and the government elite. They have been in bed together ever since.

• • •

I would like to make one last observation about the CPI. Readers who have gotten this far know that I have given many examples throughout the book of false-flag propaganda (manufactured incidents) and disinformation, both of which are designed to arouse passions and, basically, to create mass hysteria, particularly prior to and during wars.

The false-flag/disinformation techniques were very much in evidence leading up to and during World War I to arouse the passion of the American people for fighting in a war they were initially against. The CPI fed newspapers a story that ships escorting the First Division to Europe sank several German submarines. This story was proven false when newsmen interviewed the ships' officers in England. It was a manufactured, false-flag incident and disinformation.[13]

The CPI also conducted a campaign to arouse war passion with scare headlines that "the first American built battle planes are today in route to the front in France." It was later learned that the accompanying pictures were fake and that there was only one plane. Creel blamed the secretary of war for the false story.[14]

The CPI also supplied Hollywood with atrocity stories and influenced the 1918 production of cinematic classics such as *The Kaiser: The Beast of Berlin*, *The Prussian Cur*, *To Hell with the Kaiser*, and *The Claws of the Hun*.[15]

Political scientist and communications theorist Harold Lasswell wrote that "in the Great Society it is no longer possible to fuse the waywardness of individuals in the furnace of the war dance; a new and subtler instrument must weld thousands and even millions of human beings into one amalgamated mass of hate and will and hope. A new flame must burn out the canker of dissent and temper the steel of bellicose enthusiasm. The name of this new hammer and anvil of social solidarity is propaganda."[16] How many false-flag incidents have we employed to weld thousands and even millions of us into one "amalgamated mass of hate" with this new hammer and anvil of propaganda that Lasswell refers to?

CHAPTER 14

Post–World War I to the Cold War

I NOTED IN CHAPTER 2 that the father of modern propaganda, Edward Bernays, wrote a book in the twenties called *Propaganda*. He emphatically stated that there is an "invisible government" in America in the employ of the economic power elite that is secretly "pulling the wires"(as he put it) to manipulate our thoughts and behavior.[1]

I've also pointed out that Senator Robert La Follette of Wisconsin recognized the beginnings of this mass mind molding and warned several times in 1917 that the propaganda activities of the Committee on Public Information (CPI) were designed to shape our viewpoints by arousing our emotions, particularly fear.

In a Senate speech in 1917, a speech that was judged one of the top 100 Senate speeches in history, LaFollette warned: "The purpose of this ridiculous campaign (the CPI's pro-war campaign) is to throw the country into a state of sheer terror, to change public opinion, to stifle criticism, and suppress discussion. People are being unlawfully arrested, thrown into jail, held incommunicado for days, only to be eventually discharged without ever having been taken into court, because they have committed no crime. But more than this, if every preparation for war can be made the excuse for destroying free speech and a free press and the right of the people to assemble together for peaceful discussion, then we may well despair of ever again finding ourselves for a long period in a state of peace."[2]

Has LaFollette's warning come true? Has our almost endless state of war since he made that statement a century ago been "the excuse" for controlling public opinion through what he called "a state of sheer terror"? What La Follette astutely observed was the beginning of a new era in mass persuasion, an era in which pioneer propagandists had learned how to apply psychological and social engineering to manipulate public opinion. These pioneer propagandists were so good at their craft that many foreign governments began to take notice, including Nazi Germany.

The CPI was so successful in changing Americans' attitudes and behavior concerning the war that Hitler's propaganda minister, Joseph Goebbels, credited the CPI with teaching him the mass persuasion techniques he used to gain support of the German people. Byoir's contribution to the CPI's successful propaganda efforts was the major reason Nazi Germany hired him.[3]

There's a lot of mystery around Byoir. He purposely kept himself out of the limelight, but not all of Byoir's propaganda campaigns were low-profile or primarily in the interests of big business or governments.

For example, he promoted President Roosevelt's birthday balls for several years. These were local dances held each year to celebrate the president's birthday and to raise money to fight polio, from which Roosevelt suffered. In 1937 six thousand dances drew over 5 million people.[4]

The slogan for the balls was "Spare a dime so a child can walk." Who could resist donating a dime to help a crippled child? This national PR program led to the creation of the March of Dimes. Byoir once told a national radio audience during the birthday ball promotions, "You are the painters of rainbows in lives clouded by pain and sickness and lost hope."[5]

He also introduced the Montessori educational system to America. And his PR agency helped keep a generation of children glued to their TV sets watching *Sesame Street*, which was produced by his agency's client The Children's Television Workshop.. I noted in an earlier chapter that most of the information about Byoir and the CPI during the World War I era is in some obscure files tucked away in the National Archives in the Library of Congress. A few historians and others have written some about the CPI. Their information came primarily from CPI files.[6]

Interestingly most of these CPI files, as I noted, were supposedly "lost." What files do exist were written by historians who were handpicked by Byoir and the CPI. These historians, along with other leaders of academia, were able to avoid being drafted into the military by working for the CPI. This work basically involved recording the history of the period in a favorable light.

In other words, the CPI and the historians on their payroll propagandized or slanted the history of our country during and immediately after the war. Even historians who didn't work for the CPI wrote about this period with incomplete information since much of the information was in "missing" files.

Former CIA operator Victor Marchetti wrote an article in *Institute for Historical Review* in which he noted that "the CIA is a master at distorting history: even creating its own version of history to suit its institutional and operational purposes."[7]

Another reason not much is known about Byoir, the CPI, or propaganda itself is that mass persuasion and propaganda are rarely taught in schools or colleges. Another reason is that the most effective mass persuasion is done clandestinely, in secret. Still another reason is that mass persuasion techniques are not designed to target individuals, but the mass mind. Most historians or journalists have no training in mass persuasion and don't know how to even recognize it.

Another member of the CPI, Edward Bernays, had a lot to do with teaching propagandists how to draw lines in the sand and how to persuade us not to cross those lines. Bernays, like Byoir, impressed Joseph Goebbels, Hitler's propagandist. Goebbels's propaganda library is said to have included Bernays's publications.

Bernays pioneered, as noted previously, the use of psychology and social sciences to design public persuasion and mind manipulation campaigns that he called "the engineering of consent."

An example of this technique was put into play during the first world war when Bernays argued against censorship. Most countries, including the United States, implement censorship during wartime, but Bernays recommended and helped implement the very opposite of censorship: an affirmative-action approach whereby the population itself exercises voluntary censorship through a uniformity of opinion.

Bernays believed he and his CPI cohorts could manipulate the mass mind using psychological and motivational methods so that people on their own (with a lot of help from propagandists) would decide the acceptable parameters and the line in the sand not to cross. What is amazing is that Bernays and the CPI were able to vastly increase support for the war within a few months by implementing this engineering-of-consent strategy.[8]

• • •

Shortly after the CPI was created in the spring of 1917, the Czar of Russia was overthrown in the Bolshevik Revolution. The world's first Communist government came to power. The CPI immediately began a Red Scare propaganda campaign, which ran in conjunction with its propaganda to convince Americans to support the war effort.[9]

One of the first things the CPI did was to create the famous slogan "Make the World Safe for Democracy." Those six words had a major impact on the mass mind during the war and are still in today's political vernacular.

This slogan served a dual purpose. First, it enlisted support for the war effort. Secondly, it was the first salvo in our 140-year-old psychological war against all things hinting of collectivism, be it communes, socialism, or communism. Bernays and Byoir were among those at the forefront of this anti-Collectivist mass mind manipulation.[10]

Since the mid-nineteenth-century writings of Karl Marx and Friedrich Engels, the economic elite have feared anything that smacked of collectivism. The growth of unions and the growing radicalization of American labor added to their fear of the growing worldwide Socialist movement.

Shortly after he went to work for Germany in 1933, Byoir launched a campaign to convince American business leaders, many of whom he knew from his past CPI work, that fascism was an effective buffer against both communism and unionism. As a result American business leaders provided financial support for Byoir's pro-Nazi, anti-Communist activities, such as a march in Madison Square Garden shortly after Byoir took the German account.

Two-time Medal of Honor winner Major General Smedley Butler testified on November 20, 1934, before a House Committee on Un-American Activities that a group of Wall Street financiers urged him to lead a Fascist march on Washington. The 1940 *Encyclopaedia Britannica* noted the appeal of fascism to conservative business interests: "Even in the democratic countries, many conservatives have viewed with great favor the rise to power of fascism and have supported them as fighters of communism."[11]

This anti-Communist bias in the United States, which Byoir helped create, contributed to Hitler's rise to power in 1932. It helped him march into several European countries unopposed under the guise of fighting communism. One of Hitler's goals was to keep the United States out of the European fighting. Hitler saw Byoir as an ally in this effort since he was well-connected with business leaders and was staunchly anti-Communist. The success of this strategy was reflected in the 1937 German-American Neutrality Act, which stated the United States had no intention of joining the European battlefront. The United States was content to sit back and let Hitler wipe communism off the face of the earth.

However, the West's faith in Hitler's anti-communism backfired in 1939 when Germany shocked the world by entering into a nonaggression alliance with Russia. Hitler, who sold Germany as the world's savior from communism, now spoke of an "international revolution destined to put an end to Capitalist society." Byoir and American business interests felt betrayed. Hitler had pulled a fast one on them. Hitler had used the vey propaganda techniques we had taught him, such as diversion, the block and bridge, and the straw man, to manipulate the anti-Communist fervor of America's business and government leaders.

The Bolshevik Revolution in 1917 was the straw that broke the camel's back for those involved in the American mass persuasion program. The economic elite saw Communist Russia and any political or economic movement that would loosen the tight hold they had on their purse strings as something to be fought to the death. Prior to World War I, the economic elite had used red-baiting as a propaganda tool to discredit and crush labor movements, but those had been straw-hat, theoretical fearmongering. Now the real thing had happened: a Communist government had risen to power in Russia. It was time for war, a war to win people's minds and, even more importantly, their emotions.

The weapons of choice from the beginning to the end of the Cold War were the newly developed techniques of mass persuasion, tools that Byoir and Bernays had a key role in developing. Even though they would compete for clients in later years, CPI members Byoir and Bernays were cohorts in mastering and deploying newly discovered motivational and psychological techniques that would allow them and future propagandists to shape public opinion for many decades to come.

• • •

Bernays was a spin doctor long before that term was even part of our political vocabulary. He worked for the US government, a variety of special interest organizations, and numerous large corporations. He spent his entire life studying and practicing the craft of mass persuasion. He promoted products, ideas, political movements, and the art of propaganda itself. He was one of the first to recognize how the use of psychological, sociological, and motivational techniques could be applied to mass communications and how those tools could benefit the power elite. The theories and proven techniques of Bernays and his peers have become ingrained in multiple communications disciplines, ranging from public relations, marketing, and advertising to clandestine intelligence activities.

Mass persuasion is pervasive in our society. It envelops us, yet most of us aren't aware of its presence, techniques, or impact. Just about every public official, from local to state to the federal government, is surrounded by public relations or image consultants. Congress people and the president rarely speak or write a word without the message being written and/or edited by their PR advisers. Just about every medium- to large-size company in America has internal and/or external PR help. No product hits the market without branding and image considerations. Everything is staged, from products to ideas to government actions.

Stuart Ewen, American PR historian, puts it this way: "We live in a society in which nearly every moment of human attention is exposed to the game plans of spin doctors, image managers, pitchmen, communications consultants, public information officers and public relations specialists."[12]

Bernays, Byoir, and their cohorts saw themselves as providing a service to democracy. They didn't see themselves as spin doctors, but as mass psychology propagandists. Propaganda was not a dirty word, nor did it have negative connotations as today. The early propagandists believed they were caretakers of the public good. They thought their backroom, behind-the-scenes manipulations were a good thing. They took pride in their invisible spinning.[13]

The mass persuasion that Bernays and Byoir were primarily interested in was not the obvious, open advertising and public relations often associated with propaganda. They (and their cohorts) worked largely behind the scenes to influence the mass mind. While Bernays was more of a theorist, Byoir's expertise was implementing the newfound ways to influence the mass mind. Byoir was known as "the miracle man" of the CPI for his ability to get results. One of his primary activities involved persuading draft-eligible non-English-speaking Americans to join the war effort. One ethnic group he targeted was Germans. Thirteen years later he would become deeply embroiled with Germany, this time as the American PR representative for Nazi Germany's German Tourist Council.

Byoir also represented several Nazi corporations that played a major role in the Nazi regime, including one huge corporation that made the sarin gas that killed so many. Byoir's successes at the CPI, including the work he did for German Americans during the war, caught Hitler's attention, as did Byoir's conservatism and his anti-communism. So did the work he did for Lithuania and Czechoslovakia in the twenties and for a Cuban dictator in the early thirties.

Byoir's penchant for influencing public opinion also caught the attention of governments, intelligence agencies, and big business interests, all whom have adopted and employed the techniques developed by the early propagandists.

Hitler's propaganda minister, Joseph Goebbels, arduously studied the intricacies of American propaganda. In his famous book *Mein Kampf,* Hitler credited the CPI with teaching him the propaganda techniques he used in Germany to garner public support for Hitler.

I should clarify one thing before moving on. The early propagandists like Byoir and Bernays did not, as far as I know, break laws or intentionally do anything subversive. Byoir has maintained, for example, that he did not know of Hitler's intentions toward Jews when he was handling Nazi PR. Byoir or Bernays-bashing is not the purpose of this book. I'm more concerned with the techniques used by propagandists in the past and in the present.

Not only were the Nazis impressed with Byoir's PR acumen; he brought several other things to the table. Prior to joining the CPI in 1917, he worked for William Randolph Hearst, the largest newspaper and magazine publisher in the country. Hearst was also ardently anti-Socialist.[14]

Byoir became head of circulation for all of Hearst's magazines prior to World War I. While working for Hearst, Byoir learned about journalism (the yellow type) and anti-socialism. Upton Sinclair criticized Hearst's use of yellow journalism techniques to whip up popular support for US military adventurism in Cuba, Puerto Rico, and the Philippines. According to Sinclair, Hearst's newspaper employees were "willing, by deliberate and shameful lies, made out of whole cloth, to stir nations to enmity and drive them to murderous war."[15]

Sinclair also asserted that in the early twentieth century (when Byoir worked for Hearst) that Hearst's newspapers "lied remorselessly about radicals, excluded the word Socialist from their columns" and "obeyed a standing order in all Hearst offices that American socialism shall never be mentioned favorably."

Just as Byoir parlayed his CPI experience to get clients ranging from governments to large corporations, Bernays used his CPI experience as head of Latin American PR activities to later land some key south-of-the-border clients, most notably United Fruit, which, along with the CIA, played a key role in removing the democratically elected president of Guatemala in a 1954 coup that involved the highest levels of the US government. Here is how Bernays described his role in the coup: "I was struck by the thought that although I was advising a banana company, I was actually fighting the Cold War."[16]

Why would the key propagandist in the United Fruit incident say he was fighting the Cold War? Because he knew that the real reason for the coup was the anti-Communist campaign and to protect the financial interests of the elite. Like Byoir, Bernays was versatile. He could put a spin on just about anything. For example, he helped increase the sale of Ivory Soap, a product of his client Proctor & Gamble, by encouraging kids to use the soap for making creative sculptures. He may have also helped launch the women's liberation movement for client Lucky Strike.[17]

During the twenties Byoir parlayed his "miracle man" reputation at the CPI to land a contract with Lithuania. The Lithuanian National Council in the United States hired Byoir to work his magic on public opinion so that the US Senate would recognize Lithuania as a free (from Russia) and independent nation. This campaign succeeded in securing Lithuania's future as an ally with the United States. Bernays also did some work for Czechoslovakia.[18]

Both Byoir and Bernays were staunch anti-Communists. They knew that their famous slogan ("make the world safe for democracy") was more than just a rallying cry to support the war effort. It was also intended to draw the line in the sand for the real enemy: collectivism.

Besides representing countries Byoir dabbled in commercial PR ventures. For example, he promoted Blondex hair products and promoted the phrase "sexy platinum blondes." Dark hair was in fashion during the early twenties. By the end of the decade, many women clamored to become sexy blondes. How many non-natural blondes today realize that good propaganda from decades ago likely influenced them indirectly to become blond?

Byoir's campaign for Blondex was open and overt propaganda, but even overt propaganda, particularly over many years, can convince us to do things and make decisions that we believe are independent decisions or actions, but are often conditioned responses to well-orchestrated propaganda campaigns.

In 1930 Byoir traveled to Havana and published the *Havana Post* and the *Havana Telegram*. He began editorially promoting American tourism. This caught the attention of Gerardo Machado, Cuban's ruthless dictator. Byoir also caught the attention of the Mafia, which ran a lucrative gambling business in Havana's numerous casinos. His future client Howard Hughes also had a strong connection with the Mafia. Machado gave Byoir a five-year contract to attract American tourists to Cuba. Within one year Byoir's PR campaign doubled the number of American tourists. His work for Machado ended after the dictator was overthrown in 1933. Nonetheless, with his CPI successes and other PR accomplishments, such as in Cuba, Byoir was beginning to get worldwide attention.[19]

• • •

Shortly after working for a right-wing Cuban dictator, Byoir found another right-wing entity, the German Tourist Information Office, knocking on his door. The Nazis knew of Byoir's propaganda magic on the American people with the CPI and how he had used propaganda techniques to double the American tourism trade to Cuba.

They also knew that Byoir had strong right-wing political views and was adamantly anti-Communist. Besides the German tourism office, Byoir did PR work for two of Germany's largest industries, including IG Farben, one of the world's largest chemical conglomerates, and the Frederick Flick Group. Both Farben and Flick executives were Nazis. Both companies were primary suppliers to Hitler and contributed to the rise of Nazis to power in 1933.

Farben produced the sarin gas that killed so many of Byoir's fellow Jews. Between 1929 and 1939, Farben doubled in size and, besides making money off of the Nazi war efforts, also had cartel agreements with Standard Oil of New Jersey, DuPont, Alcoa, and Dow Chemical. A US War Department document noted that without Farben, "Germany's war efforts would have been unthinkable."[20]

Farben's key war records were destroyed in 1945. Interestingly, as I pointed out earlier, two thirds of the CPI's World War I files were also destroyed, as were most of the MK-ULTRA files on the CIA's mind control projects.

Ivey Lee, another pioneer American propagandist, also handled German-American relations in the United States. Lee handled public relations/propaganda for many years for the Rockefeller family. He was very successful at softening the image of Rockefeller as a hard-driving, take-no-prisoners Capitalist. By the time Lee got through with Rockefeller, the American public had a much more favorable image of the Rockefellers and the economic elite.

Because of his propaganda work for Nazi Germany, Byoir was accused of setting up front organizations in the United States to represent Nazi interests. On June 3, 1940, Texas congressman Wright Patman demanded Byoir be investigated by the House Un-American Activities Committee and the Department of Justice. The DOJ immediately began an investigation.

Byoir quickly wrote a personal letter to President Roosevelt. By June 17, two weeks later, the Justice Department cleared Byoir. It helps to know people in high places, such as the president of the United States. Roosevelt was indebted to Byoir for the work he had done for President Wilson and for his help in promoting the birthday balls to raise money for polio.

Roosevelt was also grateful for the propaganda results Byoir had obtained for some politically connected members of the elite, such as Henry Doherty, a financier and oil man who founded Cities Service Company. Cities became CITCO Petroleum and a Byoir client.[21]

• • •

In 1934 at Byoir's suggestion, Doherty donated $25K to the president's Warm Springs Foundation to establish a series of local birthday balls to double as celebrations of the president's January 30 birthday, as well as to raise funds that would benefit sufferers of polio, which Roosevelt suffered from. Byoir helped promote the nationwide dances and called them "dances so others may walk."[22]

Instead of appealing to people with wealth for donations, Byoir came up with the idea of appealing to the emotions of the average person and asking them for small donations. Who could resist, he argued, donating a dime or two so a crippled child could walk? This concept led to the March of Dimes.

Byoir had gone from someone who convinced Americans to fight in World War I, to someone who represented Nazi Germany, to someone who befriended a liberal American president, to someone who indirectly created the March of Dimes.

John Biggers, president of the glass manufacturing conglomerate Libby-Owens Ford, met Byoir in Miami when Byoir was helping promote an FDR-sponsored commission for the census of the unemployed.

Biggers was impressed with Byoir's access to FDR's press secretaries, Steve Early and Marvin McIntyre, both of whom Byoir had worked with while on the CPI. Biggers hired Byoir to represent Libby-Owens in 1938. Byoir CPI contacts had paid off again twenty years later.[23]

In the mid-forties, Byoir began representing Howard Hughes, who remained a client for nearly forty years. Hughes had a penchant for operating in secrecy. So did Byoir. Hughes was an avid anti-Communist. So was Byoir. Hughes was well-connected to the oil industry. So was Byoir. Hughes had major connections with Cuba's casino operations. So did Byoir. Hughes had numerous mob contacts. So did Byoir (from his Cuba experiences). Hughes knew how to keep secrets. So did Byoir.

After World War II, the Office of Strategic Services and the CIA concentrated on two primary objectives: anti-communism and protecting the elite's worldwide financial interests (primarily oil). The anti-Communist Cold War fervor was launched shortly after the war ended with the Truman Doctrine (1947), which basically said anything goes in the fight against communism. It set the legal groundwork for the United States to become the world policeman.

Propaganda was considered the key weapon to destroy communism and to open and maintain worldwide markets. The CIA became the world's most prolific propaganda operation. Its propaganda was highly effective because the CIA was a secret, clandestine organization that pretty much had free reign worldwide.

The best propaganda is always done in secret. The cardinal rule of the propagandist is to remain in the background. How many historians have looked into our country's covert propaganda efforts? I don't know of any. Even if they tried, where would they go for information? You can't interview someone who is invisible.

CHAPTER 15

The Cold War, Hollywood, and Organized Crime

ALBERT E. KAHN NOTED IN his book *High Treason: The Plot Against the People* that "every conceivable promotional device and propaganda technique was galvanized into an intense and incessant anti-Communist campaign which permeated every phrase of the nation's life."[1]

I have personal knowledge of the effectiveness of this Red Scare campaign. I was swept up in it. I even joined the Christian Anti-Communist Society as a teen. We had storm shelters in our neighborhood and watched TV programs like "I Led Three Lives" about a Communist masquerading as an FBI agent. We were scared.

Speaking of the FBI, it has been one of the primary enablers of the anti-Communist movement. Its head, J. Edgar Hoover, was an ardent anti-Communist. I noted earlier how Byoir and a young Hoover jointly set up a publicity bureau after World War I and issued press releases claiming Russia was planning to invade the United States.

That was a lie (disinformation) from the get-go, but such Red-Scare disinformation served a purpose in the twenties and again after the second world war, which was to scare the American people. As soon as Japan surrendered, Congressman John E. Rankin, a member of the Dies Committee on Un-American Activities, began issuing press releases on "Communist intentions to dominate the world."[2]

Winston Churchill unleashed a barrage of anti-Communist battle cries that gave great prestige to the economic elite's calculated campaign to use anti-Communism as a smokescreen for the goals of the economic elite. Some credit Churchill for coining the phrase "Iron Curtain" because it became popular after he used it in a March 5, 1946 speech, but a March 5, 2015 article in Time magazine was titled "Winston Churchill Did Not Coin the Phrase Iron Curtain." Ironically, he may have picked-up the phrase "Iron Curtain" from Hitler's propaganda minister Joseph Goebbels who used it years earlier.

On September 30, 1946, Hoover let loose a well-publicized blast against the evils of collectivism that implied that Communists were everywhere. Among those who led the Red Scare chorus were Howard Hughes, President Truman, master spy John Foster Dulles, future CIA director Allen Dulles, Senator Joe McCarthy, Under Secretary of State Dean Acheson, Secretary of State George Marshall, and Clark Clifford. Clifford was the main architect of the Marshall Plan and was secretary of defense in the Johnson administration. Clifford worked with Johnson in developing disinformation propaganda about the Gulf of Tonkin lie to garner support for increased bombing. The Truman Doctrine, according to William Appleman, was designed purposely "to promote trouble on the other side of the Iron Curtain."[3]

Truman believed promoting trouble for the Soviet Union was the best way to serve the interests of the economic elite. He believed that dropping the nuclear bombs on Japan made us "the giant of the economic world" and gave us the God-given right to determine economic relations for the entire world.[4]

The editors of *Business Week* agreed with Truman and wrote a major story in 1946, in which they reveled in the financial windfall American business would reap from our Cold War, anti-Communist scare campaign. The *Business Week* editors rightly predicted a huge economic windfall for the military-industrial complex. It took many decades to smash the Soviets into submission, but to the economic elite, it was worth every penny and every life lost. It was also worth manipulating the mass mind.[5]

For those who question that their government would unleash a calculated propaganda barrage to manipulate our innermost fears and desires to promote the financial interests of the economic elite, here is what Abraham L. Pomerantz, deputy chief counsel to the US prosecution staff at the Nuremberg trials, said in noting how the propaganda approach works:

> The press and radio first lay down a terrific barrage against the red menace. Headlines without a shred of substance shriek of atom bomb spies or plots to overthrow our government, of espionage, of high treason, and of other blood-curdling crimes. We are now ready for the second stage: the pinning of the label Red indiscriminately on all opposition.[6]

The suicide of Secretary of Defense James V. Forrestal epitomizes the anti-Communist hysteria whipped up after the war. On April 11, 1949, Forrestal ran down the streets of a Florida resort town screaming, "The Red Army has landed," after he heard a fire-truck siren. He was taken to Bethesda Naval Hospital. On May 22, he jerked away from some attendants assigned to watch him and jumped through a screen window to his death.[7]

On October 10, 1946, *Life* magazine reacted to the Soviet detonation of an atomic device by publishing an article on atomic warfare. Accompanying the article was a photograph of the damage caused by the explosion of a bomb on Wall Street next to J. P. Morgan's firm on September 16, 1920. Although no one was ever arrested for the bombing, the *Life* headline read: "In 1920 Reds Exploded Bomb in Wall Street, Killed 30, and Wounded Hundreds."[8]

Not only had no one ever been arrested for the bombing; there was no proof so-called "reds" had planted the bomb. There's considerable evidence to the contrary: that the bomb was planted by government provocateurs. Regardless of who planted the bomb, the fact remains that America's so-called objective media reached back twenty-six years into its files to send a message. The same message was delivered after the Palmer raids in the twenties to show that the reds used bombs against innocent Americans.

Besides Hoover and Byoir, another staunch anti-Communist was Howard Hughes, the world's richest man after the second world war. Byoir's PR firm represented Hughes for decades. I worked on several projects involving Hughes. The rest of this chapter will be devoted to how Hughes, as a key representative of the economic elite, used clandestine propaganda to achieve his (and the elite's) goals.

• • •

Hughes was possibly history's most successful implementer of a little-known propaganda technique called the "propaganda of silence." Keeping Hughes scarce and away from the press was the job of Carl Byoir & Associates. We did this by erecting stone walls and diversions to keep the press away. We, in effect, made Hughes invisible. You can't finger a ghost. By going into seclusion and projecting himself as a weird recluse, Hughes could avoid public scrutiny of his numerous business interests. In addition, secrecy allowed him to move seamlessly in the invisible realm of covert operatives.

Byoir was able to create a mystique about Hughes, an aura of intrigue that diverted attention from his economic and political wheeling and dealing. Hughes was a headline name throughout his early years, but was not seen publicly after 1958. There was speculation he had died or gone insane. Neither happened. Hughes simply made a calculated decision that secrecy worked best for him and his economic interests. No one was more invisible than Hughes. Both Hughes and Byoir believed that the propaganda that is seen the least is the most effective. Byoir was one of the world's leading public opinion experts by the time he teamed up with Hughes.

Like many top-level manipulators of people's attitudes, Byoir knew how to work behind the scenes to influence public opinion. Hughes was impressed with Byoir's penchant for secrecy and his propaganda successes for President Wilson, President Roosevelt, Hitler, Nazi Germany, a Cuban dictator, and some of the country's top businesses and trade associations. More importantly, Hughes was impressed with Byoir's staunch anti-Collectivism.

Byoir, until his death in the late fifties, handled most of Hughes's public relations needs personally. After his death the account was supervised by Byoir's board chairmen. Day-to-day activities were initially handled by Bill Utley and, later, for many years by Dick Hannah. Hannah died in the spring of 1976 just several weeks before Hughes passed away. Hannah, as the Byoir in-house humor told it, passed away first in order to prepare the way for his client.

No one knew Howard Hughes better than Dick Hannah. Few people have heard of Hannah, although he was the person most responsible for Hughes's public image. News articles concerning Hughes sometimes mentioned Hannah as a Hughes spokesman and, on occasion, as a source of information. I never saw Hannah's role as Hughes's exclusive propagandist explained. Hannah, like the man he served, was nearly invisible, at least as far as the public was concerned. Hannah had almost daily phone contact with the recluse and, on occasion, had secret rendezvous with Hughes at his various hideouts around the world. Anything meant for public consumption about Hughes first went through Hannah. Hannah worked out of Byoir's regional office in Los Angeles. He had little in common with other Byoir personnel.

For one thing, his offices were separated from other Byoir employees and their offices by a long corridor. For another, he didn't follow the normal 9:00 a.m. to 5:00 p.m. work schedule. Instead, he followed Hughes's haphazard schedule, which meant Hannah could be found at his desk, door closed, from 9:00 or 10:00 p.m. until 5:00 to 9:00 a.m. Hannah was rarely in the office during normal working hours. He was just about as reclusive as his client. Besides handling Hughes's personal propaganda needs, Hannah served as public relations consultant for the Hughes-owned Summa Corporation, the umbrella entity for Hughes's varied interests. The Byoir organization continued to represent Summa, along with Hughes's other holdings, through most of the seventies. The original Byoir agency was purchased in the late seventies by another agency.

I recall Hannah telling me once that the most important events are not what end up in the public domain, but those things that take place in secret, behind closed doors. He said the real news is the news behind the news.

I wasn't sure at the time what he meant, but as I became more deeply involved in the propaganda business, I understood well. Much of what ultimately ends up in the public domain, he said, is often a diversion to what is really happening. Hannah explained that journalists are trained to get quotes to give stories credibility, but what is quoted is rarely the complete story because the really important things are never quotable. He knew that the true story was not the facts, but the truth behind the facts. He knew that the truth is elusive enough when facts are available. It's nearly impossible to find the truth when facts are hidden by sophisticated propaganda techniques, such as diversions, misdirection, third-party fronts, disinformation, and many more.

Interestingly, considering his later seclusion, Hughes was one of the most visible men in America during the thirties and forties. His name, in fact, was a household word. His name and photos were frequently on front pages. Exposure was as important to Hughes's early career as was secrecy in later years.

Hughes was one of the few filmmakers who didn't feel the financial pinch of the Depression. He had the reputation of a free spender, to whom money was no object. He also had the reputation of being a dashing, debonair playboy who could have just about any woman he wanted. Hughes didn't do anything to discourage that image. Hughes was quite the lady's man, much like JFK. Both men had something else in common – they slept with some women who had ties to organized crime.

The tall, lean, and physically attractive Hughes slept with or had strong intentions toward more than 50 actresses, including just about all of the most famous Hollywood movie stars, such as Ginger Rogers, Loretta Young, Lana Turner, Ida Lupino, Ava Gardner, Katherine Hepburn, and many others, according to numerous sources, such as a Nov. 23, 2011 arti-cle at *Classic Movie Chat.com* titled "Howard Hughes the World's Greatest Womanizer?" Based on what I learned while working at the PR agency that represented Hughes, I agree that Hughes was a dedicated womanizer. Hughes, the womanizer, was quite the contrast, however, to Hughes' later image of being a weird, bearded recluse. Both images had one thing in common. They were the by-products of very successful propaganda.

His secret with women? For one thing he was rich. For another he feigned shyness as a decoy to disarm women. His romantic pursuits led to just about as many headlines as did his film and aviation exploits. Hughes was a far cry from the eccentric, bearded recluse he was alleged to have become in later years. Hughes wanted all the exposure he could get during the thirties. He had not yet entered into the secret alliances that would make clandestine operations a practical necessity. Hughes used mass persuasion techniques long before they became fashionable tools of the economic elite to protect its interests. Hughes was one of the first of the superrich to recognize how media could be manipulated to influence mass consciousness and, even more importantly, to protect the elite's profits and potential profits.

● ● ●

In the early thirties, at the age of twenty-one, Hughes began what was to become a highly successful flirtation with film production. His first movie, *Swell Hogan*, was so bad it was never distributed. Not one to give up, the young Hughes followed his initial failure with minor moneymakers such as *The Racket*, *Everybody's Acting*, and *Two Arabian Knights*.[9]

After these early movie-production experiments, Hughes was ready to apply the ingredients he thought would distinguish his work from any-thing that had ever been produced. These ingredients were the glorifica-tion of speed, violence, sex, and the pursuit of pleasure and power. These are the same ingredients on which American media, from film to televi-sion, has thrived ever since. Hughes tested these theories in *Hell's Angels*, a $4 million aerial epic that featured high-speed, real-to-life adventures of the flying aces of World War I.

Unlike most aerial movies of the time, which were filmed in movie studios using sky-blue backdrops and model airplanes, Hughes used the real thing. Hughes assembled, in effect, an air force of his own for the movie. He used some eighty World War I planes and a few hundred stunt flyers. Several of these top pilots lost their lives during filming as they tried to meet the exact standards set by the young producer.

These tragedies, it should be noted, weren't without publicity value. One critic labeled the film an artistic mess and then astutely observed that it had become one of the most exciting news stories that the cinema has ever evolved, and therein is the secret of its terrific appeal.

Therein is what made Hughes's early success as a producer and propagandist: he made his movie a news event. Not many producers have that knack anymore. The art of making a movie a news event was a lesson that would serve him well in the years to come. Hughes spent nearly as much time promoting *Hell's Angels* as he did directing and producing it. He flew many of the combat aerial scenes himself. Before long, the American public was reading almost daily news accounts of the dashing pilot-producer and his daring escapades.

In addition to the glorification of speed, violence, and the pursuit of pleasure and power that were inherent themes in the aerial combat scenes, Hughes added another ingredient to his epic film: sex. Hughes's leading lady for the film was a nineteen-year-old platinum blonde named Jean Harlow. Hughes personally discovered the shapely and sensuous young woman. He saw her as a highly marketable commodity that would conjure up the sexual fantasies of red-blooded American males and the envy of young women. The movie had fast action, violence, and sex—all the ingredients for box office success. It turned out to be one of the biggest box office hits of all time.

Film wasn't the only vehicle Hughes used to promote himself and his interests. Pretty soon the public was reading about Howard Hughes the playboy pilot. Buoyed by his promotional successes with *Hell's Angels*,

Hughes decided to apply similar promotional tactics to his airline company. If he learned nothing else from *Hell's Angels*, Hughes learned how to manufacture news for his own economic benefit. That lesson would serve him well for many decades.

The first thing Hughes did to make "news" in the airline business was to build the fastest plane in the world. In 1934 he assembled eighteen of the best young engineers and technicians in the country at a Glendale, California hangar and, pledging them to secrecy, began work on what he called "Hughes One," or "H-1." Construction of Hughes One was the beginning of one of the most powerful private companies ever assembled at the time. It was called Hughes Aircraft.

Construction of Hughes One also marked Hughes's first flirtation with the propaganda of silence, a technique he would later use extensively in his business operations. By shrouding the construction of H-1 in secrecy, Hughes was able to create an aura of suspense about what was happening behind closed doors in Glendale. This suspense served as an excellent publicity vehicle during construction and at the craft's unveiling. In order to exploit curiosity about what was happening behind closed doors in Glendale, Hughes had his press agents leak rumors about the secret aircraft. Media soon began to spread rumors about the mystery craft. The leak later became one of Hughes's favorite tactics.

The leak is known in propaganda circles as the "Saturday Night Special." Hughes was familiar with all the permutations of a leak, such as leaking negative material about yourself or your organization in order to blame the leak on someday else; the leak to stop or discredit a counter-disclosure; and the reverse buildup leak, whereby you leak good news about a competitor or enemy to embarrass them later.

In order to obtain maximum publicity for Hughes One and his fledgling aircraft company, Hughes finally unveiled his long-kept secret. He didn't simply show the craft to the world in a simple unveiling ceremony. Instead, he piloted the mystery ship on a seven-and-one-half-hour cross-country flight. Hughes set a speed record of 352 miles per hour, which stood until the introduction of jet aircraft. Hughes was a national hero.

Banner headlines proclaimed his record-breaking flight. Newspapers began running biographies of the exciting young multimillionaire. He had a ticker-tape parade in New York and was asked by Mayor LaGuardia to officiate at the National Aviation Show. In 1937 he received a national aviation award from President Roosevelt at the White House.

By 1939 Hughes had positioned himself so well in aviation circles that one of his planes was chosen to be named after the World's Fair. The aircraft was named *The New York World's Fair, 1939*. The name association between his plane and the World's Fair presented an ideal opportunity to promote his new aircraft company. Hughes later used the plane to break another flight record. This time he flew around the world. His ninety-one-hour flight was a headline story everywhere.

The Hughes name was now synonymous worldwide with the best and latest in aviation. Hughes had cleverly positioned himself as the producer of the fastest planes in the world, just as he had earlier positioned himself, through the manufacturing of news, as the producer of some of the most exciting movies ever to come out of Hollywood.

Hughes didn't fly aircraft at record-breaking speeds across country and around the world simply because of the inherent challenge of flying. Hughes, as always, had an underlying economic motive. He wanted to use the propaganda technique of association to connect his name with the best in aviation.

Hughes saw aviation as the industry of the future. The record-breaking flights were planned and carried out as promotions both for Hughes Aircraft and for a small rail and air service he bought in 1936. That small company was known as Transcontinental and Western Airlines (TWA). It grew to be one of the largest airlines in the world.

Lost in the publicity about the transcontinental flight was the fact that much of its success was attributable to a high-altitude engine that the US Air Corps had loaned Hughes. This "loan" was the first of many pacts to come between Hughes and the military.

After establishing himself as a leading producer with *Hell's Angels*, Hughes produced *Scarface*, a movie that the censorship board of the movie industry refused to grant a seal of approval because, the board claimed, it glorified crime and violence. Hughes immediately seized this censorship action as an opportunity to promote the movie. As director and producer of the film, Hughes was very much aware that the movie glorified crime and violence. Hughes had foreseen the likelihood of censorship and, using the propaganda techniques he had learned to use so well, began to blast the censorship board to obtain valuable news exposure for the film.

Hughes didn't argue the board's contention that the film glorified crime and violence. Instead, he employed the propaganda techniques of "suggestive diversion" and the "block and bridge" to divert attention from the contested issue, whether or not the film glorified crime and violence, to an issue of higher authority, freedom of expression. Hughes's tactic was to get people to dwell so much on the freedom of expression issue that the board's argument would be diffused. In short he redirected the focus.

By attaching suppression of the film to the "selfish and vicious" interests of the censors, Hughes cleverly diverted attention from his own selfish interest in using the film as a propaganda and economic tool. Hughes also diverted attention from his interests by identifying the censors with emotionally laden clichés such as "self-styled guardians of the public welfare."

Hughes was an expert at arousing popular passions by identifying emotional issues with clever phrases, slogans, and stereotypes. After Hughes milked the censorship action for all the promotion it was worth, the wealthy producer made a few minor cuts, and the film was released. It became a major box office success thanks to the pre-publicity Hughes had obtained.

● ● ●

As with *Hell's Angels* and his aircraft promotions, Hughes made a news event out of his entrepreneur involvements. *Scarface* did, as censors claimed, glorify crime and violence and made folk heroes out of racketeers.

By the time *Scarface* was in production, Hughes had met and befriended some of the top people in organized crime. One of the stars of the movie was George Raft, a tap dancer-actor who also happened to be friends with people who had top-level connections in organized crime. It was no accident that Hughes chose Raft for a key role in his movie. Raft was a friend of Meyer Lansky, one of the leaders of organized crime. Raft introduced Hughes to organized crime through an old friend, "Bugsy" Siegel.

Lansky had sent Siegel to Hollywood in search of legitimate investment opportunities for the fortune organized crime had made during the twenties and early thirties in bootlegging, extortion, labor racketeering, gambling, and other activities. Raft in later years took time off from Hollywood to become director of entertainment at one of Lansky's Cuban casinos. If you recall, I noted earlier that Carl Byoir handled travel promotion for the pre-Castro Cuban dictatorship. Mob-owned casinos were one of the biggest tourist attractions in Cuba.

Siegel advised Lansky that the film industry would be an excellent investment opportunity. Many movie houses, he told Lansky, had taken a terrible beating during the Depression and were desperate for money, no matter the source.

Lansky, who had been appointed by the Mafia's chairman of the board, Lucky Luciano, to modernize the Sicilian blood-oath family, liked what he heard from his lieutenant. Siegel was soon joined in Hollywood by other criminal luminaries, including John Roselli.

Roselli made headlines in the seventies when he told a Senate Intelligence Committee in 1975 that he and onetime Chicago Mafia chief Salvatore "Sam" Giancana were recruited by the CIA to assist in the assassination of Fidel Castro. Roselli also made headlines following his Senate testimony. His body was found floating in a 55-gallon oil drum off a North Miami Beach. Giancana was shot dead just before he was scheduled to testify before the Senate Committee.

During the thirties Hughes, Siegel, and Roselli spent a lot of time together. Privately they pursued their mutual interests; publicly they socialized with some of Hollywood's top stars, producers, and directors. It wasn't at all unusual to find Hughes and some of the top leaders of organized crime frequenting such exclusive addresses as the Friar Club, a social club for Hollywood's elite.

Scarface implanted the image of organized crime as a collection of mafiosi, cigar-smoking, foul-talking toughs. Films like *The Godfather* and *Bonnie and Clyde* have carried on this tradition of creating an aura of excitement and intrigue around organized crime.

The folk-hero image that media has portrayed of organized crime is a fantasy and, like many media myths, was designed to divert attention from the true nature of organized crime. Even to this day, American media stereotype organized crime figures as gruff and uncouth toughs decked out in pin-striped suits.

The reality is that many top organized crime figures are businessmen who dress, act, and look like most other businessmen. Today there aren't just businessmen in organized crime. There are a few women, but not many. Media, however, continue the mafioso stereotype in order to divert attention from organized crime's involvement in legitimate enterprises. Government, particularly our covert agencies, often looks the other way because they know that organized crime operates in secrecy and secrecy, as I show throughout this book, is paramount to the success of thought control and the obtaining and retention of economic power.

The phrase itself, "organized crime," conjures up Al Capone-type images of submachine gun-wielding mafioso toughs. With that stereotype etched in the mass mind, who would ever associate the churchgoing PTA member and family man next door with organized crime?

In order to insert the mafioso tough guy image into the group mind, several leaders of organized crime worked with Hughes on the script of *Scarface*. Organized crime also produced its own films to make sure the message got across. Roselli, for example, produced *Canyon City* and *He Walked by Night*, films that had the same successful ingredients as *Scarface*: high-powered action, violence, and plenty of sex.

Roselli fit the mafioso tough guy image and, for this reason, was allowed considerable visibility. Sometimes he let his street background get the best of him. He once was jailed for allegedly conspiring to extort over a million dollars from movie companies. This blunder angered his superiors because it needlessly called attention to organized crime's infiltration of Hollywood, an infiltration that had been so successful that underhanded operation was no longer necessary.

Counteracting this negative aspect of Roselli's arrest was a very positive development, that is, it continued to perpetrate the Mafioso stereotype. Up-front fall guys like Roselli divert attention from the kingpins of organized crime, most of whom appear much like any other successful businessperson. Interestingly, in nearly eighty years of trying (or giving the appearance of trying), the US government has never cracked the top leadership of organized crime. We can send people and machines into the far reaches of space, but we can't even make a dent in the activities of organized crime. Why?

• • •

The answer is that organized crime is so well-meshed into the socioeconomic system that cracking the top echelon institutions of organized crime would shake up the entire economic system.

Charles W. Wilson, president of General Motors, told Senator Richard Russell during Senate confirmation hearings on his appointment to be secretary of defense in 1953 that "what's good for the country is good for General Motors, and vice versa." Similarly it might also be said that what's good for big business is good for organized crime. And vice versa.

Organized crime's drive toward legitimacy culminated in the creation of a legitimate business association called the International Crime Syndicate or ICS. ICS is organized into numerous branches and subsidiaries. The Mafia is the best-known of these branches.

Movies like *Scarface* and *The Godfather* have created a mythical stereotype of the word "Mafia." In reality, Mafia refers more to a criminal philosophy than it does to an organizational structure. The Mafia doesn't represent all of organized crime. Members of the Italian-American branches don't even use the term "Mafia," but refer to "families." The Mafia was the dominant branch of organized crime during the twenties and early thirties, but today organized crime is a large, highly secretive international conglomerate, more so than an organization of mafioso toughs, as it is often portrayed in media.

Criminal activities have been elevated from beer running and murder for hire to Swiss bank accounts, European subsidiaries, and legitimate business operations ranging from gambling and banking to real estate and pension fund management. Al Capone-type mafiosi have been replaced by graduates of the best Ivy League business schools. The syndicate's criminal activities are so well-insulated by legitimate fronts that few ICS employees even know they are employed by organized crime. Secrecy has been the key to the success of organized crime.

Many people in white-collar and organized crime don't even consider themselves criminals because they aren't dealt with by society and law enforcement agencies in the same way as other criminals.

Edwin Sutherland has noted in *White Collar Crime* that "white collar criminals, owing to their class status, do not engage in intimate personal association with those who define themselves as criminals. Their consciences don't ordinarily bother them because they have the support of their associates in violation of the law."[10]

White-collar criminals also often have the support of the legal system in their violation of laws. The fact that no bankers or any of the major players in the banking scandals that nearly led to the collapse of our economy in 2008 have been charged is a perfect example of a long-standing hands-off approach to white-collar crime, particularly crimes involving the top echelons of the economic elite. There is an occasional sacrificial lamb, like Enron or Bernie Madoff, but overall, few white-collar crimes are pursued.

Members of the organized underworld and the respectable businessperson rarely meet publically, but their money meets often in foreign banks through secret accounts.

On February 9, 2015, the *Associated Press* noted that HSBC's Swiss private bank "hid millions of dollars for drug traffickers, arms dealers and celebrities as it helped wealthy people around the world dodge taxes, according to a report based on leaked documents that lifts the veil on the country's banking secrecy laws."

The leaked documents cover up to 2007, which was the period in which the treasuries of many countries were depleted by the financial crisis. HSBC was fined in 2012 by the United States for allowing criminals to use its branches for money laundering, but only got a slap on the wrist. There was no jail time for any of the executives involved.

Donald R. Cressey noted in *Theft of the Nation: The Structure and Operations of Organized Crime in America* that "many corporate violations are deliberate and organized."[11] Businessmen, he added, organize for the control of legislation, selection of administrators, and restrictions on enforcement of laws that may affect themselves. Organized crime has become an integral part of America's economic, social, cultural, and political life.

A top-level hands-off policy toward organized crime has prevented law enforcement agencies from doing little more than giving organized crime an occasional wrist slapping. Another thing organized crime and white-collar crime has in common is the name itself. White-collar crime is "organized" and a "crime." Thus, white-collar crime is organized crime, just by a different name. By World War II, organized crime wielded a major influence in determining the type of entertainment fed to the American public. It was for this reason, and not just economics, that organized crime went to so much trouble to gain a foothold in Hollywood. Economics were important, but not as important in the long run as the use of film as a tool for mass persuasion, primarily to create a mythological image of organized crime.

CHAPTER 16

Sex in Media and Operation Underworld

HOWARD HUGHES WAS THE WORLD's richest man for many years during the twentieth century. He was also the world's first pornographer. Hughes introduced sex to cinema, a legacy whose propaganda implications may have indirectly influenced your sexuality without you even knowing it.

Hughes was one of the first media moguls to recognize that the business of the filmmaker was to transfer the viewer from one world, his or her own, to another, the world created by film. This process, Hughes believed, would happen so completely that those undergoing the experience would accept it subliminally with little critical awareness. He knew that entertaining, fast-action media could subtly and indirectly implant themes, ideas, and concepts into the group mind that could influence people's attitudes and behavior, including what they ate and drank, what they wore, their recreational interests, their appearance, their political orientation, their sexuality, and much more.

One of the key underlying messages that Hughes pioneered was indirectly giving the American public approval to adopt a pursuit-of-pleasure ethic. Rarely are messages like this communicated directly. They're usually sent covertly, subtly, and indirectly, so that it appears that a particular propaganda message or theme is "just the ways things are." Few today object to a movie star or anyone else displaying substantial cleavage. Before

Hughes used sex to titillate the American public, overt displays of sexuality were taboo in most circles.

People didn't suddenly wake up one day and decide that it was OK to flaunt sex. Mass media manipulators gave us that approval. And Hughes was one of the first to do so. Hughes introduced the sexploitation film as a vehicle to show that sex could be fun and should not be just for procreation. Specifically, he introduced the female breast to the American public in the well-sculptured form of Jane Russell.

Hughes himself painstakingly created an uplifted bra for Ms. Russell that was designed for maximum visual effect, even though she was more than amply endowed au naturel. Ms. Russell paraded her assets before the public in *The Outlaw*, a film widely acclaimed as an artistic disaster. But Hughes was able to overcome its mediocrity by making it a major news event. Like *Scarface* had done earlier, *The Outlaw* caught the attention of censors. This was a positive development for Hughes, who was quickly learning how to be a good propagandist. Hughes believed that the press attention he would get from the censors' probe would attract public curiosity. He was absolutely correct.

The Outlaw became a box office hit, and it also became a landmark film to influence the sexual mores of the American moviegoer. Who, after all, could resist seeing a movie described by a Baltimore judge who banned it, as a picture in which "Miss Russell's breasts hung over the picture like a summer thunderstorm spread out over a landscape"?[1]

The fact there was little talent in the movie didn't bother Hughes in the least. What counted were his young starlet's full cleavage and the subtle suggestion she had rolled in the hay with Billy the Kid. Hughes inserted the pursuit-of-pleasure ethic in a cutline that he himself wrote for Ms. Russell's publicity photograph: *"How Would You Like To Tussle with Russell?"* Note: a cutline is the descriptive sentence at the bottom of a photograph.

As with his past productions, *The Outlaw* was filled with themes of action, power, and violence. The plot, if it could be called that, involved Billy the Kid meeting a girl named Rio (Ms. Russell), sexually engaging her, getting wounded in a gunfight, meeting up with a big-time gambler,

Doc Holliday, and then being nursed by Rio, who tenderly saves his life by snuggling up to him in the hay and keeping his body warm.

In *Scarface* Hughes successfully fought the censors over crime glorification and violence and used that censorship to promote the movie. Now, censors claimed, the maverick producer was exploiting and glorifying sex. As he had done so well with *Scarface*, Hughes deployed the block and bridge propaganda technique to divert attention and shift focus from the censors' claims by associating his cause (censorship) to an emotionally laden word, "sex." But he also added another propaganda technique: the bandwagon.

The bandwagon technique is just the opposite of the propaganda of silence, which Hughes later perfected when he became a recluse. The bandwagon basically uses the premise that "everyone else is doing it; you should, too." In this case everyone was curious about seeing what was so sexually explicit that it would get the censors' attention. The block and bridge technique, which I have given many examples of, allows you to shift focus from a primary issue to a secondary issues and, thus, make the secondary issue the one we focus on. In this case Hughes blocked the original issue (censorship) and redirected to the issue of sex, which became of more interest than censorship. To help implement these techniques, Hughes hired Russell Birdwell, press agent for the greatest box office hit of all time, *Gone with the Wind*.

In order to generate publicity for Hughes's production, Birdwell called newspapers, radio stations, police departments, parent-teacher associations, church groups, and even ministers. Birdwell would pretend to be an irate citizen "offended" by the new movie in town. The film, he would claim, was an affront to public morals. He urged the good people of the town to unite against the trashy movie and to publicly demonstrate their displeasure. Birdwell and Hughes even had secretaries pose as housewives and call real housewives to demand the picture be suppressed. He also had his press agents and staff call ministers and women's clubs to express shock about the "lewd picture." Birdwell wrote a news release that urged a mass protest at the Geary Theater in San Francisco. He then planted the release with a friendly newspaper editor, who ran the story without revealing its source.

Hughes and Birdwell weren't cutting their own throats by publicly encouraging public protest of the movie. They knew their reverse-psychology strategy would generate headlines and interest in the movie. By disclaiming the movie, they were, in effect, claiming it by seeking to generate interest in it. Everybody wanted to see the terrible movie that was such an affront to public morals.

Hughes's propagandists knew that the key was not to fight the censors, but to agree with them. They knew that they would get a lot more publicity and a much bigger turnout if they agreed that the movie was sexual and an affront to accepted morals and should be banned. This propaganda campaign resulted in the opposite of what Edward Bernays called the engineering of consent. This is a classic example of the engineering of dissent or deliberately stirring up public fervor against the movie in order to increase public curiosity.

With this kind of understanding of how to manipulate public opinion, it's no wonder that Hughes is the only movie producer ever to have parlayed three movies into front-page news events. He was able to get so much publicity for his films because he was a master propagandist more than he was a master filmmaker.

He was the first of the superrich to recognize the power of modern media to influence attitudes and behavior. Hughes's first three films and the first take on *Hell's Angels* were filmed before sound. The introduction of talking film turned a rather routine and not-too-enthusiastic filmmaker into a highly enthusiastic producer who saw great potential in the new medium. Hughes became one of the first of the economic elite to take the theories of social psychology, public opinion, and motivation research out of the laboratory and put them into practice to influence public attitudes.

● ● ●

Hughes's early interest in propaganda was primarily economic. Later it also became political. He saw propaganda as a necessary buffer to protect his secret involvements with groups like organized crime and the CIA. It was no accident that three of Hughes's biggest hits emphasized fast, high-speed action or that *Hell's Angels* glorified the wedding of man and machine, *Scarface* exploited the Mafioso stereotype, and *The Outlaw* introduced sex and the pursuit-of-pleasure ethic to the American public.

The Outlaw was released in 1943. One million people saw it in Los Angeles alone. It grossed $5 million, a huge amount at that time, although on the market for just a short period of time. While the American public was being turned-on by Ms. Russell's breasts, Hughes's friends in organized crime were busy getting established in Las Vegas, a small desert town that organized crime was helping make into the pleasure center of America.

Organized crime and Howard Hughes had major roles in creating the Las Vegas we know today. Remember Bugsy Siegel, organized crime's advance man in Hollywood who introduced Hughes to criminal luminaries?

During the time Siegel was busy pouring organized crime's funds into legitimate Hollywood investments, his friends decided he needed a few days of rest and relaxation. They took him on a weekend trip to a small, isolated desert town called Las Vegas. Siegel fell in love with the place. He had a dream. Siegel would turn the sleepy, isolated little town into a pleasure palace that would rival anything on earth: gambling, entertainment, and sex. And it would all be legal and legitimate. Siegel quickly called Lansky and Hughes and told them of his dream. They both agreed he had a pretty good idea.

Before long Siegel was overseeing construction of the Flamingo, the first of the large, all-purpose pleasure palaces to which Americans would soon come in great numbers to pursue their lustful yearnings for pleasure, yearnings that print media and films like *The Outlaw* would encourage by inserting the pursuit-of-pleasure ethic into the group mind. Hughes continued his movie career after World War II when he purchased RKO Studios in 1948.

While head of RKO, Hughes shocked Hollywood by his unorthodox operations. He never even entered his own studios, but kept an office at nearby Samuel Goldwyn studios. He ignored industry trends and hired and fired talented directors, producers, and actors. Some have speculated that Hughes's strange behavior at RKO was due to his search for a great blockbuster film or that it reflected his penchant for perfection. Actually Hughes had no interest at all in production notoriety. He was more concerned with learning all he could about the use of film as a propaganda vehicle.

In return for Hughes's help in Hollywood, organized crime came to Hughes's aid when he most needed it. During the mid-forties, Hughes was called to testify before a Senate committee that was investigating war profiteering. Committee chairman Ralph Brewster (R-Maine) claimed Hughes and his companies made exorbitant profits during the war through fat government contracts, which Brewster claimed Hughes had obtained by less-than-acceptable standards.

Brewster told of Hughes's close connections with top government and military officials during the thirties, when he was establishing Hughes Aircraft; he told of Hughes's penchant for wining and dining top military leaders during the war; he told of overcharging the government on projects like the Spruce Goose venture; and he told of Hughes's relationship with Carl Byoir, a propagandist, Brewster claimed, with questionable connections, including his representation of Nazi Germany during the thirties. Brewster also told of Hughes's role in arranging a marriage between President Franklin Roosevelt's son and a Hollywood actress.[2]

Hughes's airline, TWA, sought permission from the Civil Aeronautics Board during World War II for exclusive European routes. While TWA's route request was being considered, Hughes had his press agent, Johnny Meyer, set up an introductory meeting between Roosevelt's son, Elliott, and actress Faye Emerson. This meeting led, as Hughes had hoped, into a budding romance.

Hughes responded by providing the aircraft and the funds to fly the young couple to the Grand Canyon for their December 1944 wedding.[3]

Hughes had signed, sealed, and delivered a daughter-in-law to the president of the United States. President Roosevelt was a friend and confidant he had come to know from his record-breaking flights and from his close ties with military and political leaders. Carl Byoir was another shared connection.

If you will recall, Roosevelt called on Byoir for PR help in the thirties shortly after Byoir represented Nazi Germany. Byoir helped Roosevelt on numerous propaganda projects during the thirties, including the President's birthday balls, which became the March of Dimes.

One important point about the Byoir-Hughes-Roosevelt connection: both Hughes and Roosevelt used Byoir as a propaganda consultant. He was not their press agent. Hughes had numerous press agents, such as Robert Birdwell and Johnny Meyer. They were the visible, up-front representatives the press interfaced with. Byoir worked behind the scenes. He was too valuable as a ghost propagandist to handle the everyday and often mundane chores of a press agent. Byoir spent most of his career in the background. He didn't write major books on propaganda like his cohort Edward Bernays. Nor did he often write essays or give lectures. He maintained that the best propaganda is that which is seen the least. That's why he was in demand from presidents, Hitler, and the top echelons of corporate America.

Shortly after the Roosevelt marriage had been arranged, the Civil Aeronautics Board granted Hughes's request for exclusive European routes. This was a major blow to Pan American Airways, which was TWA's chief competitor for being the nation's overseas flag carrier. Hughes always understood that it helped to know people in high places.

Hughes's friend Frank Sinatra (they both slept with Ava Gardner) would use his high-level connections to also become a famous matchmaker. Sinatra arranged for Judy Campbell Exner to have simultaneous affairs with Sam Giancana and President John Kennedy. In other words, Sinatra arranged for a mobster and the president of the United States to sleep with the same woman.

She was Kennedy's mistress from 1960 to 1962. White House telephone logs uncovered during a midseventies Senate investigation into CIA-Mafia connections showed she had at least seventy contacts with the president's office. She admitted to the affair in her later years. In a February 29, 1988 article in *People* magazine, she tells of being a courier to the mob. She said Kennedy had her arrange more than 10 meetings with Giancana. She said she also shuttled messages between Kennedy and Giancana about US plans to kill Castro.

After Brewster told of Hughes's role in the Roosevelt marriage, Hughes decided he had had enough public ridicule. It was at this time that he called on Byoir for counsel. It was also at this time that he called on organized crime for help. A plumbers'-type investigative unit was created with instructions to dig up anything incriminating that could be used against this audacious senator who had the nerve to publicly ridicule the public image Hughes had worked so hard to develop.

Within a few weeks, organized crime's plumbers' unit uncovered some startling information about Senator Brewster. Hughes, ever sensitive to the propaganda value of delivering messages with maximum impact, decided to sit on his newfound information for several weeks.

Like a cat poised to pounce on its prey, Hughes sat back and absorbed more and more assaults from Brewster. Finally, on Byoir's advice, Hughes waited for the best possible time to zero in on Brewster for the kill. The good senator, Hughes proclaimed before a packed Senate chamber, had close ties with Pan Am, TWA's competitor for overseas routes. Hughes owned TWA. Brewster, Hughes revealed, had accepted numerous favors from Pan Am and, worse still, had secret ties with Pan Am's top executive, Juan Trippe.

In the final blow, Hughes produced proof that the pious senator, who for months had unleashed his holier-than-thou fury at Hughes's alleged war profiteering and his wining and dining of government and military officials, had faked affidavits against him. Suddenly it was Brewster, not Hughes, who was in trouble.

Hughes had timed his revelations so that they would carry such an emotional charge that Hughes's wartime profiteering and favor-granting would be forgotten in the excitement over Brewster's own corruption.

Hughes had adeptly covered his tracks, as he had done earlier with the censorship publicity on *Scarface* and *The Outlaw*, by diverting attention from his own activities to those of someone else. Hughes, thanks to counsel from Byoir and the undercover work of the plumbers' group from organized crime, had skillfully laundered his image by diverting attention from his own dirty clothes.

The pilot-playboy-producer-entrepreneur came out of the hearings as "Mr. Clean," an image that he later exploited in his alleged cleaning out of organized crime in Las Vegas and his alleged phobia for personal cleanliness as a recluse. Hughes also came out of the hearings determined to henceforth conduct his operations away from the public spotlight. For one thing, he didn't want a politician-puppeteer like Brewster to ever again have an opportunity to publicly ridicule him. Also, Hughes had become too powerful to subject himself to public scrutiny. His connections with government clandestine agencies and organized crime made public scrutiny extremely dangerous, both to Hughes's own interests and those of the growing covert government.

The Brewster hearings concluded in 1947, a time during which the military-industrial war machinery was being reassembled for the Cold War. It was also a time during which the CIA, the government's first permanent clandestine agency, was being formed. Although the CIA was new, government spying and clandestine activities were not something new. The Office of Secret Services (OSS) had been active for many years.

● ● ●

After the war a much larger and permanent covert agency was needed to fight the "Communist conspiracy" that threatened the assets of the economic elite and, just as importantly, to provide the justification for a postwar economic pump priming that the elite believed was needed to redirect the postwar economy.

Among those lobbying hard for an independent intelligence group to replace OSS were brothers Allen and John Foster Dulles, and Governor Thomas Dewey of New York. These three men had met during a cooperative effort between government and organized crime in the early forties known as "Operation Underworld."[4]

By the late 1930s and early forties, organized crime had found its way into respectable banking, investment, media, real estate, and labor circles as part of its cleanup campaign and also because of the need to invest large sums of money made from illegal activities like bootlegging, gambling, drugs, extortion, and labor racketeering. Legitimate enterprises were a vehicle for cleaning or laundering funds from illegal activities.

On the West Coast, Meyer Lanksy and Bugsy Siegel had bought their way into Hollywood and had begun to lay the groundwork for the development of Las Vegas as the nation's pleasure center.

Lanksy was put in charge of the effort to legitimize organized crime in 1936 when board chairman Lucky Luciano was given a prison sentence. Thanks to Lansky organized crime soon had a strong influence on both West and East Coast unions. Organized crime's influence was particularly strong in the dockworkers' unions.

When suspected Nazi saboteurs burned and sank the *Normandy*, an ocean liner that was being converted into a troopship in its Manhattan birth in the late thirties, naval intelligence/OSS offered Lansky and his men a deal. Luciano would be freed from prison if Lansky's men would patrol the docks. Lansky, with favorable input from Hughes, agreed to the government's terms. This alliance between the government and organized crime was appropriately called Operation Underworld.[5]

Besides patrolling the docks, the syndicate agreed to provide assistance to Allied troops when they landed in Sicily. As part of this agreement, New York Governor Thomas Dewey agreed to a request from OSS official Allen Dulles to transfer Luciano to a "gentleman's prison" and, later, to free him. Not a bad deal since Luciano was given a fifty-year sentence.

The significance of Operation Underworld should not be diminished. It laid the foundation for the merging of interests among the CIA and organized crime, leading industrialists, and clandestine agencies of government. All parties knew the alliance would be difficult to uncover (and it took many years to do so) because organized crime knew how to operate in secret and they also had learned the propaganda techniques of diversion and plausible deniability.

Although Operation Underworld can be seen as the first major government-organized crime alliance, it wasn't the first time officialdom had cooperated with organized crime. Numerous top government officials, for example, looked the other way during organized crime's prohibition campaign. Government also took a hands-off policy toward organized crime's forays into legitimate business operations, its Hollywood influence, and its worldwide control of drug traffic.

• • •

The CIA's primary function, as far as Hughes and others in the economic elite were concerned, was to serve as a patron and protector of the US multinational corporations that were being established after the war to serve the burgeoning defense and technology industries. One member of this multinational club was the International Crime Syndicate, which, as I noted earlier, was the legitimate business front for organized crime.

Luciano was chairman of the board and ran the firm's international operations from Sicily, where he had moved following his early release by Governor Dewey from a fifty-year prison sentence. Lansky served as ICS president. He was in charge of domestic operations. Besides clandestine operations for Hughes and other industrialists and special jobs for their CIA friends, the good ol' boys of ICS were involved in lucrative profit centers such as drugs, extortion, and murder for hire.[6]

ICS was also heavily involved in so-called legitimate businesses through respectable fronts in banking, real estate, investments (especially labor pension plans), tourism, and gambling. ICS was one of the world's wealthiest enterprises by the midfifties, although there was no way to determine its true value. Like many of Hughes's enterprises, ICS was a capitalist's dream come true. No one at ICS had to worry about letting bids for contracts, paying taxes, or answering regulators like the Securities and Exchange Commission. ISC, in the true spirit of laissez-faire capitalism, had complete freedom to generate profit as it saw fit, legal or nonlegal.

The CIA was officially established in 1947 much to the delight of Hughes and organized crime's new corporation, ICS. The Dulles brothers obtained top positions in the new intelligence community, and Hughes, owner of the nation's largest private corporation, soon began staffing his firm with people from covert agencies. Before long, Hughes Aircraft was jokingly known among covert operatives as the nation's "spook shack."[7]

From 1968 to 1975, Hughes Aircraft had thirty-two CIA contracts, worth an estimated $6.6 billion. Most of these contracts were awarded secretly, without competitive bidding, and required no public accountability. As this story unravels, we begin to see why Hughes cherished secrecy so much. Hughes Aircraft was an important part of the economic elite's power base.

For many years the nation's defense and space and communications industries largely depended on Hughes, who supplied the nation with products such as the Phoenix missile, the Hellfire missile, helicopters for use in jungle warfare in Vietnam, and police equipment, radar equipment, the moon lander, earth communications satellites, and numerous electronic intelligence-gathering devices.

Not only did the Hughes corporation have a lot of spooks on its payrolls; it also supplied clandestine agencies with numerous technology and defense products. Hughes was one of the first to recognize the future of electronic warfare. Vietnam and the Middle East wars have served as testing laboratories for this new and highly profitable form of warfare. Hughes believed strongly in electronic weaponry as the edge that would help the United States maintain military superiority at a time in which just about every major country had begun to develop nuclear capabilities.

The same year that the CIA was formed, ICS was awarded a lucrative contract. Under terms of the highly secret deal, ICS would provide the men for the CIA (which would provide the funds and the weaponry) to prevent a shutdown of the French port of Marseilles by leftist-led strikers. ICS was the CIA's third-party front. This propaganda technique basically allows someone else to do your dirty work. It also gives you plausible deniability. Although the French government had not requested US assistance in this

1947 internal matter, the entire world had become the CIA's playground. The CIA protected its multinational companies anywhere at any time.

The port of Marseilles, France, for years had been the shipping port for heroin shipments to the United States. Most of the heroin had been manufactured by the notorious Corsican gang. This heroin network became known as the "French Connection." The CIA provided protection to the Corsican drug dealers in exchange for organized crime working to halt French leftists from gaining control of the port. In short, the CIA stood down and allowed heroin to continue to flood into the United States. Standing down (or looking the other way), if you will recall, was also used in allowing cocaine to be shipped into the United States during the Contra scandal of the seventies.

In the French operation, big business was concerned that a prolonged strike would seriously affect American shipping interests. Organized crime was concerned that a prolonged work stoppage would interfere with its heroin traffic across the high seas.[8]

ICS didn't like anything or anyone to interfere with its operations. A few dockside murders were "arranged" to instill fear among the strikers. The CIA-ICS violence (the engineering of dissent) worked. The strikers went back to their jobs, and the heroin traffic continued. The astute reader will note that the operation in France was similar to Operation Underworld on the docks of Manhattan.

Plutocratic oligarchs and pseudo, pretend patriots like Hughes are excellent covers for the clandestine activities of government and organized crime, just as government covert agencies and organized crime are good covers for the economic power elite. Hughes's sensitive connections with organized crime and covert operatives made it almost mandatory that he operate in as close to total secrecy as possible.

Publicity kick-started Hughes's career. Secrecy was needed to keep him atop his throne as the world's richest man. Hughes's covert connections were of particular importance. These connections helped him cut red tape, gave him protection from other agencies, helped provide economic intelligence, and helped cover the economics of special projects like the Glomar

Explorer. Government clandestine agencies were also a good buffer against political instability.

Members of the economic power elite like Hughes know that government covert operatives can be counted on to be around when needed. They don't change office every two to four years as do many elected representatives, plus they're sworn to secrecy. The economic elite can't afford to regroup with every change of political administration or shift in ideology. That's why the elite don't care whether someone is liberal or conservative, Democrat or Republican.

The protection and growth of the elite's assets requires not only stability but, most importantly, secrecy. The biggest threat to secrecy is transparency. The elite fear transparency more than anything. They're very much aware that a truly open and democratic society would pose a great threat to their status and assets. The almost-manic obsession with secrecy to protect their financial interests has led the plutocrats and their agents to develop, deploy, and stockpile the world's largest arsenal of weapons of mass mind destruction: covert propaganda.

We, the people, need to expose and disarm these weapons before they destroy our democracy—if they haven't already done so.

CHAPTER 17

Propaganda Techniques

THROUGHOUT THE BOOK I'VE GIVEN numerous examples of propaganda techniques. This chapter will go into more detail on the ones I've discussed, plus I will introduce some new ones. Awareness of the numerous techniques available to propagandists will help you recognize at least some of the tools they've developed to manipulate your thoughts and actions and, hopefully, will give you the ability to fight propaganda's onslaught on your senses, although no matter how much knowledge we have of technique, recognizing propaganda can be a daunting task if it's covert and launched by invisible and highly trained propagandists. Here are some examples of propaganda techniques:

Appeal to Authority is a propaganda technique in which people of authority are used as sources to give credibility to positions or potential courses of action.

Association connects an idea, belief, cause, or action to a credible idea, belief, cause, or action. An example is a baseball team associating its sports franchise with love of country and patriotism by singing "God Bless America" during the seventh-inning stretch of a baseball game. A subset of association is "false association." False association connects genuine needs and desires, such as concern for the traditional values of home, marriage, and family, with false or irreverent ends, such as "the sharp tongues of revolutionary heat," as Attorney General Palmer wrote in a *Fortune* magazine article to describe the Communist menace (the article was ghostwritten by Carl Byoir).

The Bandwagon is a technique that basically uses the premise that everyone else is doing it, and so should you. This can either be an open, white type of propaganda, or it can be done behind the scenes, which is gray or black covert propaganda.

For example, after being burned during the Depression, small investors fled the stock market and didn't come back for decades. To get them back, the Securities Industry Association, Business Roundtable, and New York Stock Exchange developed a national grassroots campaign during the seventies to get small investors to return to the market. I worked on some of these campaigns. How did we lure the investor back? We blitzed local media with so-called research showing that a large percentage of people in a particular city were investing in stocks. After months and years of hearing and reading that everyone was jumping into stocks, the small investor returned. By the eighties, everyone was jumping into stocks. My own firm spent two years on a propaganda campaign to convince Americans to use fax and e-mail. My client was the International Fax and E-mail Association. The message was simply that everyone else is doing it; you should, too.

Black and White Fallacy is a way to manipulate "either-or" dualisms. This type of propaganda gives us an either-or choice, but the desired message is positioned as the better choice. For example, Bush proclaimed prior to the invasion of Iraq: "You are either for us or against us."

Block and Bridge is a technique that allows you to shift focus from a primary issue to a secondary issue. You block the key issue by bridging or shifting interest to the secondary issue so it appears to be the primary issue. This type of misdirection is difficult to spot, but highly effective. Block and bridge is often used with the bandwagon technique.

For example, Howard Hughes's movie *The Outlaw* caught the attention of the movie industry censor board because, the board claimed, it glorified sex (Jane Russell's cleavage). Rather than fight the censors' claim, Hughes's propagandists cleverly agreed with the censors that it should be banned. They even organized protests against the movie because "it was an affront to public morals." They redirected the issue so that the problem (censorship) was redirected to the issue of sex, which became of more interest than censorship. The redirection action was a diversion from censorship to sex. It also brought into play another propaganda technique called "the third-party front." The front in this case was the protestors that Hughes organized to call attention to the sexuality of the movie. Hughes's propagandists manipulated the issue so that the public wanted to see what the big fuss was over and what was so sexually explicit that it caught the censors' attention. The Hughes block and bridge strategy worked. The movie was not censored and became one of the biggest box office attractions in history.

Circuit Breaker is a technique similar to the block and bridge. It involves diverting attention from a primary source by revealing information or pulling the plug on a secondary and less sensitive source. This strategy was used throughout the Watergate hearings when Senator Sam Erwin would slam his hammer repeatedly to the desk every time the question of presidential accountability was raised. Carl Byoir also used this technique of diverting attention from top-level accountability when he provided counsel to Hughes when Hughes was the subject of congressional hearings during the forties for his war profiteering and collusion with various government agencies.

Demonization is a technique that makes a political enemy or an opposing issue or philosophy appear evil, repulsive, and even subhuman (e.g., the Vietnam War terms "gooks" and "slant eyes" for Viet Cong). Former FBI chief Edgar Hoover worked with the CIA, various national security agencies, and even the Mafia to demonize and discredit Martin Luther King. King was considered by many, including Presidents Kennedy and Johnson, as a dangerous troublemaker thanks to this campaign. The Red Scare campaign I have discussed throughout the book is one of the best examples of demonization in our history. Even death was considered better than being a Communist. "Better dead than red" was a common slogan. Pagans have been demonized as devil worshipers by various religions even though only a small percentage of pagans claim any allegiance to a so-called devil.

Disinformation is intentionally false or inaccurate information that is spread deliberately to convince someone of an untruth. The Bush administration claiming Iraq had weapons of mass destruction in order to justify an American invasion was disinformation. A lot of intelligent people, including numerous leftists, fell for the Bush propaganda and supported the invasion of Iraq. Another example is Johnson's lies about the Gulf of Tonkin. George W's father, H. W. Bush, also used disinformation to remove Saddam from power and to garner support for invading Iraq during Desert Storm. He also used it in the dead babies' hoax. (Disinformation should not be confused with misinformation, which is information that is unintentionally false.)

Diversion is one of the most common propaganda techniques and is used to divert attention from one issue to another, often with the intent to hide information. For example, all of the attention in 2013 and 2014 on spying by the National Security Agency diverted attention from routine spying by seventeen other clandestine government agencies.

A subset of diversion is suggestive diversion. Suggestive diversion transfers emotions aroused by one circumstance to another. Hughes produced *Scarface*, a movie that the censorship board of the movie industry refused to grant a seal of approval because, the board claimed, it glorified crime and violence. Hughes diverted attention from the contested issue, whether or not the film glorified crime and violence, to an issue of higher authority: freedom of expression.

Hughes's tactic was to get people to dwell so much on the freedom of expression issue that the board's argument would be diffused. It worked by employing a slightly different twist to the block and bridge that Hughes's propagandists used in the movie *The Outlaw*. Diversion is a common propaganda technique. I have numerous examples throughout the book. It's also similar to the block and bridge.

Embedded Messaging involves inserting a message or issue deep within a written or verbal communication so that the audience will tend to downplay its importance, although it is often the most important message.

Emotionally Laden Words is the use of highly charged, emotional words to discredit a person, group, issue, statement, or belief. Conservatives calling a liberal a Socialist or a Communist is a simple example. Calling someone a terrorist is another.

The Engineering of Consent is probably the most popular of all propaganda techniques. It was first formulated by pioneer propagandist Edward Bernays. I have given numerous examples. Basically this propaganda technique leads to self-censorship. It also sets boundaries of behavior or lines in the sand we learn not to cross. Subsets of this technique are conformity propaganda, conditioning propaganda, and consensus propaganda.

The Engineering of Dissent often involves deploying provocateurs to join a group, gain confidence from its members, and then stir up or directly trigger violent acts and use the violence itself as a vehicle to discredit, demonize, or destroy groups, individuals, or ideologies by blaming the violence on the party to be discredited

The False-Flag is a manufactured "incident" designed to arouse passions and to stimulate a desired response. It's a form of engineering of dissent. False-flag is sometimes applied to events that governments are aware of and could stop, but choose to let happen anyway (called "standing down"). The CIA and Italian intelligence were accused in Operation Gladio of arranging or letting happen the bombing of women and children and blaming it on Communists in order to demonize and discredit them in an election in which socialists were favored to win. False-flag terrorism is what Geraint Hughes uses to refer to acts carried out by military or security force personnel and then blamed on terrorists.[1]

Fragmentation is a euphemism for "divide and conquer." Early twentieth-century pioneer industrial psychologist Frederick Taylor told business owners they could best gain control over the workforce by dividing worker against worker through job specialization. This division of labor, he believed, would do away with demands for labor collectivization. Mass fragmentation has been used to encourage specialization because motivational researchers have shown that specialists are usually so focused on their expertise that they can't see the forest for the trees. They don't have time to think outside of their specialties, which is why some of the most educated and intelligent people are often the easiest to manipulate.

I noted earlier that the economic power elite typically is not concerned with Republican vs. Democrat or liberal vs. conservative battles, yet these ideological skirmishes are encouraged because of the divide-and-conquer effect that results from fragmentation.

Propaganda techniques like fragmentation, neutralization, and obfuscation basically serve to co-opt us and to keep us under control. These techniques can often be unleashed on us without the propagandists having to do much of anything. They can just sit back and let high-speed media and/or drugs do their dirty work for them.

Glittering Generalities are words designed to arouse emotions and to stimulate us to accept an idea without probing beneath the surface. These words often appeal to our strong convictions, but aren't really related to these beliefs. Adolf Hitler would use words in his speeches that were linked to ideas like freedom, democracy, and pride in country. He did this to stimulate a sense of nationalism. The use of this technique helped Hitler garner strong support.

The Half-Trust technique involves combining a deceptive statement with statements that have some element of truth. The statement might be partly or totally true, or it may utilize some deceptive element, especially if the intent is to deceive, evade blame, or misrepresent the truth.

Identification is similar to association, but identification usually involves connecting something to a respected person or deity (such as God) rather than a concept or product. President Obama saying "God Bless America" as he leaves the podium after a major speech is an example of connecting America with the ultimate feel-good authority, God.

A subset of identification is "upward identification." This propaganda technique encourages envy rather than resentment. Envy is a safe, nondisruptive way to channel socioeconomic and class frustrations. Celebrities and sports figures, with their grossly inflated incomes, have been particularly effective in keeping the average person's eyes turned upward, to make him or her feel there's a chance, if not for him or her, for his or her children to make it big.

Indirect Lobbying is a grassroots, bottom-up strategy in which those being lobbied usually don't know that they're being used to influence those in leadership positions. This technique, like most good propaganda, appeals to people's emotions and their innermost needs and desires more than appealing to their rational faculties. Its intent is to bypass officialdom. Hitler was particularly impressed with the CPI's success in bypassing officialdom and appealing directly to the people. This technique is, in effect, elitist. It takes advantage of what the elitist propagandist often considers the "uneducated masses."

Intentional Vagueness uses generalities that are intentionally vague so that the target audience can make their own assessments. The intention is to encourage the target audience to accept a message without digging beneath the surface or looking at all sides of an issue.

Layering involves providing numerous layers of cover (plausible deniability) so that it becomes very difficult to detect the original source. The babies on the hospital floor hoax I described in an earlier chapter is a good example.

Misdirection typically involves planting a story fairly deeply so journalists or investigators will have to dig to find it, but once they do, the writer usually feels he or she has a big scoop, but they have no way of knowing it was planted to misdirect investigative reporters.

Neutralization propaganda involves the use of drugs or other stimulants to, in effect, anesthetize people or dull their senses so they will not be motivated to take aggressive or direct action. People, for example, who are hooked on certain narcotics aren't likely to participate in socioeconomic unrest because all they can think about is obtaining and using drugs to feed their addiction. Keeping large numbers of poor people and people of color hooked on drugs or in prison has become a way to pacify and co-opt potential dissent (see prior reference to the New Jim Crow in chapter 10). The overuse of high-speed media can also numb the senses, limit critical thinking, and serve to keep people in the status quo sandbox.

Obfuscation is deliberately making an issue complex to hide the propagandist's true intentions. Bankers, Wall Street, and corporate lawyers used this technique during and after the 2007–08 banking crisis to make it very difficult for the press, the average person, and prosecutors to know what was going on. Complexity is a great way to hide intent. Obfuscation propaganda overwhelms our capacity for attention and often our capabilities for resistance.

Obfuscation has a numbing effect on our senses and can be used as a subset of neutralization propaganda. Motivational researchers learned long ago that the human brain can only deal with a limited amount of stimulus and information. Overload us, and we have a tendency to shut down and to say, in effect, "I don't want to deal with that anymore." We simply tune out. It's much easier to unleash covert propaganda when people are not tuned in. For example, we've been involved in so many Middle East skirmishes that research has shown that the vast majority of Americans don't keep up with war news. Propagandists know that one of the best forms of censorship is self-censorship. They know that if media keep bombarding us with information and high-speed stimuli, our natural reaction will be to tune out.

Plausible Deniability typically allows top officials to accomplish a goal or mission in a way that their involvement is difficult to trace. The goal is for the officials to be able to convincingly claim they had nothing to do with an action or issue. Top officials often hide behind this technique to separate themselves from lower level operatives who carry out the actions. This technique makes it very difficult to pin blame on the actual perpetuator, particularly when combined with layering.

Polar Words are either-or, us vs. them dualities or opposites often used to separate one way of thinking from another or one group from another. Polar words have opposite meanings. Good and bad are polar words.

Propaganda of Silence is a technique that is about as clandestine as it gets because its entire purpose is to keep an idea, action, or person out of public view so that everything about that concept or person is hidden from scrutiny. This gives propagandists a free hand to do just about anything they want, legal or non-legal. One of the key benefits is that the propagandist can mold a desired image so we have no idea if that image is accurate or not.

A good example of this technique is the propaganda of silence program we conducted for Howard Hughes, once the richest person in the world. For many years Hughes was one of the most visible people in the world. He sought and got front-page news coverage for many of his myriad activities, whether breaking speed records in aircraft, producing movies, or romancing many of the leading ladies of Hollywood. After World War II, Hughes determined he could garner more profits and maintain more power by operating in secrecy. Everything the press and public knew about Hughes was the result of spin by his spin doctors. He was a very powerful force in this country, but few knew about his activities because he was a ghost. How do you finger a ghost?

The Red Herring technique involves producing compelling or intriguing information or data that is not relevant to the subject being considered and then using that irrelevant information or data to validate the primary subject or issue you are trying to communicate. In other words, the red herring is the hook to catch the big fish. In the seventies I worked on a campaign to attract small investors back into the stock market.

The campaign was a red herring. The real reason for the propaganda campaign on behalf of the New York Stock Exchange was to garner public support for legislation that would provide more liberal tax treatment of capital gains, dividend income, and a central market system. This would benefit the economic elite, but not most small investors. On July 19, 1976, for example, we distributed a press announcement in Seattle that noted in the first paragraph: "Some 244,000 stockholders in the Seattle area are seen having a major stake in the restructuring of the nation's securities markets now in progress in the U.S. Congress and the Securities and Exchange Commissions."

This lead paragraph was designed to get the attention of Seattle-area editors since it specified the number of investors in the Seattle area and quoted a well-respected source, the New York Stock Exchange. The real purpose of the news announcement was found a few paragraphs later, in which it was noted that pending tax legislation "seeks to provide more liberal tax treatment of capital gains."

Garnering public support for changing capital gains taxes was the real reason for the press release. The number of investors in Seattle was irrelevant, but it was the bait to get the editor's attention. The same formula was used in cities throughout the country. In fact, the same press release was used. They just changed the number of individual investors in each city. Not one journalist (out of hundreds I talked to and met with) asked how the numbers were obtained.

An internal Byoir memo from the account executive on the New York Stock Exchange account noted, "It will not do us or the New York Stock Exchange any good whatsoever if the newspapers just run the localized leads (info about local investors) and drop the GUTS of the stories (more liberalized capital gains). The localized leads are intended only as a means of helping you get the attention and interest of the writers and editors." The red herring was the number of investors in each city. That was just the hook to catch the big fish, which was a reduction in capital gains taxes.

Sanitization allows you to put a positive spin on something by redirecting the focus. It's often used to rewrite past events to the benefit of the propagandist's client. An example is the Vietnam War Commemoration Project. It was a $65 million, thirteen-year propaganda project to clean up the image of the Vietnam War in the minds of Americans. Some say it was an attempt to rewrite history.[2]

President Obama officially launched the project on Memorial Day 2012 with a speech at the Vietnam Wall in Washington. The project was established by the National Defense Authorization Act for Fiscal Year 2008. It budgeted $5 million a year for the next eleven years. It was simply an attempt to put a better spin on the Vietnam War. If President Obama's launching language was any indication, the purpose of the Vietnam War commemoration was to create a malleable and supportive populace for future military operations, especially under the new doctrine of focused killing with drones and special-ops units now being established around the world.

Phase one of the commemoration project went through 2014 and would "focus on recruiting support and participation nationwide." There were international, national, regional, state, and local events planned, but the main focus was on the hometown level, where the personal recognitions and thanks were most impactful.

I won't go into phase two and phase three, but they last until 2025. Will our children and grandchildren get the true version of what happened in Vietnam, or will they get a sanitized version after twelve years of redefining what happened?

The Saturday Night Special involves leaking negative material about yourself, an organization, or an issue in order to attract attention. It can also be used to discredit an opponent or idea or to stop or discredit a counter-disclosure. Howard Hughes was familiar with all the permutations of a leak, such as leaking negative material about one of his movie productions in order to attract attention to the film so everyone would want to see what the fuss was about. There is also the reverse buildup leak, whereby you leak good news about a competitor or enemy to embarrass the competitor later.

The Smokescreen technique makes one cause, philosophy, or event appear to be the primary focus or interest, when in truth it is used to cover up the secondary purpose, which is really the key purpose or goal. For example, the anti-Communist Red Scare of the fifties was a smokescreen to cover up the primary goal of the economic elite (to grow and protect profits). Iran's oil was the central focus of the CIA-led coup that overthrew President Mosaddegh of Iran in 1953, but much of the discussion at the time linked it to the Cold War (the smokescreen). As I've noted several times, President Carter's national security adviser admitted that we deliberately stirred up radical Islam in Soviet Muslim countries and that was a major factor in defeating the Soviet Union in the Cold War.

We justified our actions by saying we were fighting communism, but that was just a smokescreen for our primary goals of controlling access to oil, empire building, and growing profits for the economic elite. The block and bridge technique is similar to the smokescreen in that you redirect or block one issue (our lust for oil and world economic dominance) and redirect attention to another, such as the fight against communism.

Stacking the Cards is a technique in which you use facts or ideas selectively to stack the cards in favor of or in opposition to a position or idea.

The Stereotype is one of the most widely used propaganda techniques. The word was coined by one of the leading journalists and political thinkers of his time, Walter Lippmann, whom I have quoted several times in the book. Lippmann defined stereotype as a "distorted picture or image in a person's mind, not based on personal experience, but derived culturally." In *Public Opinion* (1922) he pointed out that "the only feeling that anyone can have about an event he does not experience is the feeling aroused by his mental image of that event." Stereotypes can become deeply embedded in individuals and public opinion and are often passed down from generation to generation. These deeply ingrained stereotypes are often very resistant to scrutiny or change.

The Straw-Man technique attempts to redirect your target audience from one position or belief to another by using what are called "straw-man arguments." The straw-man technique is often used with other techniques, like the block and bridge and disinformation. It employs crafty evasions and multilayered cover stories so potentially important facts can slip into the netherworld of confusion and deniability.

It basically involves shifting focus or distracting us. An example of the straw-man technique is President Nixon's Checkers speech in 1952 while he was campaigning for vice president. A revelation that he had diverted $18,000 in campaign funds for his personal use just about derailed his campaign until he got on national television and diffused the charge by shifting focus to a cute little puppy his young daughter received as a gift from a supporter. Nixon said regardless of what anyone said about accepting gifts, his family was going to keep the dog, which they named Checkers. Nixon used the straw-man technique to shift the focus to a heartwarming story that distracted the public from the original issue. Nixon received an outpouring of public support and the Republican Party won the election by a large margin.

The Third-Party Front involves having an unidentified third party work behind the scenes to spread your message. A combination of disinformation, propaganda of silence, and the third-party front is nearly impossible to detect. The media rarely uncover these techniques because this kind of propaganda is designed to be undetectable.

Virtue Words are words in the value system of the target audience that tend to produce a positive image when attached to a person or issue. "Peace," "happiness," "democracy," "security," "wise leadership," "freedom," "truth," etc. are virtue words. These are often used with emotionally laden words.

As you can see from this small sample of techniques, mass manipulators have a lot of weapons in their arsenal. Hopefully the above examples will help you level the playing field somewhat.

CHAPTER 18

Conclusion

I HAVE GIVEN NUMEROUS EXAMPLES throughout this book of some 50 propaganda techniques, including a summary in the previous chapter of the key ways propagandists influence our attitudes and behavior. Because many of these techniques are shrouded in secrecy and are designed not to be detected, all of us face an uphill battle in trying to at least minimize covert mass mind manipulation. However, there are a few things you can do besides being aware of various propaganda techniques.

Anytime you read, hear, or see something in mass media, apply the acronym "SAM" to the information. "S" stands for "source" or "sources." "A" stands for "agenda" or "agendas." "M" stands for "money trail." Other suggestions include to keep in mind that things aren't always as they appear, to think clearly and critically so others won't think for you, and to stay away as much as possible from SOAP (sensory overload, obfuscation, awareness diversion, and pursuit of pleasure).

Knowledge of propaganda techniques and applying these suggestions will help alert you to mass mind manipulation. Unfortunately, since the molding of our minds often involves secrecy and/or deception, the problem will likely not be solved without a lot more transparency throughout government and society. For those who believe in true freedom and democracy, transparency isn't a problem. For those who feel they need secrecy to control us and to grow and protect profits and empire, transparency is the ultimate enemy.

Covert propagandists use us as their clay. They want us soft and malleable so they can shape and mold us into a controllable mass. Let's harden up so we'll be more difficult to shape. And most importantly, let's demand more transparency. True freedom and democracy depend on it.

Acknowledgments

First and foremost, I would like to thank my sons, Greg and Bret, and my wife and partner, Gloria, for their unwavering support on this project. I'm also deeply grateful to Gloria for her dedication and devotion to me, our family, and those who suffer from disabilities. She is truly a selfless, caring person, someone who paints sunlight across the canvas of lives clouded by suffering.

I would also like to thank my ten or so friends who gather once a week for a several-hour discussion of current events, religion, philosophy, and numerous other subjects. I thank them for listening to my ramblings about propaganda. Hopefully they made it through this book and, if so, have a much better idea of what I've been talking so much about.

Finally I would like to thank my past employers at four newspapers, Computer Land Corp., Arizona State University, the University of Louisville, and Carl Byoir & Associates for providing me with a wealth of experience that enabled me to write this book. I'm also grateful to the hundred-plus clients I have represented in my own public relations/propaganda business.

I've been fortunate to have been exposed to a lot of things that are hidden from most people. This book has been a chance to share with you why I often say, "Things aren't always as they appear."

Chapter 1   Whose Thoughts Are They?

1. See Robert Mann, *A Grand Delusion, America's Descent Into Vietnam* (New York, Basic Books, June 2002, Chapter One). Also see a review of the book at NY Times.com/books/first/m/mann-delusion.Vandenberg, according to Mann, urged Truman to present the threat of the Soviet Union in the strongest terms. Truman obliged and warned a joint session of Congress that the world was "teetering toward Communist domination."

2. For information of the joint meeting to explore coordination of mind control research, see "Final Report of the Senate Select Committee to Study Governmental Operations with Respect to Intelligence Activities," Book I, p. 50. Also see CIA memorandum of June 26, 1953, describing the special meeting of June 1, 1951, "Matters Relating to CIA Project BLUEBIRD." Also see "Meeting with IAQ representatives of Project BLUEBIRD," July 25, 1951.

3. For more on the secret memo sent to President Eisenhower, see "Report on the Covert Activities of the Central Intelligence Agency." The memo was prepared for Eisenhower by the CIA Special Study Group and sent to the president on September 30, 1954.

4. See the February 20 *Washington's Blog* (washingtonsblog.com) for an overview of our numerous wars. There is also a link to the number of military bases and sites. See Susan Page, *USA Today*, October 6, 2014, for information on the "endless wars."

5. See Hugh Wilford, *The Mighty Wurlitzer: How the CIA Played America* (Harvard University Press, May 2009). For more information on

Operation Mockingbird, see the 1975 "Final Report of the Senate Select Committee to Study Governmental Operations with Respect to Intelligence Activities". Also see Michael Hasty, "Secret Admirers: The Bushes and the Washington Post" (*Online Journal*, February 5, 2004).

6. See Ernest T. Imparato, *General MacArthur's Speeches and Reports* (New York: Turner Publishing Company, 2000) p. 230. Also see William Manchester, *American Caesar, Douglas MacArthur* (New York, Little Brown, 1978), p. 692.

7. See Edward Bernays, *Propaganda* (1928) p. 1 for Bernays's description of how propaganda molds our minds. He also said, "Propaganda is the executive arm of the invisible government."

8. Supreme Court Justice Felix Frankfurter made this statement in 1952. See georgewashington2blogspot.com. Also see James Perloff, *The Shadows of Power: The Council on Foreign Relations and the American Decline* (Western Islands Publishers, 1988), p. 3.

9. See *New York Times*, March 26, 1922, per Mayor John F. Hylan. He said at the head of the octopus was "a small group of banking houses generally referred to as international bankers."

10. President Franklin D. Roosevelt said this in a letter dated November 21, 1933, to Colonel Edward M. House, as quoted in *F.D.R. His Personal Letters, 1928–1945*.

11. Senator William Jenner of Indiana said this in a 1954 speech. See *www. historicwordsblogspot.com,* June 30, 2009.

12. Senator Daniel Inouye made his remarks in 1986 testimony at the Iran Contra hearings.

13. See General Smedley Butler, *War Is a Racket* (New York: Roundtable Press, 1935) 1st chapter).

14. See Daniel Yergin, *The Prize*: *The Epic Quest for Oil, Money and Power* (New York: Free Press, 1992) p. 393, and Russ Baker, *Family of Secrets, The Bush Dynasty, America's Invisible Government, and the Hidden History of the Last Fifty Years* (New York: Bloomsbury Press, 2009), p. 288. Both sources have information on the quote.

15. See Betty Medsger, *The Burglary: The Discovery of J. Edgar Hoover's Secret FBI* (New York: Knopf, 2014).

16. See August 25, 2003, *Democracynow*.org interview by Amy Goodman with author Stephen Kinzer and Baruch College professor Ervand Abrahamian. The interview was headlined, "50 Years After the CIA's First Overthrow of a Democratically Elected Foreign Government We Take a Look at the 1953 US Backed Coup in Iran, August 25, 2003." In August 2013, at the sixtieth anniversary of the coup, the CIA released some documents showing they were involved in staging the coup.

17. "The 1953 Coup in Iran," *Science & Society*, 65 (2), summer 2001, pp. 182–215. Middle East historian Ervand Abrahamian stated that Secretary of State Dean Acheson admitted the Communist threat was a "smokescreen."

18. James Risen, *New York Times*, discovered secret CIA documents that revealed the statement about anticommunism being a "rhetorical device." See "Secrets of History: The C.I.A. in Iran—A Special Report, How a Plot Convulsed Iran in '53 (and in '79)," *New York Times*, April 16, 2000.

19. Oil was focus of coup, but discourse linked to the cold war. See "The 1953 Coup in Iran," *Science & Society*, 65 (2), summer 2001, pp. 182–215, by Middle East historian Ervand Abrahamian." Also see August

25, 2003, *Democracynow*.org interview noted above by Amy Goodman with Ervand Abrahamian.

20. See Russ Baker, ibid, p. 292 for detail about the US encouraging a Saudi effort to spread the extremist Wahhabi form of Islam. For more on how we secretly supported radical Islam, see 2003 *U.S. News & World Report* cover story. Also see Carl Gibson, *Reader Supported News*, February 6, 2015.

21. A special Senate subcommittee, chaired by then-senator John Kerry, investigated the Associated Press's findings and, in 1989, released a 1,166-page report on covert US operations throughout Latin America and the Caribbean. It found "considerable evidence" that the Contras were linked to running drugs and guns and that the US government knew about it.

22. Hoover and Byoir became acquainted through Byoir's involvement in President Wilson's Committee on Public Information (CPI). They set up the News Bureau after the war to spread fear of an imminent Communist invasion.

23. For information on Nixon's comments about Hoover, see Fred Cook, *The FBI Nobody Knows* (New York: Macmillan, 1964). Also see Church Committee 1976 report on FBI abuses and Fred Cook.

24. For information on Admiral Leahy's comments, see William Leahy *I Was There (The American Military Experience)* (New York: Ayer Company, 1979), p. 441. Also see the October 12, 2014, edition of *Washington's Blog*, "The REAL Reason America Used Nuclear Weapons against Japan (It Was Not To End the War or Save Lives)."

25. The pact between President Roosevelt and the Saudi king was described by Russ Baker, *Family of Secrets*, p. 288.

26. See *U.S. News & World Report* cover story, December 2003, by David Kaplan, Monica Ekman, and Aamir Latif.

27. Truman made these comments during an address on foreign economic policy at Baylor University, March 6, 1947. See *www.trumanlibrary. org.*

Chapter 2   The Ultimate Marriage

1. See *Century of the Self,* a 2002 BBC British television documentary series written and produced by Adam Curtis. The Anne Bernays quote is from the first show of the series, "Happiness Machines," which is available online at *moresketchynotes.blogspot.com* and other sites.

2. Aldous Huxley, *Brave New World Revisited* (Harper Perennial Modern Classics, 2006). This was originally published in 1958, twenty-six years after Huxley's fiction best seller *Brave New World.*

3. Edward Bernays, *Propaganda* (1928). See pp. 9–10.

4. Water Lippmann, *Public Opinion* (Free Press, Reissue edition, June 12, 1977). This was originally published in 1922.

5. Carl Jung's quote is found numerous places, but one of the best sources is David Eagleman, *Incognito, the Secret Lives of the Brain* (Canongate UK, Pantheon US, 2011; Vintage Reprint edition, May 15, 2012).

6. See David Eagleman, *The Week* magazine, December 26, 2011, for quote on consciousness not being the center of action in the brain. Also see Eagleman's book, Ibid, for further information on his quote that "there is a chasm between what the brain knows and what our minds can fathom."

7. Bernays's quote starts his famous work *Propaganda*, 1928.

8. One of the best books on Gulf War hoaxes is John Stauber and Sheldon Rampton's *Toxic Sludge Is Good for You, Lies, Damn Lies and the Public Relations Industry* (Monroe, MA: Common Courage Press, 1995, chapter 10). Also see John R. MacArthur, *The Second Front: Censorship and Propaganda in the Gulf War* (University of California Press, June 1992).

9. The quote from Harold D. Lasswell can be found at the end of *Propaganda, Technique in the World War* (New York: P. Smith, 1938).

10. See Edward Bernays, *Propaganda*, 1928, for a description of those who "pull the wires which control the public mind."

11. See *Theodore Roosevelt, an Autobiography*, 1913 (Appendix B).

12. See Tom Engelhardt, *Shadow Government: Surveillance, Secret Wars and a Global Security State in a Single Super World* (Chicago: Haymarket Books, 2014). Also see Tom Ross and David Wise, *The Invisible Government* (New York: Random House, 1964).

13. See "Final Report of the Senate Select Committee to Study Governmental Operations with Respect to Intelligence Activities," Book I, p. 50. See CIA memorandum of June 26, 1953, describing special meeting of June 1, 1951, "Matters Relating to CIA Project BLUEBIRD." Also see "Meeting with IAQ representatives of Project BLUEBIRD," July 25, 1951.

14. For Allen Dulles quote, see *Princeton Alumni Weekly* volume 51, p. 8.

15. This quote was in "Report on the Covert Activities of the Central Intelligence Agency," prepared for Eisenhower by the CIA Special

Study Group in 1954.. Eisenhower appointed Lt. James H. Doolittle of the US Air Force as chairman of a group to study how to improve covert activities of the Central Intelligence Agency.

16. Ibid., 1954 report to President Eisenhower.

Chapter 3   "SOAP" for the Mind

1. This is from the March 1954 issue of *Public Relations Journal*, which I saw at the Stanford University Library 40 years ago. I'm not sure if it's still available.

2. See the excellent book by Glenn Greenwald, *No Place to Hide* (New York: Metropolitan Books, Henry Holt, 2014). See p. 153 for a discussion of Operation KEYSTROKE, p. 71 for the ACLU quote, and p. 173 for the "watchful eye" quote.

3. See October 29, 2014 *Guardian* article, "FBI Demands New Powers to Hack into Computers and Carry out Surveillance."

4. The description of the airplane surveillance program is in another *Guardian* article, this one on November 15, 2014, by Trevor Timm, titled "First Snowden, Now Spies on a Plane. Yes, Surveillance Is Everywhere." It was also reported in the *Wall Street Journal* on November 13, 2014.

5. See www.democracynow.org/2011/bay area rapid transit, August 16, 2011.

6. See Terrance Qualter, *Propaganda and Psychological Warfare* (New York: Random House, 1962), p. 27.

7. See Walter Lippmann, *Public Opinion* (1922). Also see Nancy Snow, *Information War: American Propaganda, Free Speech and Opinion Control Since 9/11* (New York: Seven Stories Press, 2003), p. 32.

8. See Frederick Nietzsche, www.goodreads.com/quotes//31312-there-are-no-facts-only-interpretations.

9. See Victor Marchetti, *Institute for Historical Review,* "Propaganda and Disinformation: How the CIA Manufactures History"_(2001), http://spartacus-educational.com/JFKmarchetti.htm. Also see article by Victor Marchetti, a CIA veteran, in the September 2012 *Institute of Historical Review* (www.ihr.org). Marchetti is the author of *The CIA and the Cult of Intelligence* (New York: Alfred A. Knopf, 1974). This is the first book the US government went to court to censor.

10. See Edward Bernays, *Propaganda,* 1928. See also *The Engineering of Consent,* 1947.

11. The quote about Bernays are from a book review by John Stauber and Sheldon Rampton, published in *PR Watch*, Second Quarter,1999, Volume 6, No. 2, in which they review an excellent book on Bernays, *The Father of Spin: Edward L. Bernays & The Birth of PR* by Larry Tye (New York: Macmillan, 2002).

12. For more information on the torches of freedom, see *New York Times* (April 1, 1929) "Group of Girls Puff at Cigarettes as a Gesture of Freedom."

13. I still have press releases for work we did for Radio Free Europe and Radio Liberty during the seventies. For information and details on the Crusade for Freedom, see the Crusade for Freedom newsletters in the Charles Taft paper collection, Library of Congress, Washington, DC, Boxes 153, 156, hereafter Taft collection; and Mickelson's discussion of

the crusade in America's Other Voice, 51-58. 9. See Crusade for Freedom Newsletter July 1955 Taft collection, Box 156, folder Foreign Affairs: Geographic file, Europe: National Committee for Free Europe, Inc.

14. From Ben Cohen's December 30, 2014, *Wall Street Journal* article "Why Alabama's Nick Saban Is Against Texting." Cohen wrote that Saban chides his players for using or, in Saban's opinion, overusing, smartphones. The article cited the 2013 Pew Research Center poll on texting.

15. Neil Postman 1990 speech, see http://digitalcommons.uri.edu/srhonor-sprog, and Kristina E. Hatch, "Determining the Effects of Technology on Children," May 2011. Postman is the author of *Amusing Ourselves to Death: Public Discourse in the Age of Show Business* (Penguin Books, 2005).

16. See Vance Packard, *The Hidden Persuaders* (Ig Publishing; Reissue edition, July 1, 2007). It was originally published in 1957.

Chapter 4   Manufacturing Fear and Scaring the Hell Out of Us

1. G. William Domhoff, *Who Rules America?* (New York: Prentice Hall, 1967). See pp. 84–131 for an excellent job of detailing how the economic elite control multiple areas of American life.

2. See C. Wright Mills, *The Power Elite* (Oxford University Press, USA, 2000).

3. See Nick Turse, "America's Secret War in 134 Countries" (*Nation*, January 16, 2014). This was originally in the January 16, 2014, *TomDispatch.com*, "The Special Opts Surge." Turse is the author of the best-selling *Kill Anything that Moves*.

4. Edward Bernays, *Propaganda,* 1928. Also see David Wise and Tom Rosse, *The Invisible Government* (New York: Random House, 1964).

5. *Los Angeles Times,* July 31, 1975. Robert Maheu, businessman and Howard Hughes employee, gave testimony before the Church Committee in 1975.

6. Albert E. Kahn, *High Treason: The Plot Against the People* (Lear Publishers, 1950).

7. This quote is from Abraham L. Pomerantz, deputy chief counsel to the US prosecution staff at the Nuremberg trials, in an April 21, 1947, article in *The Daily Argus*, Mount Vernon, NY, entitled "Pomerantz Deplores Anti-Red Hysteria."

8. See *Wikipedia*, "World War II casualties."

9. Geraint Hughes, "The Military's Role in Counterterrorism: Examples and Implications for Liberal Democracies," Letort Paper, Strategic Studies Institute, May 2011, p. 105. Also see *Wikipedia*, "False flag."

10. See Swiss historian Daniele Ganser's book, *NATO's Secret Armies: Operation GLADIO and Terrorism in Western Europe* (Aware Journalism, January 1, 2005). Also see Daniele Ganser's journal article, "Terrorism in Western Europe: An Approach to NATO's Secret Stay-Behind Armies," *Whitehead Journal of Diplomacy and International Relations*, Winter/Spring, 2005, Vol. 6. Another good description of Ganser's research on Gladio can be found at *Wikipedia*, "Operation Gladio."

11. This quote is from *teleSUR* (English), March 8, 2015. See Philip Agree, *Inside the Company: CIA Diary* (New York: Farrar Strauss & Giroux, 1975).

12. On October 6, 1917 Senator Robert LaFollette delivered a three hour address to the Senate in which this statement was made. See Senator Robert LaFollette, Wikipedia.

13. See firstworldwar.com, "The Drift Towards War" for an excellent overview of World War I era propaganda, including atrocity stories.

14. See www.rense.com/general17/bushhitler.htm for more about the Bush family's ties to Nazis. This article on Nazis in the Republican Party was originally published January 28, 2000 in Online Journal, but this web site provides additional information

15. Carl Gibson, *Reader Supported News*, January 8, 2015, "What Presidents Obama and Bush Have in Common with the Charlie Hebdo Shooters." The Bill Maher quote is from the January 23, 2015, program *Real Talk with Bill Maher*. The host criticized the Clint Eastwood-directed film's portrayal of the sniper as a hero.

16. Glenn Greenwald and Andrew Fishman, "Latest FBI Claim of Disrupted Terror Plot Deserves Much Scrutiny and Scepticism Celebration," *The Intercept*, January 16, 2015.

17. See January 17, 2015, *Esquire* article, "The CIA's Willingness to Lie about Our Torture Regime: The Architecture of Unbelief" by Charles Pierce.

Chapter 5   Conspiracy and Brainwashing as Propaganda Tools

1. See *Wikipedia*.org/wiki/OperationMockingbird. Also see Michael Hasty, "Secret Admirers: The Bushes and the Washington Post," *Online Journal* (February 5, 2004).

2. See Hugh Wilford, *The Mighty Wurlitzer: How the CIA Played America* (Harvard University Press, Cambridge, May, 2009).

3. This is from Ken Silverstein in a September 5, 2014, article in *The Intercept*.

4. Edward Hunter, *Brainwashing in Red China: The Calculated Destruction of Men's Mind* (New York: Vanguard Press, 1951).

5. See Walter Bowart, *Operation Mind Control* (New York: Dell Publishing, January 1978), with an introduction by Richard Condon.

6. See "Canada's Secret Spy School in the Second World War," www.canadawar.com.

7. See John Marks, *The Search for the Manchurian Candidate: The CIA and Mind Control: The Secret History of the Behavioral Sciences* (New York: W. W. Norton & Company, 1979, new edition, 1991). Marks is a former State Department reporter who goes into detail about the CIA's mind control programs. Richard Condon wrote a fiction book called *The Manchurian Candidate* (originally published in 1959 and in 2004 by Pocket Star Books and Blackstone Audiobooks).

8. See "North Korea Begins Brainwashing Children in Cult of the Kims as Early as Kindergarten," by Anna Fifield, *Washington Post*, January 16, 2015.

9. See Alan Scheflin and Edward Opton, *The Mind Manipulators* (Paddington Press, 1978).

10. Adolf Hitler, *Mein Kampf* (Reynal, 1939). See also *1940 Britannica Book of the Year*, Encyclopedia Britannica, Inc., Chicago, 1940.

11. See *Wikipedia*, "Nayirah testimony." Note: This website contains footnotes that lead to numerous publications that wrote about the hoax. See John Stauber and Sheldon Rampton, *Lies and the Public Relations Industry* (Monroe, MA: Common *Courage* Press, 1995) chapter 10. Also see John R. MacArthur's *Second Front: Censorship and Propaganda in the Gulf War* (University of California Press, updated version, 2004).

12. See "Saddam Hussein's Alleged Shredder," Wikipedia.

13. *BBC News* on October 29, 2014, reported that CIA officials were said to have turned to Nazis to help beat the Soviet Union during the Cold War. Also see Betty Medsger, *The Burglary: The Discovery of J. Edgar Hoover's Secret FBI* (New York: Knopf, January 2014) for quote from Hoover.

14. Ibid., Medsger.

15. Secretary of State Dean Acheson said anticommunism was a smokescreen.

16. See www.*historycommons*.org, Tom Huston. Also see *Wikipedia*, "The Huston Plan."

17. See historycommons.org for Reston's quote.

18. See Charles Colson, historycommons.org.

19. Seymour Hersh, December 21, 1974, *New York Times*.

20. Alexander Bolton, *The Hill*, December 1, 2014, "UN Urges U.S. Crackdown on Police Brutality."

21. *Truthout* article based on January 28, 2012, AlterNet article by Dan Bacher, "LA Police Department Conducts Joint Exercises with the Military."

22. Jennifer Golbeck, *Psychology Today*, September/October 2014.

23. "Study: US Is an Oligarchy, Not a Democracy" appeared in the April 17, 2014, on-line edition of *BBC News*. Numerous other publications publicized the study.

24. "Enough Is Enough: The President's Latest Wall Street Nominee," by Senator Elizabeth Warren, was carried on numerous news sources in November 2014, including the Nov. 19 edition of the Huffington Post.

25. Paul Krugman wrote about wealth disparity in an op-ed piece in the *New York Times* on September 28, 2014. See "Our Invisible Rich."

26. David Hapgood, *Screwing of the Average Man: How the Rich Get Richer and You Get Poorer* (New York: Bantam Books, 1974).

27. Aldous Huxley, 1962 speech at University of California, Berkeley. It can be listened to at http://sunsite.berkeley.edu/VideoTest/hux1.ram.

Chapter 6   Mind Control, Drugs, and a Malleable Media

1. Church Committee 1976 report on FBI abuses. Also see Fred Cook, *The FBI Nobody Knows* (New York: Macmillan, 1964).

2. Betty Medsger, *The Burglary: The Discovery of J. Edgar Hoover's Secret FBI* (Knopf, 2014). Also see a *New York Times* review of *The Burglary* by David Oshinsky, January 31, 2014, and the Church Committee 1976 Investigation of COINTELPRO.

3. Fred Cook, *The FBI Nobody Knows.*

4. The CIA worked with the FBI, military intelligence, and others on behavior modification and held a joint meeting in July 1951 to coordinate this campaign. See memorandum "Meeting with IAQ Representatives of Project BLUEBIRD," July 25, 1951. Also see Wikipedia, "Project ARTICHOKE."

5. Directive 5412/I is effectively authorizations by the National Security Council to up the ante in mind manipulation campaigns. Also see Final Report of the Senate Select Committee to Study Governmental Operations with Respect to Intelligence Activities, Book I, p. 50.

6. See the CIA document "Memorandum Project BLUEBIRD," March 8, 1950, and "Memorandum of Meeting, Project BLUEBIRD," May 9, 1950. Also see Wikipedia, "Project ARTICHOKE," for the CIA quote about the scope of the projects and for a good overview of these projects, which later became Project MKULTRA. This is also covered in "Project MKULTRA, the Central Intelligence Agency's Program of Research into Behavioral Modification Joint Hearing Before the Select Committee on Intelligence and the Subcommittee on Health and Scientific Research of the Committee on Human Resources, United State Senate, Ninety-Fifth Congress, First Session," US Government Printing Office. A copy of the committee report is hosted at the *New York Times* website, August 8, 1977. Also see Nicholas M. Horrock, August 4, 1977, *New York Times* article "80 Institutions Used in CIA Mind Studies: Admiral Turner Tells Senators Behavior Control Research Bars Drug Testing Now."

7. For Allen Dulles quote, see *Princeton Alumni Weekly* volume 51, p. 8.

8. See *New York Times* committee report on Project MKULTRA noted above.

9. See *Wikipedia*, "Project ARTICHOKE." Also see article by Victor Marchetti, a CIA veteran, in the September 2012 *Institute for Historical Review,* www.ihr.org.

10. Do a Google web search to find numerous articles about the Vietnam War Commemoration Project.

11. See *San Jose Mercury News's*1996 series "Dark Alliance: The Story Behind the Crack Explosion," by Gary Webb. Also see *Wikipedia, "Gary Webb."*

12. Ryan Devereaux, September 25, 2014, edition of *The Intercept,* "Managing A Nightmare: How the CIA Watched Over the Destruction of Gary Webb."

13. Ryan Grim, Huffington Post, October 10, 2014, "Key Figures in CIA Crack Cocaine Scandal Begin to Come Forward."

14. See Gary Webb's book *Dark Alliance* (Seven Stories Press; 2nd edition, June 1999). He substantiates allegations that the CIA was aware of the transactions and shipments to the United States.

15. "Managing a Nightmare: CIA Public Affairs and the Drug Conspiracy Story" by Nicholas Dujmovic, a CIA Directorate of Intelligence staffer. Note: His name was redacted in the released version of the CIA document, but was included in a footnote in a 2010 article in the *Journal of Intelligence.* Dujmovic confirmed his authorship to *The Intercept,* according to Devereaux.

16. Ken Silverstein, *The Intercept,* "The CIA's Mop-up Man: LA Times Reporter Cleared Stories with Agency before Publication," September 4, 2014.

17. A special Senate Subcommittee, chaired by then-senator John Kerry, investigated the Associated Press findings and in 1989 released a 1,166-page report on covert US operations throughout Latin America and the Caribbean. It found considerable evidence that the Contras were linked to running drugs and guns, and that the U.S. government knew about it.

18. See Nick Schou, *Kill the Messenger: How the CIA, Crack-Cocaine Controversy Destroyed Journalist Gary Webb* (Nation Books, 2006). Also see "Washington Post's Slimy Assault on Gary Webb," by Robert Parry, *Consortium News*, October 19, 2014.

19. See *Wikipedia*, "Gary Webb." See Gary Webb, "1955–2004," *Esquire* magazine, p. 1.

20. See Michael Bromwich, December 17, 1997, special report: "The CIA-Contra-Crack Cocaine Controversy: A Review of the Justice Department's Investigations and Prosecutions, USDOJ/OIG Special Report." See also *Wikipedia*, "Gary Webb."

21. Bromwich Report, "The CIA-Contra-Crack Cocaine Controversy." Also see *Wikipedia*, "Gary Webb."

22. See "The Price for Telling the Truth," *Crosslight.org.*

23. Memorandum of Understanding item 24, released on May 7, 1998, Rep. Maxine Waters.

24. Alfred McCoy, *Politics of Heroin: CIA Complicity in the Global Drug Trade* (Chicago: Chicago Review Press; Revised edition May 1, 2003). This excellent book provides meticulous documentation of

dishonesty and dirty dealings at the highest levels from the Cold War until today.

25. Nancy Snow, *Information War: American Propaganda, Free Speech and Opinion Control Since 9-11* (Seven Stories Press, 2003) pp. 61-64.

26. Snow uses the quote about stimulating emotional drives from Alfred McClung Lee, *How to Understand Propaganda* (Rinehart, 1952).

27. *Newsweek*'s Gulf War reporter, Bob Sipschen, wrote this in the *Los Angeles Times*, March 1991.

28. After leaving the *Washington Post* in 1977, Carl Bernstein spent six months looking at the relationship of the CIA and the press during the Cold War years. His 25,000-word cover story about the CIA and the media was published in *Rolling Stone* on October 20, 1977. Also see carlbernstein.com and Nancy Snow, *Information War,* p. 40.

29. See Hugh Wilford, *The Mighty Wurlitzer: How the CIA Played America* (Boston: Harvard University Press, 2009).

30. Senator Frank Church (D-ID) headed the Select Committee to Study Governmental Operations with Respect to Intelligence Activities in 1975. The congressional report was published in 1976.

31. Michael Hasty, "Secret Admirers: The Bushes and the Washington Post," *Online Journal*, February 5, 2004.

32. An article published by the media watchdog group Fairness and Accuracy in Reporting (FAIR) has the headline "Washington Post Promotes Agendas of Power Elite." Hasty was cited as the main source for this article in FAIR. See www.wanttoknow.info/secrecygraham.

33. See Paul Craig Roberts, "What We Know and Don't Know About 9/11," VDARE.com, August 16, 2006, and *Wikipedia*, "Paul Craig Roberts."

34. See *Wikipedia*, "Charles Douglas Jackson."

35. Noam Chomsky and Edward Herman, *Necessary Illusions: Thought Control in Democratic Societies* (Boston: South End Press, 1989), p. 19.

36. See *Wikipedia*, "Operation CHAOS." Also see Robert Justin Goldstein, *Political Repression in Modern America: From 1870 to 1976* (University of Illinois Press, 2001) p. 456, and *Ramparts* magazine, "Burn before Reading," Stansfield Turner, 2005, p. 118.

37. See Walter L. Hixson, *Military Aspects of the Vietnam Conflict* (Taylor & Francis, 2000) p. 282.

38. See Mark Zepezauer, *The CIA's Greatest Hits* (Odonian Press, July 2002).

Chapter 7 The Most Powerful Propaganda Message Ever Delivered

1. See "U.S. Strategic Bombing Survey Group," July 1946, pp. 52–56.

2. Rob Edwards, "Hiroshima Bomb May Have Carried Hidden Agenda," British *New Scientist* magazine, July 21, 2005.

3. Gar Alperovitz, "The Decision to Bomb Hiroshima," Weekend Edition, *Counterpunch*, August 5–7, 2011.

4. William Leahy, *I Was There (The American Military Experience)* (New York: Ayer Company, 1979) p. 441.

5. Dwight Eisenhower, *Mandate for Change*: *The White House Years, a Personal Account* (New York: Doubleday, 1963) p. 380.

6. "Ike on Ike," *Newsweek*, November 11, 1963.

7. Norman Cousins, *The Pathology of Power* (New York: W. W. Norton & Company, 1988) p.65 and pp.70–71.

8. Lewis Strauss was quoted in Len Giovannitti and Fred Freed, *The Decision to Drop the Bomb* (Coward-McCann, 1965) p.145 and p.325.

9. The quotes from the military officers in this paragraph were obtained, respectively, from three sources. See the Weekend Edition, *Counterpunch*, August 5–7, 2011, "The Decision to Bomb Hiroshima" by Gar Alperovitz; historian Doug Long (www.doug-long/quotes.htm); and *Washington's Blog and Global Research*, "The Real Reason America Used Nuclear Weapons Against Japan: It Was Not To End the War or Save Lives," October 12, 2012.

10. *Washington's Blog and Global Research*.

11. Elaine Kurtenbach and Mari Yamaguchi, "Deadly W. War II Fire Bombings of Japanese Cities Largely Ignored," March 9, 2015, *Associated Press*.

12. Nixon said this on the fortieth anniversary of the bombings. See Gar Alperovitz, *The Decision to Use the Atomic Bomb and the Architecture of an American Myth* (New York: Knopf), p. 352.

13. This is from *history.com* and *Washington's Blog*, "The Real Reason America Used Nuclear Weapons Against Japan."

14. Gar Alperovitz, "The Decision to Bomb Hiroshima."

15. Palash Ghosh, "Were Hiroshima and Nagasaki Racist Acts?" *International Business Times*, August 5, 2011.

16. I have cited all of these examples of demonization throughout the book. The German demonization statement came from Scott Cutlip, *The Unseen Power: Public Relations: A History* (Hillsdale, NJ: Lawrence Erlbaum Associates Inc., 1994) pp. 64–77.

17. "Hiroshima and Nagasaki: Worst Terror Attacks in History," *Green Leaf Weekly*, August 3, 2005.

18. Dennis J. Kucinich, sixteen-year member of Congress, was quoted in the *Huffington Post*, "The Atomic Bomb, Then and Now," August 7, 2014.

19. This editorial is from David Lawrence, founder and editor of *U.S. News & World Report*. He wrote a number of stinging editorials, the first on August 17, 1945. This was written November 23, 1945. See Australian Free Press.Org. "Suppressed History—Japan Bombing World War II."

20. Bush's quote is from the *International News*, Amir Mir, March 17, 2014, "Obama Wanted to Say Sorry for Hiroshima but Tokyo Stopped Him."

21. See J. Samuel Walker, "The Decision to Use the Bomb: A Historiographical Update," which appeared in *Diplomatic History*, Volume 14,

issue 1, winter 1990, p. 110. Also see historian Doug Long's website www.doug-long/quotes.htm.

Chapter 8 A Beautiful "BOD": The Engineering of Dissent

1. In August 2013, at the sixtieth anniversary of the coup, the CIA released some documents showing they were involved in staging the coup.

2. See August 25, 2003, *Democracynow*.org interview by Amy Goodman with author Stephen Kinzer and Baruch College professor Ervand Abrahamian. The interview was headlined, "50 Years After the CIA's First Overthrow of a Democratically Elected Foreign Government We Take a Look at the 1953 US Backed Coup in Iran, August 25, 2003."

3. "The 1953 Coup in Iran," *Science & Society*, 65 (2), summer 2001, pp. 182–215. Middle East historian Ervand Abrahamian identified the coup d'état as "a classic case of nationalism clashing with imperialism in the Third World." He stated that Secretary of State Dean Acheson admitted the "'Communist threat' was a smokescreen."

4. James Risen, "Secrets of History: The C.I.A. in Iran—A Special Report, How a Plot Convulsed Iran in '53 (and in '79)," *New York Times*, April 16, 2000.

5. See Masoud Kazemzadeh, "The Day Democracy Died: The 50th Anniversary of the CIA Coup in Iran," *Khaneh* Vol. 3, No. 34, October 2003. See also Habib Ladjevardi, "The Origins of U.S. Support for an Autocratic Iran," *International Journal of Middle East Studies*, 15 (2) (May 1983). See Stephen Kinzer, *All the Shah's Men: An American Coup*

and the Roots of Middle East Terror (New York: John Wiley and Sons, 2003) pp. 6 and 13. See Ervand Abrahamian, "The 1953 Coup in Iran," *Science & Society*, 65 (2) (Summer 2001), p. 211.

6. See 1953 Iranian coup d'état, Wikipedia.

7. See Saeed Kamali Dehghan and Richard Norton-Taylor, "CIA Admits Role in 1953 Iranian Coup," *Guardian*, August 19, 2013. Also see See 1953 Iranian coup d'état, Wikipedia.

8. Stephen E. Ambrose, *Eisenhower, vol.2, The President* (New York: Simon and Schuster, 1984), p. 111. Also see money howstuffworks. com/10-great-moments-corporate-malfeasance3 and Guatemalan coup d'état.

9. See Larry Tye, *The Father of Spin: Edward L. Bernays & The Birth of PR* (Picador, 2002).

10. See www.coldwar.org/articles/50s/guatemala.asp. It is also in *The Cold War Museum, 1950's*.

11. See *Wikipedia, "Guatemalan coup d'état."*

12. See Steve Coll, *Ghost Wars: The Secret History of the CIA, Afghanistan, and Bin Laden, from the Soviet Invasion to September 10, 2001* (New York: Penguin Press, 2004). Also see *Wikipedia*, "Ghost Wars."

13. See Betty Medsger, *The Burglary: The Discovery of J. Edgar Hoover's Secret FBI* (New York: Knopf, January 2014). Also see a *New York Times* review of *The Burglary* by David Oshinskyjan, January 31, 2014, and the Church Committee 1976 Investigation of COINTELPRO.

14. Keith Bolender, *Voices from the Other Side: An Oral History of Terrorism Against Cuba* (Pluto Press, 2010). Also see Noam Chomsky's introduction.

15. See *nypost*.com/2013/11/10/all-the-presidents-women.

16. In testimony before the Church Committee in 1975, Maheu confirmed his role in the assassination plot against Castro, saying that he thought the United States "was involved in a just war." See *Wikipedia*, "Robert Maheu."

17. See FIB FOIA files, John Roselli files. Also see "John Roselli," *Wikipedia*, and *Los Angeles Times*, July 31, 1975. Roselli made these remarks before the Church Committee.

18. See Giacanna, *Wipipedia*, and Church Committee report.

19. President Kennedy vowed to crush the CIA "into a thousand pieces." See "State of the Nation, Warren Commission Report: The Most Absurd Investigation in US History," November 14, 2013, Item #2.

20. L. Fletcher Prouty, *JFK: The CIA, Vietnam, and the Plot to Assassinate John F. Kennedy* (Skyhorse Publishing, 2011). Colonel Prouty was a CIA operative.

21. Noam Chomsky, "The Long, Shameful History of American Terrorism," *Reader Supported News*, November 15, 2014. Chomsky's comments were also in an introduction to a study by Canadian scholar Keith Bolender, *Voices from the Other Side: An Oral History of Terrorism against Cuba, in 2010* (Pluto Press, September, 2010).

22. *New York Post* wrote an article on November 10, 2013, called "All the President's Women." It appeared online at nypost.com/2013/11/10/all-the-presidents-women.

23. See Judith Exner and Ovid Demanis, *My Story* (Grove Press, 1977).

24. *New York Post*, Nov. 10. 2013.

25. See Russ Baker, *Family of Secrets*, p. 288.

26. Ibid., p. 316.

27. Christopher Simpson, *Blowback: The First Full Account of America's Recruitment of Nazis and Its Disastrous Effect on the Cold War, Our Domestic and Foreign Policy* (Collier Books-MacMillan, August 1989).

28. Ibid.

29. Ibid.

30. See Martin A. Lee, *The Beast Reawakens: Fascism's Resurgence from Hitler's Spymasters to Today's Neo-Nazi Groups and Right Wing Extremists* (Routledge, October 1999).

Chapter 9   Dead Babies and Other Propaganda Examples

1. See www.*online-literature.com*, Jonathan Swift, "A Tale of a Tub."

2. Edward Bernays, *The Engineering of Consent*, 1947. This is an essay in which Bernays defines "engineering of consent" as the art of manipulating people. He believed that entire populations were vulnerable to unconscious influence.

3. Nancy Snow, *Information War: American Propaganda, Free Speech and Opinion Control Since 9-11* (Seven Stories Press, 2003) p. 23.

4. Edward Herman and Noam Chomsky, *Manufacturing Consent: the Political Economy of the Mass Media* (Pantheon, January 2002).

5. One of the best books on the Gulf War hoax is John Stauber and Sheldon Rampton, *Toxic Sludge Is Good for You, Lies, Damn Lies and the Public Relations Industry* (Monroe, MA: Common Courage Press, 1995) chapter 10. Also see John R. MacArthur, *Second Front: Censorship and Propaganda in the Gulf War* (University of California Press, June 1992). See "Nayirah testimony" at *Wikipedia*. This site contains footnotes that lead to numerous publications that wrote about the hoax.

6. See S. Roschwalb, "The Hill & Knowlton Cases: A Brief on the Controversy," *Public Relations Review* 20, 1994, p. 268. See also Robin Andersen, *A Century of Media, a Century of War* (Peter Lang Publishing, 2006) pp. 170–172.

7. John Stauber and Sheldon Rampton, *Toxic Sludge Is Good for You,* chapter 10, p. 169.

8) J. Edgar Hoover and Carl Byoir set up a news bureau after World War I, according to notes I found while working at the Byoir agency.

9. See Adolf Hitler, *Mein Kampf* (July 1925, vol. I, Chapter X).

10. See "Pentagon Papers" at *Wikipedia*.

11. See "Canadian Prime Minister Steve Harper's address before Parliament," *The Independent,* October 23, 2014. Journalist Glenn Greenwald commented on Canada's reaction to the lone gunman incident in an excellent article in *The Intercept*, October 22, 2014, titled "Canada, At War for 13 Years, Shocked That 'A Terrorist' Attacked Its Soldiers."

12. Ibid, *The Intercept.*

13. See Steve Coll, "The Drone War in Pakistan," www.newyorker.com/magazine/2014.

14. See Greenwald article in the November 18, 2014, issue of *The Intercept,* "The Irrelevance of the U.S. Congress in Stopping NSA Mass Surveillance."

15. "Top 10 Torturer List Actually Includes Hundreds or More," by William Boardman, *Reader Supported News,* December 20, 2014.

16. See *Wikipedia* for details on the "False-flag" technique.

17. See Marc Rogers, "Fooled Again," *Daily Beast,* December 28, 2014.

18. Glenn Greenwald, "North Korea/Sony Story Shows How Eagerly US Media Still Regurgitate Government Claims," *The Intercept,* January 1, 2015.

19. Ken Klippenstein and Paul Gottinger, "The Interview Is Propaganda Masquerading as Comedy," *Reader Supported News,* January 2, 2015.

20. Mark Mazzetti, "After Scrutiny, C.I.A. Mandate Is Untouched," *New York Times,* December 26, 2014.

21. See March 9, 2013 article in the Guardian.com, "Saddam Hussein Statue Toppled in Bagdhad, April 9, 2003."

Chapter 10   War on Drugs and Jim Crow

1.   For more on Wisconsin senator La Follette's quote, see "Opposition to Wilson's War Message," http://www.mtholyoke.edu/acad/intrel/doc19.htm.

2. Russ Baker, *Family of Secrets, The Bush Dynasty, America's Invisible Government, and The Hidden History of the Last Fifty Years* (New York, Bloomsbury Press, 2009) p. 292.

3. Director Mark Levin's fall 2014 documentary *Freeway: Crack in the System* explores the corrupt foundations of the drug war and calls into question the draconian jail sentences the US justice system often metes out to the black community. The information about the jailing of drug users largely comes from an October 10, 2014, article in the *Huffington Post* by Ryan Grimm, Matt Sledge, and Matt Ferner in an article titled "Key Figures in CIA-Crack Cocaine Scandal Begin to Come Forward."

4. See *Wikipedia*, "War on Drugs."

5. See Susan Grigsby, "How the Racists of the South Have Ruled This Nation from the Very Beginning, The War on Drugs, 1980 to Present," *Daily Kos.*

6. Michelle Alexander, *The New Jim Crow: Mass Incarceration in the Age of Colorblindness* (The New Press, January 2012). See excellent introduction by Cornell West.

7. See *New York Times.com*, "Memphis Jury Sees Conspiracy in Martin Luther King Killing" (December 9, 1999).

8. See November 14, 2014, article in *Yahoo News* based on the *New York Times.com* story, "What An Uncensored Letter to MLK Reveals," Nov. 11, 2014.

9. See Nadia Kayyali, "Defending Your Rights in the Digital World," *Deeplinks Blog*, November 12, 2014, and "FBI's Suicide Letter to Dr. Martin Luther King, Jr. and the Dangers of Unchecked Surveillance."

10. See *New York Times.com*, "What An Uncensored Letter to MLK Reveals," Nov. 11, 2014.

11. See "Project MKULTRA," *Wikipedia* and the Church Committee report on MKULTRA.

12. Juan Cole, *Informed Comment*, November 9, 2014.

13. Michael Walsh, "FBI Says 76 Law Enforcement Officers Died in the Line of Duty in 2013," *Yahoo News*, November 24, 2014.

14. See jwa.org/encyclopedia/article/stokes-rose-pasto.

Chapter 11   Language and Propaganda

1. This is from the 1832 biography of *Benjamin Disraeli* by Contarini Fleming, pt. 1, Chpt. 21.

2. Laura Walker, "Snowden Docs Lead to Discovery NSA Employees Spied on Spouses, Girlfriends," *Newsweek,* December 26, 2014.

3. See Samm Baker, *Permissible Lie: Inside Truth About Advertising* (Peter Own Ltd.,1st edition, 1969).

4. See *Wikipedia*, "Robert Maheu." In testimony before the Church Committee in 1975, Maheu confirmed his role in the assassination plot against Castro, saying that he thought the United States "was involved in a just war." Also see Victor Marchetti and John Marks's book *The CIA and the Cult of Intelligence* (Alfred A. Knopf, June 1974).

5. See Norman Moss, *The Pleasures of Deception* (Random House Inc., April 1977).

6. See David Wise's book *The Politics of Lying: Government Deception, Secrecy, and Power* (Random House, 1973). Also see his other books, including *Invisible Government*.

7. Ludwig Wittgenstein was an Austrian-British philosopher who specialized in the philosophy of language. See *Wikipedia*, "Ludwig Wittgenstein."

8. See *Wikipedia*, "Neil Postman." Postman was an American author, media theorist, and cultural critic, who is best known for his 1985 book about television *Amusing Ourselves to Death* (Penguin Books, 20th anniversary edition, 2005). It was co-written by Charles Weingartner.

9. Sydney Harris was a syndicated newspaper columnist and wrote for many years for the *Chicago Daily News* and the *Chicago Sun Times*.

10. See *New York Times.com*, Nov.11, 2014,"What An Uncensored Letter to MLK Reveals." Professor Beverly Gage discovered the FBI letters.

11. Muriel Barbery, *The Elegance of the Hedgehog* (New York: Europa Editions, 2008) p. 57.

12. See Terrance Qualter, *Propaganda and Psychological Warfare* (New York: Random House, 1962) p. 17. See p. 27 for an excellent study of the nature of propaganda.

13. See Walter Lippmann, *Public Opinion* (1922 – June, 1997 re-issue, Free Press).

14. Nancy Snow, *Information War: American Propaganda, Free Speech and Opinion Control Since 9/11* (Seven Stories Press, 2003), p. 32.

15. See Wilson Bryan Key, *Subliminal Seduction* (Signet, 1974). Wilson Key wrote several books on subliminal advertising. Also see *Wikipedia,* "Wilson Bryan Key."

16. See "Classical Conditioning," *Wikipedia*. Ivan Pavlov taught pioneer propagandists how people are creatures of "conditioned reflex" in how they relate to symbols.

17. See *generalsemantics.org.* Alfred Korzybski, a Polish-American scholar, developed a field called "general semantics." Alfred Whitehead was a philosophical mathematician who often collaborated with Korzybski.

18. See Pierre Martineau, *Motivation in Advertising* (New York, McGraw-Hill, 1952, paperback, 1971).

19. See *Sugar.com* for more information on the Sugar Association.

20. See article by Peter Steinfels, *New York Times*, April 4, 1993 for a good overview of the *Journal of Christianity and Crisis*, which published its last issue in 1993.

21. See Frederick Nietzsche, www.*goodreads*.com.

22. See David Hapgood, *Screwing of the Average Man: How the Rich Get Richer and You G2et Poorer* (New York: Bantam Books, 1974).

Chapter 12   Getting Jailed for Your Beliefs

1. This was in Edward Bernays's last book, *Public Relations* (1952).

2. See Roswell Dwight Hitchcock, *Socialism*, which was written in 1879. An updated version was printed by BiblioBazaar, Dec. 2008, and is available at Amazon.com/books.

3. See *Wikipedia*, "Tompkins Square Riots."

4. The Molly McGuires were a movement of coal miners in Pennsylvania who advocated for better working conditions for miners. They were known as "Mollies."

5. See Joseph G. Rayback, *A History of American Labor* (New York: The Macmillan Company, 1959).

6. See Rev. Joseph Cooke, *Wikipedia*. He was a Free Christian and became the inspiration behind the Methodist Unitarian movement.

7. John Eaton, Jr. (1829–1906) was a US commissioner of education and brigadier general in the Civil War. He made these remarks at the 1881 National Education Association convention.

8. See *Wikipedia*, "Haymarket Affair."

9. The private detective was hired by one of the most powerful industrialists in the East. Some historians believe that information from the Pinkerton detective was used by vigilantes to unleash massive violence on anyone suspected of being a Mollie. Even the families of Mollies were attacked.

10. This editorial appeared in the *San Diego Tribune* on March 4, 1912.

Chapter 13   The Invisible Man in the Wilson Administration

1. Much of the information on Byoir in this chapter and throughout the book comes from information I gathered during ten years working for his public relations agency. I started writing this chapter and a few other chapters in the seventies while working at the agency. One of the best sources on Byoir's career and the CPI is Scott M. Cutlip's excellent book *Unseen Power: Public Relations, A History* (Routledge, March 1994).

    Note: The original Byoir agency that I worked for has been out of business since the eighties. The agency name still exists. Carl Byoir & Associates is part of the WPP, a worldwide marketing communications company. The activities of Byoir and his agency discussed in this book have nothing to do with this marketing firm or any other entity.

2. For information on the missing files and a good account of the CPI, see James R. Mock and Cedric Larson, *Words That Won the War, The Story of the Committee on Public Information* (Princeton: Princeton University Press, 1939). Also see George Creel, *How We Advertised America* (Forgotten Books, August 2012, original 1920). For Creel's career up to 1917 and an excellent overview of the CPI, see Alan Axelrod, *Selling the Great War: The Making of American Propaganda* (New York: Palgrave Macmillan Trade), pp. 1–53.

3. See *academia.edu* for the paper Robert A. Dahl, a Yale political science/sociology professor emeritus, wrote called "The Concept of Power, Behavioral Science" (July, 1957). Dahl gave an operational definition of power.

4. Robert W. Babson was the main point of contact between the Department of Labor and the CPI. He later became a well-known investment adviser.

5. See Ralph Miliband, *The State in Capitalist Society* (Merlin Press, September 1, 2009, originally published in1969). Miliband has contributed key works in social and political theory.

6. Frederick Taylor was an engineer and industrial psychologist who sought to improve industrial efficiency. Taylor summed up his efficiency techniques in his book *The Principles of Scientific Management* (Cosimo Classics, latest edition, October 2006).

7. Guy Ford headed the CPI's Division of Civil and Educational Publications (DCEP), which was most often called the "Ford Division." Ford was a liaison between the CPI and education institutions.

8. See John Sproat, *The Best Men: Liberal Reformers in the Gilded Age* (Oxford University Press, 1968).

9. This is from Creel's April 1918 letter to the *Birmingham News* Also see Ibid, Scott Cutlip.

10. See James R. Mock and Cedric Larson, *Words That Won the War, The Story of the Committee on Public Information* (Princeton: Princeton University Press, 1939).

11. See George Creel, *How We Advertised America* (Forgotten Books, August 20, 2012, original, 1920).

12. See the Nye Committee Report, which details corporation corruption and profiteering during World War I.

13. See Thomas Fleming, *The Illusion of Victory: America in World War I* (Basic Books, May 2004) pp. 119–120.

14. See Ibid., p. 173 for information on the plane incident. Also see *Wikipedia*, "Committee on Public Information."

15. See Mock and Larson, *Words That Won the War,* for more on the Hollywood movies. There are numerous other sources about these early propaganda films. For a start, see en.wikipedia.org/wiki/ DepartmentalReorganizationAct.

16. See Harold D. Lasswell, *Propaganda Technique in World War I* (MIT Press, April, 1927). Mock and Larsen also quote Lasswel in their book noted above.

Chapter 14   Post–World War I to the Cold War

1. "We are governed, our minds are molded, our tastes formed, our ideas suggested, largely by men we have never heard of…it is they who pull the wires which control the public mind," Edward Bernays said in his book *Propaganda*, published in 1928.

2. La Follette was named one of the five greatest senators in US history. His 1917 Senate Speech was titled "Free Speech in Wartime." It was named one of the top 100 Senate speeches in history.

3. See Irwin Ross, *The Image Merchants* (Garden City, NY, Doubleday and Co., 1959).

4. The FDR library has a lot on the Roosevelt dances. See docs.fdrlibrary. marist.edu/bdsptxt.html.

5. Scott M. Cutlip, *Unseen Power: Public Relations; A History* (L. Eribaum Associates, 1994). See p. 563 for Byoir quote on painters of rainbows. Cutlip's excellent book, plus several others I reference in this chapter, has provided me with invaluable information. Some of the information in these books I also learned from working at the Byoir agency. In such cases I have referenced the outside writer rather than my own observations.

6. Committee of Public Information activities are described in the National Archives files, Library of Congress. Many of the CPI files are missing, but the remaining ones are here.

7. See Victor Marchetti, *Institute of Historical Review*, "Propaganda and Disinformation: How the CIA Manufactures History"_(2001).

8. For an excellent discussion of the Committee on Public Information, see James R. Mock and Cedric Larson, *Words That Won the War, The Story of the Committee on Public Information, 1917–1919* (Princeton: Princeton University Press, 1939). The authors note that "America went under censorship during the World War without realizing it."

9. See James Aronson, *The Press and the Cold War* (Boston: Beacon Press, 1970) p. 27. Aronson's work is one of the best on America's preoccupation with anticollectivism. Aronson is particularly perceptive in his description of media's anti-Communist development.

10) Another excellent book that deals with the CPI is Robert Sobel's *The Manipulators: America in the Media Age* (Garden City, NY: Anchor Press/Doubleday, 1976), pp. 58–88.

11. Encyclopedia Britannica, 1940 edition.

12. See Stuart Ewen, *PR!—A Social History of Spin* (Basic Books, November 1996).

13. See also George Creel, *How We Advertised America* (New York: Harper & Brothers, 1920) and George Creel, *Rebel at Large* (New York: G. P. Putnam's & Sons, 1947). See also James Aronson, *The Press and the Cold War.*

14. For a good overview of William Randolph Hearst and his newspaper empire, see *Wikipedia*, "William Randolph Hearst."

15. See Upton Sinclair's *The Brass Check: A Study of American Journalism* (University of Illinois Press, November 2002/original publication, 1919). Besides what is noted in the book, Sinclair said Hearst used yellow journalism in the *New York Journal-American* newspaper to whip up popular support for US military ventures in the Philippines, Puerto Rico, and Cuba.

16. Bernays's comment about fighting the Cold War in his propaganda campaign for United Fruit in Guatemala can be found at numerous sources, including Wikipedia. One of the best overviews of Bernays and his career can be found in Larry Tye's *The Father of Spin: Edward Bernays and the Birth of Public Relations* (New York: Macmillan, 2002).

17. Larry Tye also chronicles Bernays's campaign for Lucky Strike.

18. For more information on Byoir's work for Lithuania, see "1913–1919– The Museum of Public Relations," visionaries.com/byoir/cb13-19. html.

19. For more on Byoir's work for Machado, see Scott M. Cutlip, *Unseen Power.*

20. For Byoir's work for Nazi Germany and its corporations, see Irwin Ross, *The Image Merchants* (Garden City, NY, Doubleday and Co., 1959).

21. See Scott Cutlip, *Unseen Power,* for information on Byoir's work for Henry Doherty.

22. For more information on Byoir's work for Roosevelt and the birthday balls, see Scott Cutlip, *Unseen Power*, chapter 18. Also see "Birthday Ball," www.docs.fdrlibrary.marist.edu/bdtext.htm.

23. See Scott Cutlip, *Unseen Power*, for more on Byoir's work for Libby-Owens and John Biggers.

Chapter 15   The Cold War, Hollywood, and Organized Crime

1. Albert E. Kahn, *High Treason: The Plot Against the People* (Lear Publishers, 1950).

2. See John E. Rankin, *spartacus-eduational.com.* As soon as Japan surrendered, Congressman John E. Rankin, a member of the Dies Committee on Un-American Activities, began issuing press releases on "Communist intentions to dominate the world."

3. William Appleman, *The Tragedy of American Diplomacy* (World, 1959).

4. Truman made these comments during an address on foreign economic policy at Baylor University, March 6, 1947. See *www.trumanlibrary. org.*

5. *Business Week*, March 22, 1946.

6. Abraham L. Pomerants, deputy chief counsel to the US prosecution staff, said at the Nuremberg trials that pinning the label Red "indiscriminately on all opposition" was how Red-Scare propaganda worked.

7. See James V. Forrestal, *Wikipedia.*

8. October 10, 1946, *Life* magazine.

9. See "Howard Hughes," *Wikipedia,* for a list of Hughes movies.

10. See *legal information institue.cornell.edu*, "White-Collar Crime." Edwin Sutherland coined the phrase during a speech on December 27, 1939, to the American Sociological Association.

11. Donald Ray Cressey, *Theft of the Nation: The Structure and Operations of Organized Crime in America* (Harpercollins, June 1969).

Chapter 16   Sex in Media and Operation Underworld

1. For more on the movie *The Outlaw*, see *Wikipedia,* "The Outlaw." Note: Much of the information in this chapter is based on information I learned while working for the Byoir agency.

2. See *Wikipedia*, "Ralph Owen Brewster."

3. See www.dating.famousfix.com/tpx_1719443/elliott-roosevelt-and-faye-emerson. Howard Hughes was instrumental in bringing the two together when Colonel Roosevelt visited the Hughes Aircraft Company to evaluate the proposed Hughes XF-11. Though Elliott was married, Faye and he linked up, strongly urged on by the generous efforts of Hughes and his social facilitator, Johnny Meyer. Faye later asserted that despite her doubts, Hughes urged her to advance the relationship, and she knew that she could not defy Hughes.

4. See *Wikipedia*, "Allen Dulles."

5. See *Wikipedia,* "Operation Underworld."

6. See Lucky Luciano at *britannica.com* and at *history.com.*

7. See *spartacus-educational.com* for a good overview of Hughes.

8. See an excellent book on the heroin trade and the Port of Marseilles: Alfred W. McCoy, Cathleen B. Reach, and Leonard D. Adams, *The Politics of Heroin in Southeast Asia* (Harper & Row, 1972). Also see *Wikipedia*, the "French Connection."

Chapter 17   Propaganda Techniques

1. Geraint Hughes, "The Military's Role in Counterterrorism: Examples and Implications for Liberal Democracies," Letort Paper, Strategic Studies Institute, May 2011, p. 105. Also see *Wikipedia*, "False flag."

2. A good overview of the Vietnam War commemorative program can be found at *Counterpunch.org* in the article "The Battle Still Rages Over What Vietnam Means," by John Grant, March 7, 2013.

CPSIA information can be obtained
at www.ICGtesting.com
Printed in the USA
BVHW031801150320
575073BV00001B/13